REVISION WORKBOOK

Administrative Law

CONSULTANT EDITOR: LORD TEMPLEMAN
EDITOR: CHARLES P REED
LLB, Barrister

OLD BAILEY PRESS

OLD BAILEY PRESS
200 Greyhound Road, London W14 9RY

1st edition 1997
Reprinted 1999

Previous editions published under The HLT Group Ltd.

ISBN 1 85836 229 6

British Library Cataloguing-in-Publication.

A CIP Catalogue record for this book is available from the British Library.

Printed and bound in Great Britain.

Contents

Acknowledgements

Some questions used are taken or adapted from past University of London LLB (External) examination papers and our thanks are extended to the University of London for their kind permission to use and publish the questions.

Caveat

The answers given are not approved or sanctioned by the University of London and are entirely our responsibility.

They are not intended as 'Model Answers', but rather as Suggested Solutions.

The answers have two fundamental purposes, namely:

a) To provide a detailed example of a suggested solution to an examination question, and

b) To assist students with their research into the subject and to further their understanding and appreciation of the subject of Administrative Law.

The publishers and author would also like to thank Butterworths for kind permission to reproduce extracts from the All England Law Reports.

Introduction

This Revision WorkBook has been designed specifically for those students studying administrative law at undergraduate level. Its coverage is not restricted to any one syllabus but embraces all the core topics which can be found in university and college examinations. The coverage includes emphasis on the administrative law content of constitutional law as taught at undergraduate level.

Each chapter contains an introduction which explains the scope and general contents of the topics covered. This is followed by 'key points' to assist students in studying the essential points of law to understand properly the topic. Recent cases and relevant materials are included where appropriate. Discussion of case law has been kept at a minimum for the sake of simplicity.

Additionally in each chapter there is at least one past examination question, taken from the University of London External examinations. These questions have been selected to cover the most popular issues raised in examinations. The analysis of these questions will help the student to assess the potential range of questions in a topic. Each question is followed by a suggested solution designed to bring the most important issues to the attention of the student and to suggest an appropriate method of answering.

Careful use of the Revision WorkBook will assist the student to develop a good examination technique and also enable him to deal with the wide range of subject matter required for an examination.

The final chapter contains the complete June 1996 University of London LLB (External) Administrative Law question paper, followed by suggested solutions to each question. Thus the student will have the opportunity to review a recent examination paper in its entirety, and can, if desired, use this chapter as a mock examination – referring to the suggested solutions only after first having attempted the questions.

The law is updated until 28 February 1997.

How to Study Administrative Law

The study of administrative law will assist a student to understand the organisation and functions of public authorities and the way in which the exercise of public/governmental power is controlled so as to protect the citizen from oppressive bureaucracy. Since there is also a public interest in securing efficient public administration, there is a natural tension between permitting sufficient discretion to be enjoyed by decision-makers (a 'margin of appreciation') and, on the other hand, safeguarding human rights from undue interference. Consequently, the subject of administrative law is concerned not only with the study of administrative organisation and rule-making, but also with the scope of judicial review of administrative action and the roles of extra-judicial controllers such as ombudsmen. An appreciation of the theoretical basis of administrative law (for example, the red light and green light concepts) is as important as the ability to understand and explain the practical operation of administration and the application of the ultra vires rule.

There is also a significant emphasis on the procedural rules by which judicial review must be obtained. In the view of some critics these rules have become unnecessarily complex and occasionally more dominant than the substantive issues of a particular case. Although it is easy to be put off by the prospect of having to study what appear to be turgid technicalities, it is vital to grasp that these technical rules determine access to the courts: the touchstone of all civil liberties. Hence a student concerned with safeguarding the rule of law must be prepared to demonstrate that concern by mastering the considerable amount of technical detail that forms the bedrock of administrative law.

Administrative law has been a growth area of English law over the last 40 years and continues to be a fast-moving subject here and in common law jurisdictions around the world. Students should be prepared to study many recent cases which have refined, and sometimes redefined, established principles to such a degree that some judges have recently suggested that Parliament shares its sovereignty with the judiciary in the task of calling the executive to account. Reference to the *Public Law Journal* is a useful way to keep abreast of developments and of the (often critical) reactions to them.

To summarise, the student of administrative law needs to have a good grasp of the principles of law as laid down by the cases. In addition, a good knowledge of case law is required to explain and illustrate the working of these principles in practical situations. Fortunately, both these requirements can be satisfied by a study of one set of materials, but the student should be particularly careful not to fall into the trap of memorising lists of cases with no clear understanding of the principles established by such cases.

Finally the student should, wherever possible, study the original sources, ie the original cases. However learned or illustrious a textbook author is, the textbook is essentially a secondhand version of the facts. Given the amount of material in the syllabus, this is a counsel of perfection, but it is well worth following whenever time permits. In particular, when a student encounters difficulties, a reading of the original authorities will often make not only the point being checked clear, but several others.

Revision and Examination Technique

(A) REVISION TECHNIQUE

Planning a revision timetable

In planning your revision timetable make sure you don't finish the syllabus too early. You should avoid leaving revision so late that you have to 'cram' – but constant revision of the same topic leads to stagnation.

Plan ahead, however, and try to make your plans increasingly detailed as you approach the examination date.

Allocate enough time for each topic to be studied. But note that it is better to devise a realistic timetable, to which you have a reasonable chance of keeping, rather than a wildly optimistic schedule which you will probably abandon at the first opportunity!

The syllabus and its topics

One of your first tasks when you began your course was to ensure that you thoroughly understood your **syllabus**. Check now to see if you can write down the **topics** it comprises from memory. You will see that the chapters of this WorkBook are each devoted to a topic. This will help you decide which are the key chapters relative to your revision programme, though you should allow some time for glancing through the other chapters.

The topic and its key points

Again working from memory, analyse what you consider to be the key points of any topic that you have selected for particular revision. Seeing what you can recall, unaided, will help you to understand and firmly memorise the concepts involved.

Using the WorkBook

Relevant questions are provided for each topic in this book. Naturally, as typical examples of examination questions, they do not normally relate to one topic only. But the questions in each chapter *will* relate to the subject matter of the chapter to a degree. You can choose your method of consulting the questions and solutions, but here are some suggestions (strategies 1–3). Each of them presupposes that you have read through the author's notes on key points and question analysis, and any other preliminary matter, at the beginning of the chapter. Once again, you now need to practise working from *memory*, for that is the challenge you are preparing yourself for. As a rule of procedure constantly test yourself once revision starts, both orally and in writing.

Strategy 1

Strategy 1 is planned for the purpose of *quick revision*. First read your chosen question carefully and then jot down in abbreviated notes what you consider to be the main points at issue. Similarly, note the cases and statutes that occur to you as being relevant for citation purposes. Allow yourself sufficient time to cover what you feel to be relevant. Then study the author's *skeleton solution* and skim-read the *suggested solution* to see how they compare with your notes. When comparing consider carefully what the author has included (and concluded) and see whether that agrees with what you have written. Consider the points of variation also. Have you recognised the key issues? How relevant have you been? It is possible, of course, that you have referred to a recent case that *is* relevant, but which had not been reported when the WorkBook was prepared.

Strategy 2

Strategy 2 requires a nucleus of *three hours* in which to practise writing a set of examination answers in a limited time-span.

Select a number of questions (as many as are normally set in your subject in the examination you are studying for), each from a different chapter in the WorkBook, without consulting the solutions. Find a place to write where you will not be disturbed and try to arrange not to be interrupted for three hours. Write your solutions in the time allowed, noting any time needed to make up if you *are* interrupted.

After a rest, compare your answers with the *suggested solutions* in the WorkBook. There will be considerable variation in style, of course, but the bare facts should not be too dissimilar. Evaluate your answer critically. Be 'searching', but develop a positive approach to deciding how you would tackle each question on another occasion.

Strategy 3

You are unlikely to be able to do more than one three hour examination, but occasionally set yourself a single question. Vary the 'time allowed' by imagining it to be one of the questions that you must answer in three hours and allow yourself a limited preparation and writing time. Try one question that you feel to be difficult and an easier question on another occasion, for example.

Mis-use of suggested solutions

Don't try to learn by rote. In particular, don't try to reproduce the *suggested solutions* by heart. Learn to express the basic concepts in your own words.

Keeping up-to-date

Keep up-to-date. While examiners do not require familiarity with changes in the law during the three months prior to the examination, it obviously creates a good impression if you can show you are acquainted with any recent changes. Make a habit of looking through one of the leading journals – *Modern Law Review, Law Quarterly Review* or the *New Law Journal*, for example – and cumulative indices to law reports, such as the *All England Law Reports* or *Weekly Law Reports*, or indeed the daily law reports in *The Times*.

The leading law journal for the subject of Administrative Law is the *Public Law Journal.*

Journald mentioned in this WorkBook:

CLJ	Cambridge Law Journal
LQR	Law Quarterly Review
L Teach	Law Teacher Journal
MLR	Modern Law Review
NLJ	New Law Journal
PL	Public Law

(B) EXAMINATION SKILLS

Examiners are human too!

The process of answering an examination question involves a *communication* between you and the person who set it. If you were speaking face to face with the person, you would choose your verbal points and arguments carefully in your reply. When writing, it is all too easy to forget *the human being who is awaiting the reply* and simply write out what one knows in the area of the subject! Bear in mind it is a person whose question you are responding to, throughout your essay. This will help you to avoid being irrelevant or long-winded.

The essay question

Candidates are sometimes tempted to choose to answer essay questions because they 'seem' easier. But the examiner is looking for thoughtful work and will not give good marks for superficial answers.

The essay-type of question may be either purely factual, in asking you to *explain the meaning* of a certain doctrine or principle, or it may ask you to *discuss* a certain proposition, usually derived from a quotation. In either case, the approach to the answer is the same. A clear programme must be devised to give the examiner the meaning or significance of the doctrine, principle or proposition and its origin in common law, equity or statute, and cases which illustrate its application to the branch of law concerned.

The problem question

The problem-type question requires a different approach. You may well be asked to advise a client or merely discuss the problems raised in the question. In either case, the most important factor is to take great care in reading the question. By its nature, the question will be longer than the essay-type question and you will have a number of facts to digest. Time spent in analysing the question may well save time later, when you are endeavouring to impress on the examiner the considerable extent of your basic legal knowledge. The quantity of knowledge is itself a trap and you must always keep within the boundaries of the question in hand. It is very tempting to show the examiner the extent of your knowledge of your subject, but if this is outside the question, it is time lost and no marks earned. It it inevitable that some areas which you have studied and revised will not be the subject of questions, but under no circumstances attempt to adapt a question to a stronger area of knowledge at the expense of relevance.

When you are satisfied that you have grasped the full significance of the problem-type question, set out the fundamental principles involved. You may well be asked to advise one party, but there is no reason why you should not introduce your answer by:

'I would advise A on the following matters ...'

and then continue the answer in a normal impersonal form. This is a much better technique than answering the question as an imaginary conversation.

You will then go on to identify the fundamental problem, or problems posed by the question. This should be followed by a consideration of the law which is relevant to the problem. The source of the law, together with the cases which will be of assistance in solving the problem, must then be considered in detail.

Very good problem questions are quite likely to have alternative answers, and in advising A you should be aware that alternative arguments may be available. Each stage of your answer, in this case, will be based on the argument or arguments considered in the previous stage, forming a conditional sequence.

If, however, you only identify one fundamental problem, do not waste time worrying that you cannot think of an alternative – there may very well be only that one answer.

The examiner will then wish to see how you use your legal knowledge to formulate a case and how you apply that formula to the problem which is the subject of the question. It is this positive approach which can make answering a problem question a high mark earner for the student who has fully understood the question and clearly argued his case on the established law.

Examination checklist

1 Read the instructions at the head of the examination carefully. While last-minute changes are unlikely – such as the introduction of a *compulsory question* or *an increase in the number of questions asked* – it has been known to happen.

2 Read the questions carefully. Analyse problem questions – work out what the examiner wants.

3 Plan your answer *before* you start to write. You can divide your time as follows:

   (a) working out the question (5 per cent of time)

   (b) working out how to answer the question (5 to 10 per cent of time)

   (c) writing your answer

Do not overlook (a) and (b)

4 Check that you understand the rubric *before* you start to write. Do not 'discuss', for example, if you are specifically asked to 'compare and contrast'.

5 Answer the correct number of questions. If you fail to answer one out of four questions set you lose 25 per cent of your marks!

Style and structure

Try to be clear and concise. Basically this amounts to using paragraphs to denote the sections of your essay, and writing simple, straightforward sentences as much as possible. The sentence you have just read has 22 words – when a sentence reaches 50 words it becomes difficult for a reader to follow.

Do not be inhibited by the word 'structure' (traditionally defined as giving an essay a beginning, a middle and an end). A good structure will be the natural consequence of setting out your arguments and the supporting evidence in a logical order. Set the scene briefly in your opening paragraph. Provide a clear conclusion in your final paragraph.

Table of Cases

Table of Statutes

Rules of the Supreme Court

Regulations

1 Introduction to Administrative Law

1.1 Introduction

Administrative law determines the organisation, powers and duties of administrative authorities and is essentially concerned with controlling the manner in which public authorities exercise their functions. The heart of the subject is judicial review of administrative action, although some control is exercised by parliamentary institutions. It is through the development of common law principles that the doctrine of ultra vires has become a constitutional fundamental in preventing misuse of public power.

The doctrine of ultra vires is the product of the constitutional doctrines of the sovereignty of Parliament and the rule of law. The judges presume that Parliament intends in every statute conferring discretionary power that such power should not be unfettered or uncontrollable, for otherwise its own sovereignty would be imperilled. The rule of law encourages judges to exercise vigilance in reviewing the exercise of wide discretionary power so as to safeguard individual rights.

The inevitable tension between the doctrines of parliamentary supremacy and the rule of law has resulted in academic and judicial debate over the precise scope of the doctrine of ultra vires. Whilst it is generally agreed that the ultra vires rule is concerned with review of the legality of public decisions, rather than with an appeal on the merits of such decisions, there is a conflict of opinion over whether review should be primarily concerned with ensuring the protection of human rights through effective challenges to the decisions of public bodies (the 'red light theory'), or whether review should be exercised upon the primary consideration that public bodies need protection from unnecessary numerous challenges in order to ensure efficient public administration (the 'green light theory').

The red light theory contends that judges should be activists in developing liberal grounds of review so as to safeguard human rights from the many varieties of misuse of public power. Red light theorists concede that such development of the common law might blur the distinction between review and appeal by allowing judges to come closer to examining the merits of administrative decisions. They argue that such development of common law principles is essential in the absence of a modern Bill of Rights to control an over-powerful executive.

A red light approach to review requires the judge to take a 'hard look' at the quality of the decision being challenged and to require the public body to demonstrate a substantively rational decision based on moral and ethical values. Supporters of the red light theory argue that such an approach is essential where fundamental rights are under threat from executive action.

The green light theory contends that the judiciary must permit the executive to enjoy a wide measure of discretion in order to provide efficient services to the community in a modern welfare state. The executive should be given the go-ahead by the judges to make generous use of discretionary power without the fear of constant challenges in the courts. The interests of the individual or group of individuals who is or are adversely affected by administrative action must give way to the collective public interest in ensuring that the business of administration is not brought to a standstill. The green light theory is favoured by constitutional purists because it emphasises the supremacy of Parliament and the separation of law from politics. It also finds favour with some judges as a means of ensuring that the floodgates are not opened to applications for review which might exhaust scarce judicial resources.

A third approach to judicial review, sometimes described as the 'amber light' approach, may occur where a judge treats judicial review as context-based in order to vary the scope of review according to the pragmatic demands of the case before him rather than according to fixed principles. For further discussion of the theoretical basis of judicial review see Harlow and Rawlings, *Law and Administration: Text and Materials* (2nd edn 1997), chapters 1 and 2.

1.2 Key points

a) Administrative law is mainly concerned with procedures and judicial review. It does not include the substantive law produced by state agencies such as housing law, social security law or immigration law. However, it is concerned with the manner in which discretionary power in these and other fields is exercised, and with the effectiveness of judicial review generally.

   There has been a tendency for some judges to adopt a green light approach to applications for judicial review in the field of social welfare law, apparently on the ground that the executive may have to make sensitive policy choices in situations of scarce resources, eg public housing: see *R v Hillingdon London Borough Council, ex parte Puhlhofer* [1986] 2 WLR 259; [1986] 1 ALL ER 267 (HL).

   However, even green light enthusiasts among the judiciary are reluctant nowadays to declare particular executive areas to be totally non-justiciable: see especially the growth of judicial review in the field of prerogative powers in chapter 3.

b) Judicial review is essentially concerned with review of the legality of administrative decisions, and not with exercising a form of appeal on the merits of such decisions, for otherwise the supremacy of Parliament and the separation of law from politics would be undermined. It is for Parliament to enact a Bill of Rights if one is needed, not for the judges to import one through the back door by over-zealous development of common law principles: per Lord Ackner in *R* v *Secretary of State for the Home Department, ex parte Brind* [1991] AC 696 (HL). However, red light theorists contend that the common law is capable of further evolution, for example by developing a doctrine of proportionality, and they cite Lord Diplock's dicta in *Council of Civil Service Unions* v *Minister for the Civil Service* [1985] AC 374 (HL).

c) Historically English administrative law has been much influenced by Dicey's view (1885) that the rule of law requires that public and private law should be treated as if they were the same, with the consequence that public bodies are answerable to the same system of courts as the private citizen. By way of contrast, in continental countries such as France a separate system of public law courts exists to adjudicate on public law disputes between citizen and state. English administrative law may be moving in that direction through the continuing development of general principles of judicial review and as a result of the creation of a special and exclusive procedure for dealing with pure public law applications in the Divisional Court of the Queen's Bench Division of the High Court: RSC O.53 and s31 Supreme Court Act 1981. Modern supporters of Dicey oppose such developments as a threat to the Rule of Law, eg Harlow 'Public and Private Law: Definition without Distinction' (1980) 43 MLR 241.

d) 'Public law' may be defined as the system which ensures the proper performance by public bodies of the duties which they owe to the public. 'Private law' may be defined as the system which protects the private rights of private individuals or the private rights of public bodies. A dispute involving purely public law must be brought under O.53 procedures: *O'Reilly* v *Mackman* [1983] 2 AC 237 (HL), as interpreted in *Roy* v *Kensington and Chelsea and Westminster Family Practitioner Committee* [1992] 1 All ER 705 (HL). The distinction between public law and private law has been justified as being in the public interest, eg Lord Woolf 'Public Law – Private Law: Why the Divide? A Personal View' [1986] PL 220.

e) The denial of the existence of public law by Dicey inhibited the growth of the subject to such a degree that in 1964 Lord Reid declared that England still had no developed system of administrative law: *Ridge* v *Baldwin* [1964] AC 40 (HL). However, the rapid development of the common law throughout the 1960s and 1970s led Lord Diplock to declare in 1982 that the progress towards a comprehensive system of administrative law was the greatest achievement of the judges during his judicial lifetime: *IRC* v *National Federation of Self-Employed and Small Businesses* [1982] AC 617 (HL). The developments included:

   i) the evolution of natural justice into a general duty on administrators to act fairly: *Ridge* v *Baldwin* [1964] AC 40;

   ii) the birth of the doctrine of legitimate expectation: *Schmidt* v *Secretary of State for Home Affairs* [1969] 2 Ch 149;

   iii) the formulation of a new, rational concept of ultra vires which led to the effective abandonment of the artificial doctrine of error of law on the face of the record and the equally artificial distinction between jurisdictional and non-jurisdictional error, with the result that today all errors of law are jurisdictional and subject to review: *Anisminic Ltd* v *Foreign Compensation Commission* [1969] 2 AC 147 (HL), as explained in *Page* v *Hull University Visitor* [1993] 1 All ER 97 (HL);

   iv) a new, robust approach to the interpretation of statutory exclusion clauses so as to prevent the exercise of unfettered discretion: *Padfield* v *Minister of Agriculture* [1968] AC 997 and *Anisminic*, above;

   v) the reinterpretation of the rules on remedies so as to liberate them from old procedural limitations and to render them effective weapons in the battle against abuse of power, eg by allowing certiorari to be granted to quash an administrative decision by removing the rule that it lay only against a body with a duty to act judicially: *Ridge* v *Baldwin*, above;

   vi) the evolution of Crown privilege into public interest immunity so as to prevent the Crown claiming an exclusive, unchallengeable right to suppress evidence that might be needed by litigants in their quest for justice: *Conway* v *Rimmer* [1968] AC 910 (HL).

These developments led Lord Denning to declare in 1971 that 'it may truly now be said that we have a developed system of administrative law': *Breen* v *AEU* [1971] 2 QB 175.

f) The development of administrative law continued throughout the 1980s, notably with Lord Diplock's re-classification of the grounds of ultra vires in *Council of Civil Service Unions* v *Minister for the Civil Service* [1985] AC 374. During the 1990s there has also been a noticeable trend toward relaxing the locus standi test so as to permit challenges by individuals or interest groups with a sincere concern for public interest questions: *R* v *Secretary of State for Foreign and Commonwealth Affairs, ex parte Rees-Mogg* [1994] 2 WLR 115; *R* v *Inspectorate of Pollution, ex parte Greenpeace Ltd (No 2)* [1994] 4 All ER 329; and *R* v *Secretary of State for Foreign and Commonwealth Affairs, ex parte World Development Movement* [1995] 1 All ER 611.

1.3 Recent cases and articles

The following case illustrates the contrast between the red light and green light approaches to judicial review.

R v *Cambridge District Health Authority, ex parte B* [1995] 2 All ER 129 – a girl of 10 suffering from leukaemia was refused further medical treatment on the grounds that the likelihood of a successful recovery was very small (about 10 per cent), that the treatment itself would cause her great suffering, and that the total cost of the treatment was £75,000 which was too much to bear in the light of other demands on medical services. At first instance in the Queen's Bench Division, Laws J quashed the Health Authority's decision. He laid emphasis on the need to protect fundamental human rights, in this case the right to life. The failure of the Authority to consult the girl's parents as to whether she ought to undergo the risk of treatment was significant. Further, where life was at stake 'the responsible authority had to do more than toll the bell of tight resources'. This judgment can be described as a 'red light' judgment because the judge took a 'hard look' at the quality of the decision being challenged.

However, on the immediate appeal to the Court of Appeal the decision of Laws J was reversed. Sir Thomas Bingham MR (at pp136a–137f especially) gave a 'green light' judgment in which he expressed sympathy for the difficult and agonising judgments that medical authorities had to make in such cases. On the facts he found that although the girl's parents had not been directly consulted, the Authority was well aware of their views and had not disregarded them in coming to its decision. Further, the costs factor was a very relevant one because in an imperfect world of finite resources priorities had to be set and it was not for the courts of law to substitute their views on such questions for those of the responsible authority:

'the courts are not ... arbiters as to the merits of cases of this kind. Were we to express opinions as to the likelihood of the effectiveness of medical treatment, or as to the merits of medical judgment, then we would be straying far from the sphere which under our constitution is accorded to us. We have one function only, which is to rule upon the lawfulness of decisions. That is a function to which we should strictly confine ourselves' (at p136b).

See further chapter 11 for the traditional *Wednesbury* unreasonableness test used in this case.

The following articles analyse the decision in *R v Cambridge DHA, ex parte B*, above:

Brown, '*ex parte B*' (1995) 29 L Teach 365

James and Longley, 'Judicial Review and Tragic Choices: *ex parte B*' [1995] PL 367

Morgan, 'Reasons for Decisions: *ex parte B*' [1995] NLJ 428

Mullender, 'Judicial Review and the Rule of Law: *ex parte B*' (1996) 112 LQR 182

Parkin, '*ex parte B*' (1995) 58 MLR 867

The following articles explore the implications of judicial review for parliamentary sovereignty and the separation of powers:

Forsyth, 'Of Fig Leaves and Fairy Tales: the Ultra Vires Doctrine, the Sovereignty of Parliament and Judicial Review' [1996] CLJ 122

Gordon, 'The New Sovereigns?' [1995] NLJ 529

Lord Irvine, 'Judges and Decision-makers: the Theory and Practice of *Wednesbury* Review', [1996] PL 59

Sir John Laws, 'Law and Democracy' [1995] PL 72

Lord Woolf, 'Droit Public – English Style' [1995] PL 57

The following article contains a useful discussion of the 'margin of appreciation' doctrine:

Jones, 'The Development of Human Rights under the European Convention of Human Rights' [1995] PL 430 at 445–449

The following article contains an analysis of the general impact of judicial review:

Richardson and Sunkin, 'Judicial Review: Questions of Impact' [1996] PL 79

1.4 Analysis of questions

Usually essay-type questions are set requiring conceptual analysis of the foundations of public law and judicial review, in particular of the distinctions between appeal and review. In recent years questions have been set directly on the red light and green light theories and require a critical analysis of the scope of review, the objectives of the ultra vires doctrine, and the functions of the judge when exercising a review jurisdiction. A knowledge of the historical background, the influence of Dicey, and of the modern expansion of public law is essential to tackling such questions. Ability to identify the landmark cases is also important. The general themes covered in this chapter run throughout this syllabus, so that later questions on specific subject areas may also require an account of the concepts behind the legal rules.

1.5 Questions

QUESTION ONE

Assess the usefulness of 'red light' and 'green light' theories in explaining the constitutional dimension of administrative law.

University of London LLB Examination
(for External Students) Administrative Law June 1994 Q1

General Comment

This question concerns the structure and content of administrative law. Should administrative law focus upon the principles of judicial review, or should it take a broader view of the different ways in which administrative power is conferred, exercised and controlled? How adequate are the different types of theory in describing and explaining administrative law? The constitutional dimension of administrative law relates to the way in which powers are conferred upon inferior bodies and the justification for the courts' interference in the decisions of those bodies. This requires familiarity with the concepts of parliamentary sovereignty and the rule of law. (Recommended reading on this question includes P P Craig, *Administrative Law* (3rd edn, 1994), chapter 1, and Harlow and Rawlings, *Law and Administration* (2nd edn 1997), chapters 1 and 2).

Skeleton Solution

- Narrow 'red light' theories summarised:
  - parliamentary sovereignty;
  - rule of law;
  - ultra vires.
- The inadequacy of 'red light' theories.
- 'Green light' theories – the need for a broader approach.
- Difficulties with the 'green light' approach.
- Judicial review as the basis of administrative law.

Suggested Solution

It has been said that administrative law 'is about power and its allocation' (P P Craig, *Administrative Law*). 'Red light' and 'green light' theories are attempts to describe the limits of administrative law and its content in relation to the allocation of power and the way in which the exercise of power is controlled. The steady expansion of administrative law throughout this century, coupled with fundamental tensions at the heart of the British constitutional system, means that it is extremely difficult for any one theory to explain adequately all of the many facets of administrative law.

Traditional theories tend to adopt a narrow approach to describing administrative law. These 'red light' theories focus upon judicial review as the principal means of control over the exercise of power, and as the main source and expression of administrative law. According to such theories, administrative law is really concerned with the general principles governing judicial intervention in administrative action. Justification for such a narrow focus is based upon Diceyan models of parliamentary sovereignty and the rule of law. These models justify judicial review in relation to the manner in which power is allocated.

One consequence of parliamentary sovereignty is that all power flows from and is regulated by Parliament. Thus inferior bodies only enjoy those powers conferred upon them by Parliament, and those powers will be necessarily limited. A particular body will only have jurisdiction over a certain area of public life, and it will only be able to exercise its powers in certain circumstances. For example, a particular body may be given responsibility for health, or for transport, or for education. The exercise of its powers will be dependent upon certain criteria which must be fulfilled before those powers may be exercised. It should be noted that this description of the allocation of power instinctively disapproves of broad discretions and prefers powers to be subject to more or less precise rules. This description also concentrates upon statutory powers; it does not recognise the existence of power other than that flowing from Parliament.

The rule of law requires that all inferior bodies be subject to the ordinary law of the land, and thus that there be the possibility of judicial scrutiny of the legality of their actions. The justification for judicial review lies in the notion that the judiciary are giving effect to parliamentary sovereignty by ensuring that inferior bodies neither exceed the limits of their powers nor usurp powers that have not been conferred upon them. This notion finds its expression in the doctrine of ultra vires, which, according to 'red light' theories, is the heart and soul of administrative law. These theories adopt a narrow, generalist approach, assuming that the content of administrative law can be described in terms of a set of principles of judicial review applicable to all inferior bodies.

It is clear from the case law that the ultra vires principle is indeed the foundation for judicial intervention. The cases also contain many references to jurisdiction and parliamentary intention. It might be thought then that 'red light' theories are correct in focusing so narrowly upon judicial review as the source of administrative law. But such theories provide an inadequate description and explanation of the way in which public power is allocated, expressed and controlled. Hence it may be argued that what is required is a broader 'green light' theory which takes account of all of the expressions of public power and the various means of controlling it, and which adopts a more specific approach to the various organisations involved.

The inadequacy of 'red light' theories as a description of administrative law in a modern democratic state arises in part from their foundation upon the Diceyan traditions of constitutional law. The description of power-allocation inherent in such traditions is naive and inaccurate. For a number of reasons, it cannot be said that all power flows from Parliament. Within the British democratic system, the government, or executive, will invariably be able effectively to dominate Parliament. Thus, in a very real sense, the origins of power lie in the heart of the executive. The allocation of power may also be a matter of purely executive intent. Powers may be conferred on a particular branch of the executive that enable it to make delegated legislation. Some delegated legislation may be far-reaching and yet may not be adequately scrutinised by Parliament.

Furthermore, as has been pointed out, there is a tendency to devolution inherent in the increasing privatisation of large public organisations (Fredman and Morris [1994] PL 69). Such devolution effectively places power in the hands of private companies, in other words in the hands of their shareholders and directors, although they may be subject to statutory regulation. There is, then, an increase in the administration of public duties by private bodies on the basis of market principles (P P Craig, *Administrative Law,* chapter 1). On other occasions, a private body may acquire powers as a result of a bargain made with the executive for the express purpose of evading parliamentary control through legislation (for instance, *R* v *Panel on Take-overs and Mergers, ex parte Datafin plc* (1987)). Private bodies in the form of pressure groups may also have a more or less strong influence on the formation of policy by the executive; this influence may then find its way into the legislative process, and may be in some ways more determinative of the exercise of Parliament's power than the participation of citizens through their MPs.

If 'red light' theories break down in their description of the allocation of power, they are also inadequate in their analysis of its control. One reason for this is that the failure of the theory to explain the origins of power also casts doubt upon the justification for judicial intervention. How can the courts be said to be implementing parliamentary intention when such intention is not even apparent in the powers possessed by a particular body, as in the *Datafin* case? Even on occasions where the courts have been faced with express parliamentary intention, in the form of legislation purporting to oust the jurisdiction of the courts while conferring broad discretion on a particular body, the courts have used the ultra vires doctrine to evade that express intention (for instance, *Anisminic Ltd* v *Foreign Compensation Commission* (1969)). This places strain on the traditional or 'red light', view that accords supremacy to the notion of the judiciary applying general principles so as to enforce parliamentary intentions.

Furthermore, just as public powers may be acquired and exercised in a variety of ways, some of which operate independently of Parliament, so their exercise may be controlled in a variety of ways. 'Green light' theories suggest that administrative law should look at the whole picture of the exercise and control of public powers. The 'green light' description of administrative law shifts the focus away from a general list of principles of judicial review towards more specific, or functionalist, considerations. Rather than assuming that the same principles are appropriate to every kind of decision, the administrative lawyer needs to look closely at each type of decision to determine what specific principles apply to that decision. Entirely different considerations will apply to decisions in the sphere of immigration and decisions in the sphere of town planning. These considerations all form part of the content of administrative law. Thus there is a need to analyse the workings of different tribunals, inquiries, government and local government departments, pressure groups and corporate bodies in order to produce an adequate description of administrative law.

These 'green light' theories have merit. They recognise the diversity of administrative law, and its expansionist tendencies. They adopt a useful pragmatic stance, which moves away from the inadequate assumptions of nineteenth century constitutional lawyers. But the difficulty they present is that there is no theoretical limit to the expansion of administrative powers or to the different ways in which decisions may be made. A 'green light' description of administrative law must be assembled, piecemeal, by a lengthy process of investigation. But at the end of the day, such investigation may be unnecessary. It is submitted that it is more worthwhile to search for the common elements of the different kinds of administration body. One thing that nearly all such bodies have in common, despite their diversity, is that they are subject to the principles of legality, reasonableness and procedural fairness laid down by the courts. Although 'red light' theories are flawed in their assumptions about the allocation and control of power, they are right to place judicial review at the centre of their description of administrative law. The truth of the matter is that neither of the theories presents an entirely adequate description of administrative law, but that is not surprising given the rapid expansion of public administration that has been noted.

QUESTION TWO

In what manner and to what extent does Judicial Review of administrative action uphold the sovereignty of Parliament?

University of London LLB Examination
(for External Students) Constitutional Law June 1993 Q7

General Comment

Essentially the question requires detailed conceptual analysis of judicial review. Do the grounds for review undermine sovereignty and legitimate executive discretion? There is a wealth of case law available to illustrate the discussion, but it is probably sensible to concentrate on two or three leading cases in order to demonstrate depth of knowledge and research. This is an area which requires specialist study and a student will fail if he or she indulges in general waffle or superficial analysis. Reference should be made in the solution to specialist texts or articles in order to satisfy the examiner that the student has looked at appropriate sources.

Skeleton Solution

- The red light and green light concepts of judicial review explained and defined.
- Reasons for the predominance of the green light approach among the judiciary.
- The established grounds of review and their emphasis on procedure rather than substance.
- Lord Denning's attempts to broaden the scope of judicial review in defence of individuals.
- Jurisdictional error.
- Proportionality.
- Conclusions.

Suggested Solution

The rapid development of the principles of judicial review over the last 40 years has been marked by a continuing debate as to how far judges should go in controlling the exercise of administrative discretion and in protecting the rights of citizens against the ever-growing power of the state. Those who subscribe to the 'red light theory' of judicial review contend that judges must become activist in putting a stop to the misuse of executive power, so that grounds of judicial review should be drawn liberally and widely to encompass not only all sources of state or public power but also to permit examination of the content and manner of public decision-making. Those who subscribe to the 'green light theory' argue that judges must respect parliamentary delegation of executive discretion even where it is couched in very wide terms; in this way judges would be giving the go-ahead to the executive to provide community services in an efficient and effective manner.

When one examines judgments in some of the leading cases of judicial review in the last four decades it is apparent that the majority of judges have followed a 'green light' approach and consequently adopted a carefully restricted role for judicial review, probably because of their sensitivity to the delicate constitutional relationship between Parliament, the executive and the judiciary. Respect for parliamentary sovereignty and the separate functions of administrator and judge have deterred judges from entangling themselves in what in essence are political or administrative decisions dressed up in legal clothing. Such an approach has been criticised as too timid in defence of individual rights by red light theorists, but it has been applauded by Diceyan followers of the Rule of Law, sovereignty and the traditional constitutional boundaries between law and politics.

Typical of the green light approach is Lord Brightman's dictum that 'judicial review is concerned not with the decision but with the decision-making process ... unless that restriction on the power of the court is observed, the court will ... under the guise of preventing the abuse of power be itself guilty of usurping power': *Chief Constable of North Wales Police* v *Evans* (1982).

The established classification of the grounds of judicial review (procedural impropriety, illegality and irrationality: per Lord Diplock in *CCSU* v *Minister for the Civil Service* (the GCHQ case) (1984) therefore puts the emphasis on review of procedural decision-making rather than the merits, policy or wisdom of the decisions themselves. As Sir John Laws commented:

'... "substance" may be said to be "hands off"; "procedure" is definitely "hands on". This distinction reflects a constitutional awareness that the power and responsibility of making decisions on their merits is given by Parliament not to the courts but to the Executive ...

Interference with substantive decisions usurps the democratic element in our constitution' ([1989] PL 27 at p29).

Such an approach can be further supported by the argument that other checks exist on the exercise of political and executive power which may be more appropriate than the formal judicial process, eg MPs and the Select Committee system; Ombudsmen; tribunals and inquiries, etc. However, red light theorists contend that there can be no substitute for independent judicial review as a safeguard for the citizen against misuse of public power and discretion, and among the minority of judges who subscribed to this view probably the most famous was Lord Denning when Master of the Rolls in the period 1962–82. Some of his judgments became landmarks for their attempts to widen the scope of judicial review into (from some perspectives) almost an appellate process. Some of the landmarks did not stand for long, eg his attempt to abolish the distinction between jurisdictional error of law and error of fact made by courts of law, such as the High Court and county courts: rebuffed by the House of Lords in *Re Racal Communications Ltd* (1980), which restated and explained the law on excess of jurisdiction laid down by the *Anisminic* case (*Anisminic Ltd* v *Foreign Compensation Commission* (1969)).

Other Denning judgments lasted longer, eg his use of the concept of proportionality as part of the traditional test of total unreasonableness to strike down a grossly excessive penalty imposed on a market trader in *R* v *Barnsley Metropolitan Borough Council, ex parte Hook* (1976). In the GCHQ case (above) Lord Diplock, in reformulating the test of unreasonableness under the test of irrationality, had doubts as to whether a test of proportionality would one day become part of English law. Those doubts were dispelled to some degree by some robust judgments in *R* v *Secretary of State for the Home Department, ex parte Brind* (1991), which upheld reporting restrictions imposed by the Government on media interviews with supporters of the Irish Republican Army. Lords Ackner and Lowry rejected a test of proportionality because it would transform judicial review into an appellate process: judges were not equipped by training, experience or expert knowledge to determine whether a Minister or other public official had stuck a proper balance, unless the decision was so grossly out of balance as to be irrational. But red light critics of such reasoning would point to the risks to freedom of the press created in the Brind case by apparent judicial reluctance to test the quality of the decision against, for example, the international standards set by the European Convention on Human Rights. The two Law Lords had taken, perhaps, an unduly restrictive approach to use of the Convention in the area of executive discretion that compares unfavourably to their more liberal use of the Convention in the areas of ambiguous statutory construction or ambiguous common law. The other three Law Lords were less hostile to the possible future introduction of proportionality as a test for review.

So until Parliament incorporates the European Convention into English law (or perhaps until the European Court of Justice does so indirectly through rulings on EC law) it seems as if judges will continue to use judicial review as a process in which they may blow the whistle when the ball goes out of play but desist from taking part in the game or from telling the players how to play when the game restarts: per Lawton LJ in the *Laker* case (*Laker Airways Ltd* v *Department of Trade* (1977)).

2 Delegated Legislation

2.1 Introduction

The use of delegated legislation to confer administrative discretion on ministers and other public officials is inevitable in a modern welfare state. It would be impossible to regulate everything by individual Acts of Parliament; there are far too many problems of detail and far too many matters which cannot be decided in advance. However, Dicey's warnings against the exercise of wide discretionary power have led to attempts to regulate such power by political control through Parliament and by judicial review through the courts.

2.2 Key points

a) The main types of delegated legislation are orders in council, statutory instruments and bye-laws. There is also a wide range of regulations, rules and directions which may or may not be put in any of those main forms. Sometimes they are found in 'quasi-law', a term which covers all sorts of administrative rule-making and guidance which, depending on the context, may or may not be legally binding, but which nevertheless is applied by officials to structure their discretionary decision-making.

b) The dangers of delegated legislation were pointed out by Dicey (1885) and Lord Hewart CJ (1929). Apart from infringing the separation of powers by allowing the executive to legislate, delegated legislation tends to authorise the use of wide discretionary power ('blank cheques') by ministers and other public officials. Lord Hewart said that delegated legislation tended 'to subordinate Parliament and evade the courts' (*The New Despotism* (1929)). These warnings led to the setting up of the Donoughmore Committee on Ministers' Powers, which reported in 1932: Cmd 4060.

c) The principal finding of the Donoughmore Report was that delegated legislation provided useful flexibility in areas of rapid change and permitted a degree of judgment and experiment to specialists. Parliament was not suited to the technicalities involved, nor was it sufficiently responsive to deal with unforeseen contingencies. The Report encouraged political and judicial supervision over the exercise of delegated power as the main safeguards for the rule of law. The Report gave a specific warning against the use of Henry VIII clauses in primary legislation, ie clauses under which ministers are given power to amend primary laws without consulting Parliament (described as similar to Henry VIII's despotic authority to legislate by decree). The Report concluded that Henry VIII clauses were 'inconsistent with the principles of parliamentary government' and 'should be abandoned in all but the most exceptional cases'. These views have been echoed by the Hansard Society Commission on the Legislative Process (the Rippon Report) 1993: 'Henry

VIII clauses are of their nature undesirable. Unless absolutely necessary a single minister should not be given power to change the law made by Parliament as a whole.'

d) The volume of delegated legislation has grown with the expansion of the administrative apparatus required to run a modern welfare state. In 1995 to 1996 approximately 8,000 statutory instruments were issued. For many years Her Majesty's Stationery Office (HMSO) has contracted out the production of statutory instruments to third parties. HMSO was privatised in 1996 and its functions are now performed by private profit-making organisations. The Statutory Instruments Act 1946 will be amended so as to confirm (retrospectively) the validity of all statutory instruments issued under the contracting out arrangements and so as to authorise the new publication arrangements. The sheer volume of modern delegated legislation and the demands of executive necessity have led to the revival of the use of Henry VIII clauses which can be found in many modern statutes, eg in the fields of local government law and social security law.

e) Parliamentary controls over delegated legislation include:

   i) negative and affirmative resolution procedures;

   ii) general debates and parliamentary questions;

   iii) scrutiny by the following Parliamentary committees:

   - the House of Commons Standing (Merits) Committee: on Statutory Instruments, which have been operating since 1973 and which examine the substantive merits of SIs;
   - the House of Commons Deregulation Orders Committee, established in 1994 to examine the vires and merits of deregulation orders;
   - the House of Lords Delegated Powers Scrutiny Committee, which has been operating since 1992 examining the vires and merits of delegated powers;
   - the Joint Committee of Commons and Lords on Statutory Instruments (the Joint Scrutiny Committee), which has been operating since 1973 examining SIs for technical defects only. Its functions in regard to deregulation orders have passed to the new Deregulation Orders Committee, above, since 1994.

It has been argued that these methods of control are weak simply because of the huge volume of delegated legislation passed each year and the pressures on parliamentary time. MPs can only scramble about on the tip of a very large iceberg. Modern legislation, especially in such fields as local government law and social security law, has become a skeletal enabling framework conferring on ministers not only the functions of detailed implementation but also the power to determine major policy questions. In *R* v *Secretary of State for Social Services, ex parte Stitt* (1990) The Times 5 July the judge expressed surprise and concern at the amount of wide discretionary power conferred on the Secretary of State to administer the system of social security benefits. It may be that recent reforms to parliamentary procedures, such as the introduction of more morning sittings, will give MPs more time to scrutinise such measures.

f) An important step to securing better publicity for delegated legislation came with the enactment of the Statutory Instruments Act 1946. The Act sets out requirements as to the laying before Parliament of statutory instruments, their issue and publication. However, the effectiveness of the Act has been undermined by conflicts of authority as to whether the requirements are mandatory (legally binding) or directory (advisory only). The balance of authority suggests that non-issue and/or non-publication will not affect the validity of the instrument in question since the Act gives a special defence to the citizen under s3(2) in the event of being prosecuted under an instrument which has not been issued and/or published, unless the Crown can show that it took reasonable steps to bring the purport of the instrument to public notice or to the notice of the citizen in question: *Blackpool Corporation* v *Locker* [1948] 1 All ER 85 and *R* v *Sheer Metalcraft Ltd* [1954] 1 QB 586.

Some authorities suggest that non-laying of an instrument before Parliament will also not affect its validity: *Bailey* v *Williamson* (1873) LR 8 QB 118, though there are contradictory dicta in *R* v *Sheer Metalcraft*, above.

Only statutory instruments are covered by the provisions of the 1946 Act. Other kinds of delegated legislation and quasi-law escape the requirements as to publicity and consequently pose a threat to the rule of law since the maxim that ignorance of the law is no excuse is based on the assumption that the law is readily accessible to every citizen, or at least to his/her legal advisers: *Blackpool Corporation* v *Locker*, above.

g) Judicial control exists over delegated legislation and, to a lesser degree, over quasi-law.

   i) Judicial control over delegated legislation

   The scope of judicial review depends on the type of delegated legislation being challenged. In regards to bye-laws and other kinds of very inferior and routine delegated legislation the normal grounds of judicial review are available, ie for procedural impropriety, illegality and irrationality (total unreasonableness): *Kruse* v *Johnson* [1898] 2 QB 91. Additional grounds for the review of bye-laws include inconsistency with the general law, vagueness and uncertainty of contents: *Kruse* v *Johnson*, above. See also *Percy* v *Hall*, section 2.3 below.

   However, in regard to statutory instruments and other kinds of delegated legislation which have been laid before Parliament and approved by a vote of MPs, the grounds for judicial review are restricted to cases of 'obvious' ultra vires (ie an instrument which on its face purports to do what is not authorised by the enabling statute), or bad faith on the part of the minister who laid the instrument before Parliament, or where the consequences of the instrument are so absurd that the minister must have taken leave of his/her senses: per Lord Scarman in *Nottinghamshire County Council* v *Secretary of State for the Environment* [1986] AC 240. However, these dicta were described as a warning on the need for judicial sensitivity in this area, rather than as a fixed rule excluding judicial scrutiny: *R* v *Secretary of State for the Home Department, ex parte Oladehinde* [1990] 3 All ER 393 (HL).

   The rules of natural justice and fairness do not apply to the making of delegated legislation in the absence of a statutory duty of consultation: per Megarry J in *Bates* v *Lord Hailsham* [1972] 1 WLR 1373 at 1378.

   If parts of an instrument or bye-law are found to be ultra vires it may be possible for the court to sever the invalid parts from the valid parts so as to enforce the latter if it can be done without altering the substance or policy of the whole instrument or bye-law, and provided that a sensible instrument or bye-law is left for enforcement: *DPP* v *Hutchinson* [1990] 2 AC 783 (HL). Similarly, if there is a statutory duty of consultation, breach may render the instrument invalid only in respect of those who should have been consulted, because the reviewing court can declare the enforceable extent of the imperfect instrument: *Agricultural, Horticultural and Forestry Industry Training Board* v *Aylesbury Mushrooms Ltd* [1972] 1 All ER 280.

ii) Judicial control over quasi-law

Examples of quasi-law include codes of practice, circulars, memoranda and special tax concessions. Judges are willing to declare a piece of quasi-law invalid and unenforceable if it is in clear conflict with primary or delegated law, eg the Secretary of State's 'guidance' to the Civil Aviation Authority in *Laker Airways Ltd* v *Department of Trade* [1977] QB 643, in which Lord Denning MR said of such guidance: 'It cannot be used so as to reverse or contradict the general objectives of the statute. It can only be used so as to explain, amplify or supplement them.' In *Gillick* v *West Norfolk and Wisbech Area Health Authority* [1986] AC 112 (HL) Lord Bridge opined that a court could grant a declaration if a circular contained wrong legal advice, even though no ultra vires might be involved because of the lack of legal force of the circular; such control was important because of the practical reliance placed on such a circular by administrators.

Provided the piece of quasi-law keeps to the function of explaining and guiding, the judges will be prepared to concede that it has a legitimate foundation for the exercise of discretionary power and, indeed, they may sometimes find grounds for enforcing it as if it were an ordinary kind of delegated legislation, eg the circular in *Coleshill and District Investment Co Ltd* v *MHLG* [1969] 2 All ER 525.

h) *The role of the Parliamentary Commissioner for Administration*

Under s5(1) of the Parliamentary Commissioner Act 1967, in order to be eligible for investigation by the Commissioner complaints must be directed against actions taken in the exercise of administrative functions. Therefore, the creation of delegated legislation is beyond his jurisdiction, though he may investigate maladministration arising out of the exercise of administrative functions under a piece of delegated legislation. It can also be argued that the making of quasi-law falls within his jurisdiction.

2.3 Recent cases

R v *Secretary of State for Social Security, ex parte Joint Council for the Welfare of Immigrants* [1996] 4 All ER 385 (CA) – the Secretary of State had made regulations in 1996 under the Social Security Contributions and Benefits Act 1992 with the aim of discouraging asylum claims by limiting the right to income support for urgent cases to those who submitted claims 'immediately' on arrival in the UK. The applicants contended that the regulations were ultra vires. *Held* (CA, Neill LJ dissenting) that the regulations were ultra vires because they conflicted with the statutory rights granted to asylum seekers under other primary legislation (the Asylum and Immigration Appeals Act 1993):

'The principle is undisputed. Subsidiary legislation must not only be so drawn as not to conflict with statutory rights enacted by other primary legislation ... the effect of the 1996 Regulations upon the vast majority [of asylum seekers] will be to leave them without even the most basic means of subsistence. The stark question that has, therefore, to be answered is whether [such] regulations ... have the effect of rendering their ostensible statutory right [under the 1993 Act] to a proper consideration of their claims in this country valueless in practice by making it not merely difficult, but totally impossible for them to remain here to pursue those claims ... the answer to the question, when it is so expressed, can only, in my view, be Yes' (per Waite LJ at p402).

Simon Brown, LJ, observed (at p399 a–b):

'Specific statutory rights are not to be cut down by subordinate legislation passed under the vires of a different Act'.

Simon Brown LJ went on to describe the regulations as 'uncompromisingly draconian' and likely to result in a life for asylum seekers that was 'so destitute that no civilised nation could contemplate it.'

Comment: The strong condemnation of the regulations might be seen as another example of a 'red light' approach by the judiciary and a further challenge by the judiciary to the omnipotence of Parliament, since the regulations had been approved by Parliament and strongly defended by the Secretary of State at the time of their making.

Percy v *Hall* [1996] 4 All ER 523 (CA) – the plaintiffs had been arrested on numerous occasions for trespassing on Ministry of Defence land contrary to 1986 bye-laws. They sued the arresting officers for wrongful arrest, contending that the bye-laws were invalid for uncertainty and therefore provided no defence. *Held* the bye-laws were not void for uncertainty, and that even if they had been void the arresting officers would not have been deprived of the defence of lawful justification if they could show that they were acting in the reasonable belief that the plaintiffs were committing a bye-law offence. The Court of Appeal compared two common law approaches to the issue of invalidity on the ground of uncertainty. In *Kruse* v *Johnson* [1898] 2 QB 91 it had been said that a bye-law would be invalid if it did not contain adequate information as to the duties of those who were required to obey it, but in *Fawcett Properties Ltd* v *Buckinghamshire County Council* [1961] AC 636; [1960] 3 All ER 503 it was said that mere ambiguity was not sufficient and that the court should not set aside the instrument unless it was impossible to give it any sensible meaning. This latter approach was preferred by the Court of Appeal. Simon Brown LJ observed (at p537c):

'... so long as in certain circumstances an offence will undoubtedly be committed, bye-laws should (subject to any issues of severance such as arose in *Hutchinson*) be upheld and to that extent enforced.'

2.4 Analysis of questions

It is often assumed by examiners that delegated legislation, as a topic, is open to examination in first year constitutional law examination papers and therefore it is irregularly examined on its own in administrative law. Instead questions on the grounds for judicial review are often set in the context of the exercise of delegated law and discretionary powers. Occasionally the topic of quasi-law comes up for scrutiny.

2.5 Questions

QUESTION ONE

In addition to Acts of Parliament and statutory instruments the following methods of promulgating general principles of conduct are now being commonly used:

a) Codes of practice;

b) Circulars and memoranda of government departments;

c) Bye-laws.

Describe these methods and give examples of each of them.

Compare the effect of each with that of Acts of Parliament and statutory instruments.

University of London LLB Examination
(for External Students) Administrative Law June 1986 Q5

General Comment

Each matter is best dealt with separately under its own heading. Care should be taken to differentiate between the different measures and, where possible, to provide examples.

Skeleton Solution

- Character of codes of practice – examples of such codes – advantages – justiciability and judicial control.
- Character of circulars and the like – examples – justiciability.
- Character of bye-laws – political and judicial controls.

Suggested Solution

The traditional method by which change is promulgated by government is through legislation, primary legislation and delegated legislation. There may be a number of reasons why, in any given case, use of these traditional methods is inconvenient or inappropriate; hence the use of codes, circulars, and by-laws, each of which will now be considered in turn.

a) *Codes of practice*

A code of practice, in very general terms, is a guide as to how certain individuals or other legal bodies are to conduct themselves or their business. A code will normally be drawn up by civil servants acting at the behest of a minister, and its existence will be publicised amongst those likely to be affected, by the relevant government department.

Interested parties may be consulted before codes of practice are finalised.

Many examples of codes of practice can be found. The most well known must be the Highway Code, issued now under the Transport Act 1982. Unlike some other codes of practice, the Highway Code must be approved by Parliament. The Police and Criminal Evidence Act 1984 introduced sweeping reforms of police powers and arrested persons' rights in detention. Under many provisions of this Act, police officers are given discretion as to how they should proceed in any given case. A code of conduct has been drawn up by the Secretary of State indicating how and on what grounds such discretion should be exercised.

It can be seen that codes of practice are useful administrative tools in that they allow legislators to draft primary legislation in broad terms, leaving the more subtle aspects of the aims and objects of the legislation to be promulgated through the code of practice. Codes are also more flexible, in that they may be easier to update than primary or delegated legislation, and they certainly have the advantage of being written in an easily comprehended, non-technical style, to the benefit of those readers without any legal expertise.

Unlike primary or delegated legislation codes of practice have no judicial status, and thus cannot be cited as the source of rights or duties, but may be referred to by a decision maker as a relevant consideration to be taken into account before the exercise of a discretion. The Highway Code does not impose criminal or civil liability if its provisions are breached, but it can be cited in evidence in legal proceedings to establish what constitutes good and bad road behaviour.

A further point of comparison is that unlike the procedure for enacting primary legislation, or the laying procedures for delegated legislation, no set procedure exists whereby Parliament is enabled to scrutinize and comment upon codes of practice before they are published; should any procedure be required it will be prescribed in the relevant enabling Act.

It is trite law that an Act of Parliament cannot be declared invalid by the courts (see *British Railways Board* v *Pickin* (1974)).

Delegated legislation, on the other hand, can be declared ultra vires its parent Act. Codes of practice may be declared ultra vires on similar grounds, particularly if they purport to impose a financial burden, or interfere with private property rights.

b) *Circulars and memoranda of government departments*

The distinction between circulars and codes of practice is not always clear. Both are extra-statutory, and both are intended to explain in less technical language the way in which other statutory provisions should be implemented. One possible distinction is that circulars are much more narrowly targeted than codes of practice and deal with much more specific points, as may become clearer from consideration of the examples below.

Some circulars simply contain information that central government considers those affected ought to have; others may be used to explain, in general terms, the effect of recently enacted legislation. Frequently circulars are issued by government departments indicating the current central government policy on a particular topic. In the sphere of town and country planning, the Department of the Environment makes frequent use of circulars to indicate its view to local planning authorities on matters such as the imposition of conditions on grants of planning permission.

Other notes, bulletins and memoranda of government departments may perform functions very similar to that of circulars, albeit on a rather more ad hoc basis. Frequently there is little more in the distinction than a matter of nomenclature. Under this heading one might even include advertisements placed by government departments, for example, warning parents of the dangers of certain medicines when given to children.

In theory circulars differ from primary and secondary legislation in that they have no legal status, but in a number of decisions the courts have regarded circulars as if they had the force of delegated legislation, in that they could confer powers and impose duties, see *Jackson Stanfield & Sons Ltd* v *Butterworth* (1948), *Blackpool Corporation* v *Locker* (1948). Circulars are certainly regarded by the courts as relevant considerations in the exercise of statutory powers: see *Bristol District Council* v *Clark* (1975).

c) *Bye-laws*

The power to create bye-laws is conferred upon bodies such as local authorities, or nationalised industries, so that they can introduce specific controls, creating criminal liability in the event of breach; and which are of limited geographical application. Bye-laws have more in common with delegated legislation that any other administrative procedure considered above; they can give rise to legal obligations, and can be challenged in the courts on grounds very similar to those upon which delegated legislation may be challenged. These grounds include substantive ultra vires, uncertainty and unreasonableness. Whereas delegated legislation emanates from the minister and may then be subject to parliamentary scrutiny, bye-laws usually emanate from the promoting body that has been given the power to draw them up, after which the proposed bye-laws will then be subject to ministerial approval. The precise procedure for issuing bye-laws will depend on the enabling Act. Similar to delegated legislation, bye-laws are subject to publicity requirements. Examples of bye-laws would be those drawn up by local authorities relating to the use of public parks.

QUESTION TWO

'The adequacy of Parliamentary scrutiny of primary and secondary legislation is defective. Procedural reform is urgently needed.'
Discuss.

University of London LLB Examination
(for External Students) Constitutional Law June 1993 Q5

General Comment

A straightforward question but one involving a considerable amount of material, so selectivity of issues for discussion is important. Equal emphasis should be given to primary and delegated legislation; it is tempting for students to revise only one of these areas and hence produce a one-sided approach. Such a question should be attempted only if the student is confident of having enough material to produce a balanced and critical analysis.

Skeleton Solution

- Control of primary legislation by the Executive.
- Effect of whips and patronage.
- Uses of the guillotine.
- Weaknesses of parliamentary control.
- Proposals of the Hansard Society.
- Critical evaluation.
- Types of delegated legislation and weaknesses of parliamentary control.
- Special problem of EC legislation.
- Threats to the rule of law.
- Conclusions.

Suggested Solution

In regard to primary legislation the Executive controls business not only by setting a general timetable for discussing Bills but also the length of debates on individual issues through the use of its (in normal times) party majority to ensure the closure, guillotining or adjournment of debates. The control extends beyond the debating chamber to the Standing Committees in which Bills are scrutinised line by line. The effect of the whip and patronage systems to ensure party loyalty enables the efficient passage of legislation but at the price of reducing the independence of action of MPs, who may be unable to object to hasty or ill-conceived measures, or even simply poorly drafted ones, because of the priority given to complying with the Government's timetable. An article by Ganz ([1990] PL 496) contains a devastating analysis of the frequency of the use of the guillotine during the 'Thatcher Years': more use was made of it than in the entire period of 1945–1979 (the Thatcher Years were May 1979 to November 1990).

In 1993 the Hansard Society, a non-party group, published proposals for reform of parliamentary procedures to ensure better examination of legislation. The price would be an agreed timetable with Opposition parties in which the latter would have to surrender their most valuable weapon, delay (filibuster) of Government proposals. It may be that the price is one an Opposition will not be prepared to pay.

Among the Hansard Commission proposals (published 3 February 1993) are pre-legislative enquiries by MPs into the preparation of Bills and evidence-taking sessions after their publication. In this way more open consultation of interested parties could take place, which should be continued at later stages with more open meetings of standing committees. For this purpose the current minimum intervals between stages of Bills should be increased and more information should be made publicly available. A two year legislative programme should be designed to replace the current one year programmes to allow greater time for drafting Bills.

Such proposals are unlikely to go down well with the Government civil service, which tends to view the passage of primary legislation like a military operation. The reforms might also be unpopular with MPs, who would be faced with more work on standing committees, stretching into mornings, evenings and weekends if all interested groups are to be heard fairly. As Peter Riddell commented:

'The trouble with proposals like those from the Hansard Society ... is that they take too idealistic a view of what MPs can, and want, to do. Most see themselves primarily as party politicians and ministerial aspirants. Only a minority regard themselves as legislators and champions of Parliament.' ((1993) The Times 3 February)

The scrutiny process is probably just as unsatisfactory when it comes to review of delegated legislation. The sheer quantity of such legislation makes it impossible for an amateurish group of 650 individuals (Speaker omitted) with other diverse responsibilities to exercise anything like detailed scrutiny of the content and effect of statutory instruments, orders in council, ministerial regulations, etc. Indeed, the flood of EC delegated laws in the form of Directives from the Council of Ministers and European Commission is so great that not even the specialist select committee of the House of Lords on the European Communities can cope with it and the Hansard Report gives warning of this. Probably a joint committee of both Houses with co-opted experts is needed. The parliamentary joint committee on domestic delegated legislation in the form of statutory instruments seems to work reasonably well, but its reports are rarely read in the whole House and MPs simply do not seem to have the time to devote to such issues. Experiments with morning sittings devoted entirely to such scrutiny have been tried and proved failures, probably because, as Riddell said in his article above, many MPs are 'too old, too idle, too maverick or too preoccupied with their constituencies or outside business interests to play an active part'.

Yet the problem of inadequate scrutiny of delegated legislation has always been a considerable one, one not to shy away from, if one follows the Diceyan attitudes on the rule of law and accepts the need for curtailment of wide executive discretion:

'There is a clear threat to parliamentary government if power is delegated to legislate on matters of general policy or if so wide a discretion is conferred that it is impossible to be sure of what limit the legislature intended to impose.' (*Wade & Bradley* (10th edn, 1985), p612)

Consequently reformers should go on trying to persuade MPs of the need to devote more time and energy to this subject and to stop providing blank cheques for the Government of the day. If MPs need more resources to do this, by way of expert researchers and other assistants, so be it. Most modern legislatures, from the American Congress to the Australian and New Zealand Parliaments, spend enormous sums on ensuring proper scrutiny of subordinate legislation: finding, Hansard Report, above.

A new Select Committee on the Scrutiny of Delegated Powers was established as an experiment by the House of Lords in 1992 to report whether the provisions of any Bill inappropriately delegate legislative power, or whether they subject the exercise of legislative power to an inappropriate degree of parliamentary scrutiny. Greater use of the second chamber as a means of scrutinising delegated legislation may therefore be a partial solution to an intractable problem.

3 Prerogative Power

3.1 Introduction

The royal prerogative is important historically as being the original source of what we would now term governmental power. Before Parliament came into existence all government power came from and was administered by the monarch. Since 'the King could do no wrong' it was the rule that the courts could not question the exercise of such prerogative power.

Some personal prerogatives are still, in theory, retained by the monarch, eg the power:

a) to award knighthoods and other honours (ie patronage);

b) to dissolve Parliament;

c) to appoint/dismiss ministers;

d) to assent to Acts of Parliament.

In practice such personal prerogatives are theoretical rather than real in the sense that today the monarch would not exercise any of them without the advice of the Prime Minister, save in exceptional circumstances, such as a hung Parliament, where the monarch may need to exercise a personal discretion in the choice of Prime Minister or in deciding whether to dissolve Parliament.

All other prerogative powers have passed to and are exercised by the government of the day and, perhaps, should more properly called executive prerogatives. These are useful instruments of executive power because decisions can be taken without the need to obtain parliamentary approval, though for this reason Dicey (1885) warned of the threat to the Rule of Law arising from extensive use of prerogative powers. Of course most of the areas of power once governed by the prerogative have now been overtaken by Acts of Parliament which take precedence over the prerogative (*Attorney-General* v *De Keyser's Royal Hotel* [1920] AC 508). Since most government power has today been given by statute, the exercise of governmental powers are controllable by the courts by way of judicial review.

But what of those areas of government power that have not been overtaken by Act of Parliament and remain, therefore, within the prerogative? Can an individual complain to the courts about the way in which such powers have been exercised? This is the most topical aspect to the prerogative and the most likely examination area.

The major areas of such executive prerogative powers today are law and order, defence and foreign affairs. Sensitive matters of law and order, foreign policy, state security and decisions of the Attorney-General on questions of public interest are probably still outside the scope of judicial review. For example in *Gouriet* v *Union of Post Office Workers* [1977] 3 All ER 70 (concerning the refusal of the Attorney-General to take civil action against post office workers refusing to sort mail going to South Africa); *China Navigation Co* v *Attorney-General* [1932] 2 KB 197 (concerning the manner in which the Government chose to protect its overseas nationals); and *Chandler* v *DPP* [1964] AC 763 (concerning the Government's nuclear defence policy) the courts felt unable to intervene.

However, the courts are naturally jealous of powers that cannot be challenged and in *BBC* v *Johns* [1965] Ch 32 the House of Lords stated that no new prerogative powers would be recognised by the courts. Indeed the 1970s onwards have seen a much more robust attitude by the courts towards the exercise of prerogative powers at least in matters of a more domestic and less sensitive nature. In *Laker Airways Ltd* v *Department of Trade* [1977] 2 All ER 182, which concerned the making of a treaty pertaining to air routes available to UK operators, Lord Denning boldly stated:

'Seeing that the prerogative is a discretionary power to be exercised for the public good it follows that its exercise can be examined by the courts just as any other discretionary power which is vested in the executive.'

Equating prerogative with statutory powers was going too far, but the statement illustrates the court's dislike of unfettered powers. In *CCSU* v *Minister for Civil Service* [1985] AC 374, which is usually referred to as the GCHQ case (or sometimes *CCSU* case) a majority of the Law Lords indicated, obiter, that in principle prerogative powers are justiciable and reviewable. Lord Diplock said that it was for the courts to decide on a case-by-case basis whether the area in question is one upon which the courts are competent to intervene. Subsequent case law indicates that the following factors are relevant in determining questions of justiciability and reviewability:

a) whether the matter is one of high policy more suitable for parliamentary or other extra-judicial supervision;

b) whether the court has sufficient information and expertise on the matter in issue;

c) whether there are objective standards by which to measure the exercise of the prerogative power in question; and

d) whether judicial review would inhibit government efficiency.

In the GCHQ case itself, involving a matter of national security, all the Law Lords agreed that such a matter was non-justiciable. Other similarly sensitive policy areas are likely to remain non-justiciable, eg the ratification of treaties: *R* v *Secretary of State for Foreign and Commonwealth Affairs, ex parte Rees-Mogg* [1994] 2 WLR 115; [1994] 1 All ER 457. By contrast other previously non-reviewable areas have been opened up for potential review as a result of the change of approach signalled in the GCHQ case, eg the issue of passports (*R* v *Secretary of State for Foreign and Commonwealth Affairs, ex parte Everett* [1989] 1 All ER 655), and to identify errors of laws in the exercise of the prerogative of mercy (*R v Secretary of State for the Home Department, ex parte Bentley* [1994] 2 WLR 101; [1993] 4 All ER 442). In *ex parte Bentley* Watkins LJ observed:

'The *CCSU* case made it clear that the powers of the court cannot be ousted merely by invoking the word "prerogative". The question is simply whether the nature and subject matter of the decision is amenable to the judicial process. Are the courts qualified to deal with the matter or does the decision involve such questions of policy that they should not intrude because they are ill-equipped to do so? Looked at in this way there must be cases in which the exercise of the royal prerogative is reviewable, in our judgment. If, for example, it was clear that the Home Secretary had refused to pardon someone solely on the grounds of their sex, race or religion, the courts would be expected to interfere and, in our judgment, would be entitled to do so. We conclude, therefore, that some aspects of the exercise of the royal prerogative are amenable to the judicial process. We do not think that it is necessary for us to say more than this in the instant case. It will be for other courts to decide on a case by case basis whether the matter in question is reviewable or not'.

See further section 3.3 Recent cases and articles, below, especially the distinguishing of *ex parte Bentley* in *Reckley's* v *Minister of Public Safety and Immigration (No 2)* [1996] 2 WLR 281.

3.2 Key points

It is important that students understand the following issues regarding the prerogative:

a) *Classification of the prerogative*

There are two traditional categories of prerogative:

i) Personal prerogatives being those enjoyed by the Sovereign personally;

ii) Political prerogatives being those exercised by or on the advice of the Crown.

Political prerogatives arise in both domestic and foreign affairs. In foreign affairs the exercise of the prerogative is known as Act of State and may provide a defence for the Crown to proceedings brought against it in UK courts in respect of such exercise.

b) *The effect of statute on the prerogative*

i) Parliament is supreme. A prerogative can therefore be expressly abolished or restricted by statute.

ii) The prerogative may not, however, be impliedly abolished by statute. The prerogative is merely placed in abeyance and if the statute is repealed the prerogative will be revived.

iii) If a statute conflicts with a prerogative without expressly abolishing the prerogative, the courts must give effect to the statute and treat the prerogative as being in abeyance: *Attorney-General* v *De Keyser's Royal Hotel* [1920] AC 508.

iv) A statute which conflicts with a prerogative may expressly provide that the prerogative be left intact.

v) Sometimes the court may find that although prerogative powers and statutory powers overlap in a particular case they do not precisely coincide, with the result that there is no conflict between them and the prerogative power can therefore continue to co-exist with the relevant statutory power: *R* v *Secretary of State for the Home Department, ex parte Northumbria Police Authority* [1988] 1 WLR 356. This decision may be classified as a 'green light' one because it appears to be generously favourable to the executive.

c) *Prerogative and the courts*

Where the exercise of a prerogative directly affects the rights of an individual the courts may be asked to determine the following issues:

i) Does the prerogative claimed by the Crown exist? The courts will not recognise the existence of new prerogative powers. Only those already recognised at common law will be upheld: *BBC* v *Johns*, above.

ii) Is the official or public body concerned entitled to benefit from the prerogative?

iii) Has the existence or exercise of the prerogative in question been affected by statute?

v) What is the extent of the prerogative power?

vi) Is it a prerogative which because of its nature and subject matter the court is competent to review? The traditional approach of the courts has been that while they may consider the existence, scope and extent of the prerogative they may not go further and review the manner of the exercise of the prerogative power. However modern cases indicate a shift in favour of granting judicial review in respect of the exercise of the prerogative in certain circumstances.

3.3 Recent cases and articles

R v *Criminal Injuries Compensation Board, ex parte P* [1995] 1 All ER 870 (CA) – prior to 1 October 1979 the Board had a policy of not compensating victims of crime who were continuing to live under the same roof as the perpetrator of the crime, eg a victim of domestic violence in the family home. This 'same roof rule' was modified as from 1 October 1979. The applicants argued that it was irrational and unfair to deny their applications in respect of injuries occurring before 1 October 1979. It was *held* that the denial was not irrational or unfair. The court had jurisdiction to consider the legality of the revisions to the Criminal Injuries Compensation Scheme, even though such revisions were in the exercise of prerogative functions. Neill LJ relied not only on dicta in *Council of Civil Service Unions* v *Minister for the Civil Service*, above, but also on Lord Templeman's speech in *M* v *Home Office* [1993] 3 All ER 537 (HL), from which he concluded that the courts have jurisdiction to review *all* exercises of executive functions unless the courts are expressly excluded or limited by statute from doing so. This approach represents another boost for the rule of law theory.

However, having jurisdiction and exercising it are separate issues. Having established the court's jurisdiction, the judges were then divided on whether to exercise it in this case. Neill LJ held that the policy revisions were non-justiciable, being high-level decisions of government policy which were a 'judicial no-man's land'. He continued: 'These decisions involve a balance of competing claims on the public purse and the allocation of economic resources which the court is ill-equipped to deal with' (at p881h). He also observed, obiter, that even if the revisions of policy were justiciable they were probably not unlawful. Evans and Peter Gibson LJJ thought that the policy revisions were justiciable but that they were not unlawful on the grounds of unfairness or irrationality.

R v *Secretary of State for the Home Department, ex parte Fire Brigades Union* [1995] 2 All ER 244 (HL) – in 1964 the government had introduced a non-statutory, voluntary (ex gratia) scheme for compensating victims of violent crime. The amount of compensation was based on common law principles. The Criminal Justice Act 1988 put the scheme on a statutory basis for the first time, but left it to the discretion of the Secretary of State as to when to bring the scheme into force. The Home Secretary decided not to bring it into force but instead to use his prerogative power to introduce a modified and less expensive version of the original ex gratia scheme. The effect was to use his prerogative power in order to legislate contrary to existing legislation not yet in force. The Union challenged the legality of the new scheme.

The House of Lords held (3 to 2, Lords Keith and Mustill dissenting) that the Home Secretary had abused his prerogative powers. He could not lawfully establish a new scheme radically different from the existing but unimplemented provisions which Parliament had enacted and intended to be in force at some future date. Whilst he had discretion not to implement these provisions, he was under a duty to keep the matter under review and would need Parliament's approval to introduce any *new* scheme different from these provisions:

'It would be most surprising if, at the present day, prerogative powers could be validly exercised by the executive so as to frustrate the will of Parliament expressed in a statute, and, to an extent, to pre-empt the decision of Parliament whether or not to continue with the statutory scheme even thought the old scheme has been abandoned': per Lord Browne-Wilkinson (at p254b).

The decision is therefore an *extension* of the principles of *Attorney-General* v *De Keyser's Royal Hotel* [1920] AC 508 (HL), because in the present case statute affected the exercise of prerogative powers in the same field even though the statute had not been brought into force. It was this point that caused Lords Keith and Mustill to dissent on the ground that a statute not yet in force was incapable of creating rights or duties, so that the prerogative powers in the same field continue to exist unimpaired. The two Law Lords were also concerned about judicial interference in the political process: 'To grant the applicants the relief which they seek, or any part of it, would represent an unwarrantable intrusion by the court into the political field and a usurpation of the function of Parliament': per Lord Keith (at p248h). Lord Mustill refused to accept that it must have been Parliament's intention to have the 1988 scheme in force at some future date because practical politics decides such matters and further study may have revealed flaws in the scheme which would make it undesirable to implement it (at p262h–j). Consequently, in Lord Mustill's view, the courts had no jurisdiction to review the non-implementation of the scheme. Further, the possibility of substituting one non-statutory scheme for another was well within the contemplation of Parliament and would not be an abuse of the Home Secretary's prerogative powers (at p265b). The prerogative powers remained intact because Parliament had chosen to allow the statutory scheme to enter the field only at some future date, if at all, at the choice of the Home Secretary: 'Until he chooses to call the parliamentary scheme into existence there is a legislative void and the prerogative subsists untouched' (at p265e). Lord Mustill concluded with a strong warning on the need for judges to keep to their places in the unwritten British Constitution: 'As the judges themselves constantly remark, it is not they who are appointed to administer the country' (at p268d).

This case is of great importance because it illustrates aspects of several constitutional doctrines (sovereignty, separation of powers, rule of law, review of prerogative powers) and, in administrative law, provides a fascinating contrast between the majority judgments ('red light' judgments) and the dissenting judgments ('green light' judgments).

R v *Ministry of Defence, ex parte Smith and Others* [1995] 1 All ER 257 (CA): see chapter 11, section 11.3.

Reckley v *Minister of Public Safety and Immigration (No 2)* [1996] 2 WLR 281; [1996] 1 All ER 562 (PC) – Reckley had been sentenced to death in the Bahamas in 1990. Following the dismissal of another person's appeal to the Privy Council on the lawfulness of the death penalty, Reckley was granted a further stay of execution in order to challenge the refusal of the prerogative of mercy in his case. The Judicial Committee of the Privy Council *held*, inter alia, that the discretion of the minister in death sentence cases was a personal discretion and not justiciable. Lord Goff observed: 'Mercy is not the subject of legal rights. It begins where legal rights end'. He went on to distinguish *ex parte Bentley*, at section 3.1 above, on the ground that *Bentley's* case was 'exceptional': [1996] 1 All ER at 572 c–h.

Lord Goff's view seems to confirm the cautious approach taken by Watkins LJ in *ex parte Bentley*, since Watkins LJ was careful to emphasise that a review was being granted in that case only on the narrow ground of error of law so that the Home Secretary could be properly informed of the types of pardon available under the prerogative of mercy. The decision, he said, should not be regarded as authority permitting other kinds of challenge to the exercise of the prerogative of mercy.

The following articles analyse the *Reckley* case, above:

Hare, 'Death Row and the Privy Council' [1996] CLJ 401

Pannick, 'Tempering Justice with Mercy' [1996] PL 557

The following articles analyse the implications of the *Fire Brigades Union* case:

Allan, 'Parliament, Ministers, Courts and the Prerogative: Criminal Injuries Compensation and the Dormant Statute' [1995] CLJ 481

Barendt, 'Constitutional Law and the Criminal Injuries Compensation Scheme' [1995] PL 357

Ganz, 'Criminal Injuries Compensation: the Constitutional Issue' (1996) 59 MLR 95

Thomas, 'Parliamentary Supremacy and the Judicial Function: *ex parte Fire Brigades Union*' (1996) 112 LQR 177

3.4 Analysis of questions

The general topic of the royal prerogative is usually examined directly in first year constitutional law examination papers. In administrative law examination papers the emphasis is on judicial review, so many of the cases on the royal prerogative tend to be examinable (eg *Council of Civil Service Unions* v *Minister for Civil Service* (above), *Laker Airways Ltd* v *Department of Trade* (above), *R* v *Criminal Injuries Compensation Board, ex parte Lain* [1967] 2 QB 864 and *R* v *Secretary of State for the Home Department, ex parte Bentley* (above)) in the context of the application of the grounds for review and the rules on remedies. The decision in *ex parte Fire Brigades Union*, above, is so significant and controversial that it is likely to be examined in second/third year administrative law examinations, as well as in first year constitutional law examinations. In the latter, questions are most likely to be essay type requiring the student to show an understanding of the extent to which the courts are prepared to control the exercise of prerogative power.

3.5 Questions

QUESTION ONE

Critically assess the respective roles of the House of Commons and the courts in regulating the royal prerogative

University of London LLB Examination
(for External Students) Constitutional Law June 1993 Q8(a)

General Comment

Questions on the royal prerogative have become familiar in recent years and almost predictable as far as judicial review is concerned. However, this question places equal emphasis on the role of the Commons in regulating the prerogative, so it is important that a balanced approach is adopted. There is the opportunity to use topical examples from the field of government and politics and also to make use of recent cases and academic research.

Skeleton Solution

- Definition and scope of the royal prerogative.
- The threat to the rule of law.
- Examples and effect of the prerogative in domestic affairs.
- Examples and effect in foreign affairs.
- Problems of weak Commons scrutiny and control.
- Scope and development of judicial review culminating in the breakthrough in the GCHQ case.
- Limited scope of that breakthrough.
- Critical conclusions.

Suggested Solution

The royal prerogative covers the residue of discretionary executive powers left to the monarch after the establishment of the constitutional monarchy in the period 1688–9. Most of the powers concern matters of state and government policy and these are exercised by the monarch, by convention, on the advice of her ministers. A few powers may be exercised at the monarch's personal discretion.

The essential character of the royal prerogative is such as to make parliamentary and judicial control almost impossible. Hence the Diceyan view that the prerogative, like all wide discretionary power, is a threat to the rule of law. Reformers like Tony Benn MP wish to see a codification of the prerogative which, whilst allowing the monarchy to remain, would strip the monarch and her government of the ability to take fundamentally important decisions without prior approval of Parliament. Such codification would also make it easier to obtain judicial review, which is a system much more appropriate to the construction of statutes to discover whether delegates have exceeded the statutory discretions conferred on them.

In domestic affairs of state the royal prerogative covers such areas as the regulation of the armed forces; the administration of justice through the supervision of public prosecutions and 'public interest' civil actions; the release of prisoners under the prerogative of mercy; the regulation of the civil service; the granting of honours such as peerages; the issue and revocation of passports; and there are others. Many of the powers (eg over the civil service and peerages) are exercisable by the Prime Minister, giving the Prime Minister a position of special authority within the Constitution and raising fears that, from time to time, a Prime Minister is able to enjoy an almost presidential type of authority. Indeed Tony Benn, when presenting his Commonwealth of Britain Bill to the Commons a few years ago, argued that a British Prime Minister enjoys more power to act unilaterally in many fields than an American President, who is confined by a written constitution, a rigid system of checks and balances in his relationship with Congress, and vigorous judicial review from the Supreme Court.

In foreign affairs the royal prerogative covers even more far-reaching decisions such as the power to declare war and peace or other hostilities (fleets were sent to the Falklands and the Gulf under prerogative power: parliamentary consent was sought only after the fleets had been despatched); the power to sign international treaties so as to bind the United Kingdom in international law; the power to recognise foreign states and their diplomats; and to commit hostile acts on foreign soil under protection of 'Act of State', which protects the Crown from civil action in domestic courts.

Commons control over such decisions is comparatively weak because of the absence of normal methods of parliamentary scrutiny found in the processing of legislation. Nevertheless political pressures are normally sufficient to ensure that at least a debate is held on the exercise of particularly important decisions, although at one point in recent times, during the passage of the legislation to ratify the Maastricht Treaty, the Prime Minister had indicated a readiness to use the prerogative if he lost the vote on the Social Chapter element, provoking accusations of unconstitutional and undemocratic behaviour from the Opposition (and some of his own backbenchers). He did not lose the vote so the threat did not materialise but the ability of the Executive to bypass Parliament or ignore a parliamentary vote is still there.

Until the late 1970s and the 1980s judicial review of the royal prerogative appeared to be confined to ensuring that decisions were taken under established prerogatives and not in conflict with statutes: *BBC* v *Johns* (1965), *Attorney-General* v *De Keyser's Royal Hotel* (1920). It appeared to be well established that judges could not investigate the manner of prerogative decision-making or the policy wisdom of such decisions: *Chandler* v *DPP* (1964). Then, in the *Laker* case (1977) Lord Denning MR suggested, obiter, that the prerogative is a discretionary power exercisable for the public good and that judges could intervene if it is exercised 'improperly or mistakenly'. Hence he was suggesting that the 'ultra vires' concept, used in relation to statutory powers, was capable of extension to prerogative powers. Indeed, Lord Denning applied the concept to the exercise of the Attorney-General's prerogative powers in the *Gouriet* case (1977). Although the Denning views were rejected by the House of Lords on the appeal in *Gouriet*, they were revitalised when the Law Lords reviewed the development of administrative law in *Council of Civil Service Unions* v *Minister for the Civil Service* (1985), where a majority suggested, obiter, that judicial review should depend not on the source of executive power but on the subject matter, so that if the latter was of a justiciable kind, judges would have the power of review.

Although this was a major breakthrough in extending a form of control over what previously had been almost uncontrollable power, it has been argued that the traditional, natural reluctance of judges to involve themselves in political decisions has resulted in very limited use of the review power, which has been confined either to non-contentious political decisions, such as the revocation of a passport (*Everett*'s case (1989)) or clearly justiciable decisions involving the administration of justice, such as the exercise of the prerogative of mercy (*R* v *Secretary of State for the Home Department, ex parte Bentley* (1994), though contrast *Reckley* v *Minister of Public Safety and Immigration (No 2)* (1996)). It is doubtful whether judges in the United Kingdom will be tempted to review prerogative decisions relating to defence and foreign policy in the way Canadian judges have been prepared to do: see analysis by Walker ([1987] PL 62). In cricketing terms it is up to Parliament to assert itself as the wicket-keeper; the courts can only be a long stop and may be unable to catch executive hits which offend democratic principles and the rule of law.

QUESTION TWO

'The uncertainties surrounding the scope and exercise of the royal prerogative give rise to serious constitutional questions concerning the rule of law in a democratic society.'

Critically assess this statement.

University of London LLB Examination
(for External Students) Constitutional Law June 1994 Q5

General Comment

A question that illustrates the dangers in question-spotting, since it requires knowledge of both the rule of law and of the royal prerogative. A tricky question, too, since both these areas must be discussed – and linked – in the context of the quote. However, given this overlap and that it is not an easy question, candidates familiar with the areas should not be dissuaded from an attempt; a good answer to a difficult question should gain a good mark. As ever, the success of the attempt depends largely on actually answering the question – critically assessing the statement; and to do this, the introduction is crucial.

Skeleton Solution

- Definitions of the rule of law, the royal prerogative and their relationship.
- Prerogative and statute: Bill of Rights 1688; *Attorney-General* v *De Keyser's Royal Hotel; Northumbria Police Authority*; *BBC* v *Johns*.
- Political control: ministerial responsibility.
- Judicial control: GCHQ case; *Everett*; *Bentley*.
- Conclusions.

Suggested Solution

It is doubtful whether Dicey's traditional exposition of the rule of law, focusing on government in accordance with law and equality before the law, remains wholly adequate. In a modern democratic society the rule of law means more: it requires, inter alia, clarity and certainty in law, so that individuals know what it is they can and cannot do. To the extent, therefore, that there are 'uncertainties surrounding the scope and exercise of the royal prerogative', it would be hard to disagree with the statement in the quote. But it will be argued below that the scope of the prerogative today is relatively well-defined and that recent developments, particularly in judicial review of the prerogative, have clarified many of the uncertainties surrounding its exercise.

Blackstone (in his *Commentaries*) defined the prerogative in terms of the special pre-eminence enjoyed by the King over and above all others, so that prerogative powers were those enjoyed by the King alone and not shared with the ordinary subject. Such a definition does seem to offend the requirement of equality before the law, but it is important to recognise the justification for the existence of prerogative powers – that they are necessary to enable the Crown to perform its function of governing the country. Some inequality may thus be tolerable, provided adequate controls exist to prevent abuse of power. It is submitted that the controls available, both political and legal, are indeed adequate to ensure that the government, in exercising prerogative powers, is subject to the rule of law.

Certain propositions about the prerogative are, in modern law, quite clear: it has been settled law since the Bill of Rights 1688 that the prerogative is subordinate to statute; Parliament may thus abolish prerogative powers. Even when Parliament has not chosen to abolish a prerogative, *Attorney-General* v *De Keyser's Royal Hotel* (1920) establishes that, where prerogative and statutory powers co-exist, the Crown is precluded from relying on the former and must act under its statutory powers. While it is arguable that the *application* of this principle may give rise to some uncertainties – see, eg, *R* v *Secretary of State for the Home Department, ex parte Northumbria Police Authority* (1988) – the principle itself is clear. Similarly, prerogative powers are residual: in Diplock LJ's memorable phrase, 'It is 350 years and a civil war too late ... to broaden the prerogative'; its limits 'are now well settled and incapable of extension' (*BBC* v *Johns* (1965)).

That government is carried out in accordance with law is also ensured, at least in theory, through political controls; although in law prerogative powers vest in the Monarch, they are by convention exercised on her behalf by ministers of the Crown. Those ministers are, by convention, responsible to Parliament in respect of any exercise of prerogative powers. Should ministers abuse their powers, Parliament may remove those powers by statute. It is, however, arguable that the ability of Parliament adequately to control ministers is, at least in modern law, something of a fiction. To this extent it is true that the dominance of Parliament by the executive does pose serious questions concerning the rule of law in a democratic society – and not merely in the context of the prerogative.

It is perhaps in recognition of this 'democratic deficit' that the past ten years have seen remarkable developments in judicial control of the prerogative. The traditional rule was that the courts exercised jurisdiction to determine the existence of a prerogative power – they could thus decide that a claimed prerogative did not exist – but once its existence was established, they would not rule on the manner of its exercise. This traditional approach was abandoned in the GCHQ case (*Council of Civil Service Unions* v *Minister for the Civil Service* (1985)), where the House of Lords opined that, in principle, the exercise of prerogative powers was subject to judicial review, although their Lordships did add that not all prerogative powers were reviewable: in particular, where the exercise of the power gave rise to a 'non-justiciable issue', it would still be immune from review.

It is noteworthy, however, that in the case of *R* v *Secretary of State for the Home Department, ex parte Bentley* (1994), the Court of Appeal was willing to review the exercise of the prerogative of mercy, treating as obiter its inclusion in the list of non-justiciable issues given in GCHQ. Moreover, in *R* v *Secretary of State for Foreign and Commonwealth Affairs, ex parte Everett* (1989), the Court was prepared to review the prerogative power to issue passports on the basis that its exercise involved 'administrative decisions affecting individuals'.

In conclusion, it remains true to say that, in so far as the exercise of some prerogative powers remains unreviewable, primarily those that operate in the sphere of foreign affairs, serious constitutional questions concerning the rule of law do still arise – although it is, of course, always open to Parliament to intervene in case of abuse. It is however submitted that recent years have seen considerable clarification of the uncertainties surrounding the scope and exercise of the prerogative and, while some do remain, the existence of the royal prerogative does not, in general, offend against the rule of law.

4 Crown Liability

4.1 Introduction

The Sovereign in her personal capacity is exempt from liability because of the ancient principle that the monarch can do no wrong, ie has no legal power to commit wrongdoing. The Sovereign in her public capacity acts through her ministers and agents as a corporation sole. Hence the Crown in the public, official sense may be broadly defined as the central government and agencies under its direct control: per Lord Diplock in *Town Investments* v *Department of the Environment* [1978] AC 359 (HL).

A judgment against the Crown is therefore a judgment against the taxpayers of the state. In a modern welfare state the need for the government to enjoy certain immunities from the ordinary law is inescapable if its responsibilities are to be discharged efficiently. Complete equality under the law as between citizen and government might have an inhibiting effect on the discharge of governmental functions causing a defensive attitude on the part of government, ie a fear of doing anything in case liability should arise. Hence what the rule of law requires is that the government should not enjoy unnecessary privileges or exemptions from the ordinary law.

4.2 Key points

a) *Crown liability in contract*

i) Crown Proceedings Act 1947, s1 allows the Crown to sue or be sued in contract as if it were a private individual of full age and capacity, provided that a petition of right would have been available under the prior common law. The result is that s1 preserves certain common law privileges of the Crown.

ii) A petition of right was not available where a government contract expressly stated that it depended on the grant of funds voted by Parliament and where no funds were in fact granted: *Churchward* v *R* (1865) LR 1 QB 173. The case is no longer authority for the more general proposition that contractual liability is contingent upon funds being voted by Parliament: *New South Wales* v *Bardolph* (1934) 52 CLR 455 (Australia).

iii) A petition of right was not available to enforce government contractual obligations where the breach had resulted from a change of government policy taken in the general public interest. It was said that the Crown 'cannot by contract hamper its freedom of action in matters which concern the welfare of the state' because 'it is not competent for the Government to fetter its future executive action which must necessarily be determined by the needs of the community when the question arises': per Rowlatt J in *Rederiaktiebolaget Amphitrite* v *R* [1921] 3 KB 500. This rule survives today, though there is controversy over its scope since Rowlatt J relied on no authority for his view and went on to say that the immunity from contractual liability did not extend to the breach of ordinary commercial contracts which do not affect the welfare of the state. No definition was given of 'ordinary commercial contracts' or of 'the welfare of the state'.

In later cases attempts were made to restrict the *Amphitrite* principle. For example in *Robertson* v *Minister of Pensions* [1948] 2 All ER 767 Denning J said: 'The defence of executive necessity is of limited scope. It only avails the Crown where there is an implied term to that effect or that is the true meaning of the contract.' In *Crown Lands Commissioners* v *Page* [1960] 2 QB 274 Devlin LJ (at p293) said that the *Amphitrite* principle should not be regarded as an easy escape route from contractual liability merely because the fulfilment of the contract turns out to be disadvantageous to the Crown.

The *Amphitrite* principle probably has its origins in the special rules on Crown service (below).

iv) Since the Crown can act only through its employees or agents contractual liability will arise only where the employee/agent had express or ostensible authority to make the contract on behalf of the Crown. Ostensible authority will arise if the employee/agent made the contract whilst 'performing a regular and recognised activity of government': *New South Wales* v *Bardolph*, above. However, since the doctrine of ostensible authority rests on the principle of estoppel there may be difficulties pleading it against the Crown (or any other public body), especially where the contract involves the exercise of power outside the statutory powers of the Crown and the employee/agent, since estoppel in public law cannot be used to circumvent the ultra vires rule: *Attorney-General for Ceylon* v *Silva* [1953] AC 461.

b) *Crown service*

i) A civil servant has the right to sue the Crown for unfair dismissal before an industrial tribunal which may order compensation or reinstatement, with compensation payable if the reinstatement order is not obeyed. This statutory action for unfair dismissal is independent of any breach of contract and therefore avoids the traditional problems of the extent to which a contract of employment can be created by Crown service. Civil servants are also given the same rights as ordinary employees in respect of rights granted by the Sex Discrimination Act 1975.

ii) At common law a Crown servant cannot sue in the ordinary courts for wrongful dismissal because he is 'dismissable at pleasure'. It was regarded as being unconstitutional and against the general welfare of the state for the Crown to tie its hands by employing particular individuals for fixed periods. The *Amphitrite* principle (above) was probably based on this principle. Dicta in old cases go even further by suggesting that no contracts can exist between the Crown and its employees on the ground that the Crown has no capacity to fetter its freedom of action by employment contracts, although an action for debt (independent of contract) was available to civil servants (not military ones) to recover arrears of pay: *Dunn* v *R* [1898] 1 QB 116.

Modern authorities have produced conflicting judicial opinions as to whether contractual obligations on matters other than tenure can exist between Crown and employee. In *Kodeeswaran* v *Attorney-General of Ceylon* [1970] 2 WLR 456 the Judicial Committee of the Privy Council held that enforceable obligations could arise on such matters as conditions of service and holiday pay since these matters do not affect the welfare of the state and were separate from the issue of dismissal. In *R* v *Civil Service Appeal Board, ex parte Bruce* [1989] 2 All ER 907 (CA) it was held that no contract could exist because of the absence of the intention to create legal relations on the part of the Crown. However, the Court of Appeal did not disapprove the view expressed at first instance ([1988] 3 All ER 686 at p694) that there was nothing unconstitutional about civil servants being employed under contracts of service. In *McClaren* v *Home Office* [1990] ICR 824 (CA) it was held that a contract of employment existed between the Crown and a prison officer because the Crown's intention to enter into legal relations was evidenced by the statutory framework and codes of practice regulating his employment. Finally, in *R* v *Lord Chancellor's Department, ex parte Nangle* [1992] 1 All ER 897 (QBD) it was held that all the ingredients of a contract could be found in the documentation and relationship between an executive officer and the department employing him, even though one paragraph of the Code of Civil Service Pay and Conditions expressly stated that there was no contract of employment enforceable in the courts. It was also held that the contract was subject to the Crown's right to dismiss the officer at pleasure, so that the decision does no more than give the civil servant the right to sue for arrears of pay and for breach of other terms not connected with tenure.

iii) The uncertainties and anomalies created by the common law rules on Crown service may be resolved as the government continues its present review of the Civil Service by building on the Next Steps Programme of the 1980s. This will involve a gradual reduction in the number of civil servants and a transfer of obligations to semi-autonomous bodies and privatised utilities which will be able to create ordinary contracts of employment so as to embrace modern concepts such as performance-related pay: White Paper (1994) Cmnd 2627. The position of military servants has only recently received a statutory framework but this has probably not affected the non-contractual situation in which military servants find themselves, ie where everything depends on voluntary discharge of obligations by the Crown under its prerogative powers.

It should be noted that the jurisdiction of the Parliamentary Commissioner for Administration is excluded so far as contracts of Crown service and conditions of employment are concerned.

Note: Judges are not Crown servants because their security of tenure is secured by statute and constitutional convention.

c) *Crown liability in tort*

i) Crown Proceedings Act 1947, s2 allows the Crown to be sued for the torts of its servants or agents on the ordinary principles of vicarious liability. It should be noted that vicarious liability can arise even in respect of the tort of misfeasance in a public office, ie where a public official acts maliciously with the intention of injuring someone or knowingly and in bad faith exceeds his powers knowing that it may injure someone: *Racz* v *Home Office* [1994] 2 AC 45 (HL).

A Crown servant or agent is one who is paid wholly from public funds (other than a judge, above), and who has actual or ostensible authority to act on behalf of the Crown. There is no Crown liability for the police, who are paid partly out of local taxes.

ii) The Crown, like any other public body, will benefit from the common law rule that no liability in negligence can arise in respect of the policy-making process. Tortious liability will attach only to the negligent operation or implementation of policy: *Home Office* v *Dorset Yacht Co Ltd* [1970] AC 1004 (HL). Whilst this rule has been justified on the ground that public bodies need complete freedom in order to formulate policy, it has been criticised for undermining the principle of equality under the law and for presenting the courts with a complex reasoning process when trying to resolve the policy/operation dichotomy in specific cases. Judicial dissatisfaction with the rule was expressed in *Rowling* v *Takaro Properties Ltd* [1988] AC 473 (JCPC), notably by Lord Keith who said that the issue was one of 'an intensely pragmatic character, well suited for gradual development but requiring most careful analysis'. Exemption from liability based on 'public policy' alone was rejected in the *Dorset Yacht* case, above: see further chapter 7, section 7.2.

iii) Crown Proceedings Act 1947, s10 prevented members of the armed forces and their dependants from suing the Crown for death or personal injury negligently inflicted by another member of the armed forces who was on duty at the time or where the victim was on duty or on military property at the time of the incident. This immunity was based on the assumption that military pensions would provide adequate compensation. The immunity could only be invoked if the Crown certified to the court that the death or injury would be attributable to service for pension purposes. The certificate was conclusive. Following dissatisfaction with the amount of military pension paid in some cases compared to the damages awarded by the courts for comparable acts of negligence, s10 of the 1947 Act was suspended (though not retrospectively) by the Crown Proceedings (Armed Forces) Act 1987. The Ministry of Defence subsequently established an internal tribunal for assessing compensation in the hope of avoiding litigation from injured servicemen. The existing system of pension benefits was continued, again in the hope of deterring litigation, with the result that there is a dual system of compensation within the Ministry. Under the 1987 Act the Secretary of State for Defence has power to reactivate s10 by order in council if he thinks it necessary or expedient to do so in the event of actual or impending hostilities or other warlike operations, or at a time of great national danger or emergency.

iv) The Crown is not bound by a statute unless expressly named in it or unless it should be bound by necessary implication. This imposes a severe restriction on the opportunity to sue the Crown for the tort of breach of statutory duty. There are many statutes which do not expressly name the Crown, eg the Crown does not need planning permission to develop Crown land because it is not named in the Town and Country Planning Act 1947 (now consolidated by the 1990 Act): *Town Investments* v *Department of the Environment*, above.

The Crown can claim the *benefit* of statutes even though not expressly named in them.

v) Crown Proceedings Act 1947, s2(5) provides that the Crown is not liable for the acts or omissions of judges or those exercising judicial functions or executing judicial process.

vi) The Crown may sometimes be able to rely on the prerogative defence of Act of State: see chapter 3, section 3.2(a).

d) *Remedies against the Crown in private law proceedings*

The Crown Proceedings Act 1947 provides a uniform procedure for all actions against the Crown, including interlocutory matters such as discovery of documents and interrogatories. Section 21 of the 1947 Act provides that no compulsory order, eg in the form of an injunction or decree of specific performance, may be granted against the Crown. However, no execution of judgment, whether for money or possession of land or the recovery of a chattel can be granted against the Crown. Consequently, a Declaration is the traditional remedy against the Crown and is invariably respected by the Crown because of the mutual trust and confidence that exists between the government and the judiciary.

e) *Remedies against the Crown in public law proceedings*

See chapter 13, sections 13.2(g) and 13.4.

4.3 Recent cases

Mulcahy v *Ministry of Defence* [1996] 2 WLR 474; [1996] 2 All ER 758 (CA) – a soldier sued the Crown for injuries caused by the alleged negligence of a fellow soldier when firing a shell from a howitzer at the Iraqis during the Gulf War. It was *held* that the soldier's action must be struck out as disclosing no cause of action. Although s10 Crown Proceedings Act 1947 had not been reactivated for the purpose of the war, the position at common law still had to be considered. At common law it would not be fair, just and reasonable to impose a duty of care on one serviceman towards another during 'battle conditions'.

4.4 Analysis of questions

The topic of Crown liability involves the discussion of many special rules and anomalies, some of which can only be explained in terms of the history of the Crown in the British Constitution. One basic theme is the need to reconcile Crown liability with the rule of law: to what extent should the latter be modified in order for government to discharge its services to the community in an efficient manner? Hence essay-type questions on this theme are common. The topic of Crown liability is not usually examined directly in first year constitutional law examinations, though it provides a source of material for general questions on the rule of law. The topic of Crown liability is often merged with general public authority liability for administrative law examinations: see further chapter 7 for local authority liability.

4.5 Questions

QUESTON ONE

To what extent should public authorities be granted special treatment under the law of tort and contract?

University of London LLB Examination
(for External Students) Administrative Law June 1989 Q2

General Comment

Students should not make the mistake of providing merely a factual outline of the existing state of the law. What is required is a discussion of the underlying policy considerations.

Skeleton Solution

- Contract – doctrine of ultra-vires – policy of preventing bodies contracting out of statutory duties.
- Tort – requirement to carry out tortious acts – operational/policy distinction – negligent ultra vires/failure to perform a statutory obligation.

Suggested Solution

In considering first the extent, if any, to which public authorities should receive special treatment under the law of contract it is necessary to focus on the operation of the doctrine of ultra vires. A public authority, like any other corporate body, must derive its powers from some specific legal source – most commonly an Act of Parliament – which defines the scope of its powers. It must therefore act within the limits of its powers and will not be bound by any contract which goes beyond those limits.

Public authorities, however, differ from private corporations in that they are usually vested with powers and subject to legal obligations to take actions or make decisions which are designed to fulfil specific or general public interest objectives. There will therefore usually be some justification for treating as unenforceable contracts which, while prima facie within the limits of their powers, have the effect of preventing proper exercise of such powers and obligations. To do otherwise would be to allow such bodies to contract out of their legal duty to act in the manner required of them as public bodies and would be clearly contrary to the public interest. It is not surprising therefore that this is the approach which has been taken by the courts in the context of the contractual liability of the crown. See for example, *Crown Lands Commissioners* v *Page* (1960).

Furthermore it is arguable, in the case of local authorities, that any contract which is in breach of their general fiduciary duty to ratepayers (as opposed to some specific duty to act in a particular way) should be similarly unenforceable.

In the case of the law of tort there are other entirely different factors which may justify special treatment for public authorities. First, there may be cases where a public authority may be directly or indirectly required to carry out some action which results in a nuisance or a trespass. It is clearly inappropriate for a body to be subject to tortious liability in respect of actions which it is required by law to carry out and this has been clearly recognised by the courts in the cases concerning the defence of statutory authority (see, for example, *Goldberg & Sons Ltd* v *Liverpool Corporation* (1900)).

Secondly, in the context of negligence, it is arguable that public authorities should only be liable in respect of their operational as opposed to policy activities. This is because any assessment of liability in respect of a policy decision; for example, a decision to run certain prison institutions on an open basis (see *Home Office* v *Dorset Yacht Co Ltd* (1970)) must necessarily involve an assessment of the policy's merits. It is generally accepted that the courts are not properly equipped to decide issues of merit as opposed to legality. The validity of the operational/policy dichotomy has been confirmed in the courts in cases such as *Dorset Yacht Co* supra and *Anns* v *Merton London Borough Council* (1978).

Finally, because of their public nature, it is arguable that public authorities should be liable to persons who are adversely affected either by an action which is ultra vires or by a failure to perform some statutory duty. The courts have, however, so far not been prepared to award damages on the basis that a public body has negligently acted ultra vires (see *Dunlop* v

Woollahra Municipal Council (1982)). Similarly a plaintiff will generally be unable to sue for breach of statutory duty unless he can show that the duty is owed to a particular class of which he is a member (see *Cutler* v *Wandsworth Stadium Ltd* (1949)) and that the relevant act does not provide for any other means of enforcing the performance of the duty (see, for example, *Southwark London Borough Council* v *Williams* (1971)).

QUESTON TWO

'Public authorities should be treated like any other body or individual.'

Discuss with reference to ONE of the following: contract, tort.

Adapted from University of London LLB Examination
(for External Students) Administrative Law June 1990 Q4

General Comment

The question requires a general overview of the law relating to public bodies and the problems thrown up by the conflict between their private contractual obligations and their public law duties, and by the imposition of tortious liability. It is important first of all to establish whether or not they are treated like other bodies, and then to consider whether or not they should be. In each version of the answer to this question one has to make certain generalisations concerning what is a public law body.

Skeleton Solution

a) What is a public law body? Consider the Crown and other public bodies separately. First, consider what special rules apply in each case. Second, consider what justifications there are for such special rules as do exist.

b) Consider the meaning of public body. Look at the problems of the public/private dichotomy. Explain how the courts have developed the policy/operational dichotomy in relation to governmental powers. Assess the reasons for the immunities in tort.

Suggested Solution

a) *Contract*

For the purposes of this answer the term 'public body' is taken as encompassing both government departments and public corporations such as local authorities.

i) *Government departments*

It is inevitable that in the conduct of the business of government, government departments are going to have to enter into contractual relationships with other parties. The first part of this inquiry is concerned with the question of whether or not any special rules apply to such contracts.

Historically, the idea that the Crown could be bound by a contract with another legal entity would have seemed odd, if for no other reason than the fact that no procedure for bringing proceedings for breach of contract, other than the archaic petition of right process, existed. This situation appeared to have been remedied with the enactment of the Crown Proceedings Act 1947. Section 1 of the 1947 Act provided that where previously litigants could have proceeded gainst the Crown by way of petition of right, they could now do so by way of writ.

The shortcoming of the reforms of 1947 was that they did nothing to alter the law relating to the Crown's liability. An examination of the law relating to the Crown's contractual liability does reveal significant areas where normal liability cannot be imposed.

Three areas in particular are worthy of note. First, those situations where a contract depends for its performance on money being voted by Parliament so that it can be appropriated to the discharge of that contract. In *Churchward* v *R* (1865), the court held that it could not compel performance of a contract by the Crown if such performance required the voting of money by Parliament. Constitutionally it would be improper for the courts to tell Parliament how to vote. The later case of *New South Wales* v *Bardolph* (1934) indicates that the correct analysis of this situation is that a contract does exist between the parties, but obtaining a remedy depends upon the availability of funds. Hence in the latter case funds had been appropriated to pay for a series of tourism advertisements. A change in government policy resulted in a decision to withdraw the adverts after an agreement had been signed to purchase the advertising space. The plaintiff succeeded in his action for breach of contract.

Secondly, the Crown will not be held to a contract if it is no longer in the public interest for it to observe it. This is the doctrine of executive necessity, whereby the interests of the state override the desirability of requiring the Crown to perform its promises. *Rederiaktiebolaget Amphitrite* v *R* (1921) is often cited as an authority for this proposition, but it is doubtful whether there was actually a contract in that case. A better example is provided by *Crown Lands Commissioners* v *Page* (1960), where the Crown leased property and then requisitioned it for troop accommodation. The tenant refused to pay rent in respect of the period of requisition, claiming that the Crown was in breach of its covenant to permit him quiet enjoyment of the property. The courts held that there was no such covenant in the lease and that none would be implied. If the Crown needed to repossess the property during the currency of the lease it should be free to do so in the public interest.

The third area concerns Crown employment. It is doubtful whether civil servants have any contract of employment with the Crown. The conventional wisdom is that they are dismissible at will, and such a state of affairs is inconsistent with the existence of a contract: see *R* v *Civil Service Appeal Board, ex parte Bruce* (1988). It would appear that while civil servants have terms of employment, and can sue for unfair dismissal, they have no contractual rights such as would enable them to sue for non-payment of wages.

Whether the Crown should enjoy any of these privileges in respect of its contractual liabilities is to some extent a matter of opinion. If one accepts that the Crown should be free to renege on contracts, and dismiss its servants whenever it takes the view that it is in the interests of the state for it to do so, then these privileges flow as a consequence of that freedom of action. What should be borne in mind is that in the vast majority of cases the Crown enters into perfectly normal commercial contracts in respect of which these immunities and privileges are irrelevant. The courts assume that if a contract is of a normal commercial nature the Crown is bound by it.

ii) *Public corporations*

Public corporations, in this context typically local authorities, do not enjoy the same privileges in relation to contractual liability as the Crown, largely because of their constitutional position, and the nature of their responsibilities.

One can start from the basic premise that local authorities are treated just like any other corporate bodies when it comes to contractual liability, and thus the argument becomes more narrowly focused on the few areas where different rules apply.

Local authorities are required to observe certain formalities before entering into contracts for the supply of goods and services, especially with regard to competitive tendering. The purpose of these statutory requirements is to ensure that those funding local authority services get value for money. Similarly local authorities cannot use their contractual powers to achieve an ulterior purpose: see *Wheeler* v *Leicester City Council* (1985).

As regards contractual liability, local authorities and other bodies created by statute will not be held to contracts which are void because they are ultra vires. Such invalidity can result where a public body enters into a contract which is incompatible with its other statutory powers and duties: see *Ayr Harbour Trustees* v *Oswald* (1883). In the case of a local authority such incompatibility may be more difficult to establish since it has a wide range of powers and duties: see *Stourcliff Estates* v *Bournemouth Corporation* (1910). Modern cases on incompatibility are few and far between. Today, the courts take a broad view of the nature of contractual obligations that a local authority can incur, even to the point of upholding an agreement by a housing authority not to let out empty council owned flats to persons on its waiting list: see *R* v *Hammersmith and Fulham London Borough Council, ex parte Beddowes* (1987).

In conclusion it can be said that public corporations enjoy few, if any, privileges in relation to contractual liability. The ultra vires rules is of more theoretical than practical significance, and is not relied upon to allow such bodies to relieve themselves of liability at will. If anything, such bodies are more constrained in the manner and form of the contract making powers than private corporations would be .

b) *Tort*

For the purposes of this answer the term 'public body' is taken as encompassing both government departments and public corporations such as local authorities.

The suggestion that public bodies receive preferential treatment in relation to tortious liability prompts the thought that such a situation would be inconsistent with the rule of law, a doctrine encompassing at least two significant concepts. The first of these is that there should be government according to ascertainable rules, as opposed to arbitrary decision making. The second is that the same law should be obeyed by, and apply to, all legal entities equally, in the sense that no one should be above the law. It is frequently stated that one of A V Dicey's fundamental objections to the development of administrative law was his fear that it might result in public bodies not being subject to the laws applicable to ordinary citizens, and thereby being placed in a preferential or advantageous position.

Whilst the development of administrative law since 1945 has resulted in public bodies being brought firmly within the control of the courts, by means of judicial review, thus proving Dicey's fears to have been somewhat unfounded, liability in tort remains an area in which public bodies continue to enjoy certain immunities not afforded to other individuals and organisations.

The problem arises in the following way. The French system of administrative law (much criticised by A V Dicey), known as the 'droit administratif', recognises two systems of law, namely public and private. It is the former which regulates the rights and liabilities of public bodies. As mentioned above, Dicey's objection to the French system was based on his conclusion that it provided public bodies with: '... a whole body of special rights, privileges, or prerogatives as against private citizens ...' (*The Law of the Constitution* (10th edn, p336)).

The truth of the matter is that the French system is, if anything, more generous than our own in compensating those who suffer loss as a result of the actions of public officers.

English law by comparison is a unitary system based on the common law which historically has never recognised any distinction between the rights and liabilities of public or private bodies. In *Davy* v *Spelthorne Borough Council* (1983) Lord Wilberforce stated:

'The expressions "private law" and "public law" have recently been imported into the law of England from countries which, unlike our own, have separate systems concerning public law and private law. No doubt they are convenient expressions for descriptive purposes. In this country they must be used with caution, for, typically, English law fastens not on principles but on remedies. The principle remains intact that public authorities and public servants are, unless clearly exempted, answerable in the ordinary courts for wrongs done to individuals ... we have not yet reached the point at which mere characterisation of a claim as a claim in public law is sufficient to exclude it from consideration by the ordinary courts of law; to permit this would be to create a dual system of law with the rigidity and procedural hardships for the plaintiffs which it was the purpose of recent reforms to remove.'

While, therefore, one would have to accept that there is a conceptual difficulty in English law in actually determining public and private law distinctions, it equally has to be accepted that agents of central and local government frequently have to perform tasks which have no direct equivalent in private law, such as the detention of prisoners, the granting of planning permission, or the approval of a programme of vaccination, and in this regard it might be contended that rules granting public bodies preferential treatment in the law of torts as regards the discharge of these functions are justifiable. As Wade comments (*Administrative Law* (5th edn, p24)):

'What the rule of law requires is that the government should not enjoy unnecessary privileges or exemptions from the ordinary law ... (I)n principle all public authorities should be subject to all normal legal duties and liabilities which are not inconsistent with their governmental functions.'

The essence of the preferential treatment in relation to tortious liability afforded to public bodies lies therefore in the governmental nature of their functions. The courts have been reluctant to impose liability in negligence upon public bodies, where the damage complained of by the plaintiff has resulted from an exercise of discretion by the public body. In this regard a distinction has to be drawn between what are referred to as 'policy' decisions of public bodies on the one hand, and 'operational' activities on the other. A policy decision might be whether to provide street lights in a particular road; an operational matter might be the way in which those street lights are actually installed. If a plaintiff is injured in a fall at night as a result of the local authority deciding not to provide street lighting, he is unlikely to succeed in an action in negligence. The view of Lord Diplock in *Home Office* v *Dorset Yacht Co Ltd* (1970) was that in exercising its discretion in relation to policy decisions a public body owed no private law duty of care to any individual, and that the proper method of challenge in such cases was for the litigant to test the legality of the policy decision by an application for judicial review.

By contrast, suppose the plaintiff is injured by an inadequately installed street light falling on him. Here the claim in negligence clearly relates to a matter that is more within the 'operational' sphere, and on the basis of Lord Wilberforce's speech in *Anns* v *Merton London Borough Council* (1978), the courts are more likely to accept that a private law duty of care arises. It would still be necessary for the plaintiff to show, however, that the local authority employees carrying out the installation acted outside the scope of any discretion delegated to them as to the manner of installation.

While a private law action for damages might lie against a public body in respect of its giving negligent advice, it seems very doubtful whether an action will succeed on the basis that the public body has negligently acted ultra vires. In *Dunlop* v *Woollahra Municipal Council* (1982) Lord Diplock went so far as to doubt whether any private law duty of care was owed by a public authority when exercising its powers. Similar doubts are raised by the Privy Council in *Rowling* v *Takaro Properties Ltd* (1988), a case involving consideration of the circumstances in which an individual might be able to bring an action against a government minister for negligently acting ultra vires, and causing economic loss as a result. Lord Keith, delivering judgment on behalf of the Board, commented that, on the broader issue of when a private law duty of care would arise in relation to the exercise of public law powers, the distinction between policy and operational decisions was not the only relevant factor. The question should be approached pragmatically, with reference to the availability of judicial review in respect of the action, the likelihood of negligence actually being established, and the danger of inducing undue caution amongst administrators. The assumption underlying his Lordship's speech seems to be that if the exercise of discretion by a public body appears to have been invalid, the matter can be rectified quickly by way of an application for judicial review. Any losses resulting from this delay should be minimal, given the speed with which a ruling can be obtained. As a result, there should be no need for a plaintiff to launch, in addition, an action for negligence. This 'pragmatic' approach side-steps the more difficult question of when a duty of care arises, and if it does, with what result.

Are these exceptions to tortious liability justifiable? As always the answer to such questions is largely a matter of opinion. To the individual who suffers loss the answer will be in the negative. One might also contend that the imposition of tortious liability might concentrate the minds of administrators. Thought must be given, however, to the issue of compensation. Any damages awarded would have to be funded by the taxpayer. Should the loss suffered be spread across the community or left to lie where it falls? Whilst the immunities afforded to public bodies might seem unfair, one returns to the point that such immunities frequently arise in relation to activities that have no parallel in private law, and, as such, to describe them as resulting in preferential treatment for public bodies, is inaccurate. Secondly, the exceptions are not arbitrary, but subject to supervision by the courts.

5 Public Interest Immunity

5.1 Introduction

The topic of public interest immunity involves a classic conflict of interests: on the one hand there is the public interest in ensuring the proper administration of justice, which requires full and frank disclosure of all relevant information to the trial court; on the other hand there is the public interest in ensuring the proper functioning of the public service, which may require certain information to be protected from disclosure. The trial judge will be the ultimate arbiter of whether disclosure should be made in the event of a contest over disclosure. The trial judge must conduct a balancing exercise by weighing the various factors pointing for or against disclosure. The character of the balancing exercise will vary, depending on whether the claim is made in civil or criminal proceedings. The topic of public interest immunity (PII) also needs to be set within the context of the rules relating to discovery of documents.

5.2 Key points

a) *Discovery of documents*

Although discovery is made available in judicial review proceedings by RSC O.53, r8, general discovery is not available as it is in an action by writ or originating summons. In judicial review proceedings an application for discovery may be refused if the court decides that it is not necessary for disposing of the case fairly: RSC O.24, r8. Since judicial review is usually concerned with issues of law, not fact, it is rare for discovery to be ordered, particularly as the court will not order discovery to allow the accuracy of evidence to be checked without a prima facie case suggesting that the affidavit or other evidence in question is false or inaccurate. Discovery may be ordered if the affidavit or other evidence only deals partially and not sufficiently adequately with an issue: *R* v *Secretary of State for the Home Department, ex parte Harrison* [1988] 3 All ER 86.

In *R* v *Secretary of State for Foreign and Commonwealth Affairs, ex parte World Development Movement Ltd* [1995] 1 All ER 611 the Court of Appeal declined to order discovery on the ground that, when viewed with the totality of the other evidence, the applicants had been provided with 'highly valuable ammunition' to which it seemed unlikely that discovery would materially add: see chapter 8, section 8.3 for the full facts of this case.

In its report on judicial review the Law Commission decided not to recommend any change to the current rules on discovery: Report no 226 (1994). It could be argued that this is a timid response since public bodies already rely on confidentiality and public interest immunity to prevent disclosure of inappropriate information, and therefore do not require further special protection under the rules of discovery.

b) *Public interest immunity*

Public Interest Immunity certificates (PII certificates) are authorised under the Crown Proceedings Act 1947, which permits discovery of documents in proceedings against the Crown but is subject to any common law rule permitting the Crown to withhold documents in the public interest.

i) The *Air Canada* test

The burden is on the applicant to establish at least an arguable case on his own evidence without the aid of discovery *and* to show reasonable grounds for requesting disclosure of the documents in question. Reasonable grounds include a reasonable likelihood that the documents will assist his case; or that the documents will put him on enquiry as to further evidence to assist his case; or that disclosure will damage the other side's case. These rules were laid down in *Air Canada* v *Secretary of State for Trade (No 2)* [1983] 1 All ER 910 (HL) and place a heavy burden of proof on the applicant, since he may not know whether any of the grounds for disclosure can be established without first examining the documents in question.

ii) The balancing exercise

If the applicant discharges the *Air Canada* burden of proof the trial judge will embark on a balancing exercise to determine whether to order disclosure. He must weigh the competing public interests and may need to inspect the documents to decide the outcome. It would be rare for him to inspect a claim to PII based on the specific contents of a document since it will usually be obvious from the nature of the document whether disclosure would harm the public interest, eg a document involving national security: *Duncan* v *Cammell Laird & Co Ltd* [1942] AC 624 (HL), and *Balfour* v *Foreign and Commonwealth Office* [1994] 2 All ER 588 (CA) per Russell LJ at p596 esp.

The claim of the Crown or any other public body to PII is no longer conclusive on the matter: *Conway* v *Rimmer* [1968] AC 910 (HL), overruling *Duncan*'s case on this particular point. Public interest immunity is not a privilege personal to a party in a case and in that sense cannot be 'waived' since the court may of its own motion forbid the giving of evidence which in its view would harm the public interest: per Lord Simon in *Rodgers* v *Home Secretary* [1972] 2 All ER 1057 (HL) and per Lord Fraser in *Air Canada*, above.

It is more common for the judge to inspect documents where the claim relates to a class of documents because blanket protection may appear prima facie unnecessary and modern trends towards openness in public administration have encouraged judges to treat such claims with more vigorous scrutiny than during the 1940s–1960s period. In a recent leading authority the view was expressed that the class categories of PII are now well settled and new ones should not be recognised unless there is 'clear and compelling evidence' that non-disclosure is necessary in the public interest: per Lord Woolf in *R* v *Chief Constable of West Midlands Police, ex parte Wiley* [1994] 3 All ER 420 (HL) at p446 especially. Lord Woolf's judgment can be regarded as 'red light' in character because it appears to introduce a presumption in favour of disclosure, and this approach was applied in a recent case so as to defeat a claim to the confidentiality of reports by a banking institution to a regulatory body: *Kaufmann* v *Credit Lyonnais Bank* (1995) The Times 1 February.

iii) Established class categories of PII

The informant cases, eg *D* v *NSPCC* [1978] AC 171 (HL); the character reference cases, eg *Rodgers* v *Home Secretary*, above; and the proper functioning of the public service cases, eg *Evans* v *Chief Constable of Surrey* [1989] 2 All ER 594, applied in *O'Sullivan* v *Metropolitan Police Commissioner* (1995) The Times 3 July. Public interest immunity no longer attaches to the class comprising witness statements and other statements made during an investigation of a complaint against a police officer since otherwise the objectives of the police complaints system might be defeated by denying to complainants access to evidence they might need in a later civil claim: *ex parte Wiley*, above, overruling *Neilson* v *Laugharne* [1981] 1 QB 736 and similar authorities. However, the possibility of PII attaching to police complaints documents was not completely ruled out in *ex parte Wiley*, which was later distinguished in *Taylor* v *Anderton* [1995] 2 All ER 420 (CA) in order to grant PII to reports and working papers prepared by investigating officers during an inquiry into a complaint against a police officer. The need to safeguard the proper functioning of the public service was emphasised by Sir Thomas Bingham MR at All ER 437g–j:

'I am fully alive to the existence of a current of opinion strongly flowing in favour of openness and disclosure. I am also, however, mindful of the fundamental public interest in ensuring that those responsible for maintaining law and order are themselves uncorrupt, law-abiding, honest and responsible. ... In very many cases where an investigating officer is appointed, there must be a real prospect of civil, criminal or disciplinary proceedings. I have no difficulty in accepting the need for investigating officers to feel free to report on professional colleagues or members of the public without the apprehension that their opinions may become known to such persons. I can readily accept that the prospect of disclosure in other than unusual circumstances would have an undesirably inhibiting effect on investigating officers' reports. I would therefore hold that the reports of investigating officers ... form a class which is entitled to public interest immunity.'

This 'green light' judgment should be contrasted with the 'red light' approach of Lord Woolf in *ex parte Wiley*, above.

c) *Public interest immunity in criminal cases*

Although a class or contents claim to PII is possible in respect of documents required for production in a criminal trial, the balancing exercise must be carried out more rigorously by the trial judge than in a civil case because the liberty of the individual may be at risk, and therefore the need to avoid a miscarriage of justice will be a very great factor in favour of full and frank disclosure of all relevant material.

The collapse of the Matrix-Churchill trial at the Old Bailey in 1993 led to the setting up of an inquiry under Sir Richard Scott, Vice-Chancellor, who examined the rules on PII and whose report was published in February 1996. During the trial the Crown had claimed PII on various grounds for government guidelines on arms sales to Iraq. The trial judge, Smedley J, inspected the documents, found that some would have been helpful to the defence and ordered disclosure of parts of the materials. This led to the prosecution dropping its case against the three businessmen accused of selling machine tools to Iraq which could have used them to make weapons.

In the political drama that followed the collapse of the trial the Attorney-General (Sir Nicholas Lyell QC) revealed in a statement to Parliament that he had advised the relevant ministers that they had a duty in law to sign the PII certificates, even though they were naturally concerned that innocent men might go to prison on the basis of incomplete trial evidence. The Attorney-General argued that it was for the trial judge to decide the issue of PII. Although there is some support for this view in the authorities, there are also opposite views to the effect that ministers enjoy a political discretion on how much information about the operation of government should be made public, and a recent leading judgment seems to support this view, although no concluded opinion is expressed: see per Lord Woolf in *ex parte Wiley* [1994] 3 All ER 420 at 437–438, where Lord Woolf seems to favour a ministerial discretion to claim PII, rather than a duty, probably on the ground that Ministers are ideally placed to conduct the sensitive political balancing exercise involved in weighing the conflicting public interests. Since a private individual would lack such political judgment it was more likely that a duty to claim PII would be imposed, where relevant, on such an individual rather than upon a Government Minister.

d) *The Scott Report (February 1996)*

Briefly, the most significant finding in this area was that Sir Nicholas Lyell's view that there was a duty on Ministers to claim PII was 'based on a fundamental misconception of the principles of public interest immunity law'. Scott found that prior to the Matrix-Churchill trial there had been no precedent for the use of PII in a serious criminal trial before a judge and jury. He also found that it would rarely, if ever, be right to withhold evidence in criminal proceedings though he conceded that there might be 'very exceptional circumstances' where a PII claim might be feasible. He did not indicate what those circumstances might be.

It followed that, in Scott's view, ministers have a policy discretion not to claim the immunity if satisfied that there is a clear balance in favour of disclosure for the administration of justice. Scott went on to find that the Attorney-General's view, though mistaken, had been taken in good faith and that there had been no government conspiracy to send innocent men to prison.

The Government's response to these findings has been to issue Ministers and civil servants with new guidelines restricting the use of PII certificates by emphasising that the presumption for release of documents in court proceedings is on disclosure not secrecy. The guidelines say that Ministers must take personal responsibility by using PII certificates. They will no longer be able to argue that they had a duty to use such certificates. If a Minister concludes that documents should not be disclosed in the public interest he must say why when signing the certificate and those reasons must reveal substantial countervailing considerations of public interest which outweigh the new presumption in favour of disclosure. It will then be for the court to decide whether to uphold the Minister's view on this issue.

It is interesting to note that, although the Government accepted the Scott findings on PII and has issued guidelines which represent a significant step towards more open government, Sir Nicholas Lyell, the Attorney-General, defended his position by arguing that his advice to Ministers had been 'fully in accordance with the law as it then stood' and on this he was supported by several distinguished lawyers and judges, including Sir Thomas Bingham MR (as he then was).

5.3 Recent articles

The following three articles contain excellent comprehensive reviews of the law on public interest immunity:

Jacob, 'From Privileged Crown to Interested Public' [1993] PL 121

Simon Brown LJ, 'Public Interest Immunity' [1994] PL 579

Zuckermann, 'Public Interest Immunity' [1994] 54 MLR 703

The following article examines the impact of Matrix-Churchill trial:

Ganz, 'Matrix-Churchill and PII: a Postscript' [1995] 58 MLR 417

The following article examines the background leading up to the Scott Report:

Oliver, 'The Scott Report' [1996] PL 357

The following articles analyse the findings of the Scott Report on PII, the first article being by Sir Richard Scott himself.

Scott, 'The Acceptable and Unacceptable Use of PII' [1996] PL 427

Leigh and Lustgarten, 'Five Volumes in Search of Accountability: the Scott Report', (1996) 59 MLR 695 at 716–723

Pavlou, 'Public Interest and Scott' [1996] NLJ 345

5.4 Analysis of questions

Public interest immunity will remain topical for some time following the publication of the Scott Report. Whilst in the past examination questions have tended to concentrate on PII in civil cases it is likely that after the Scott Report questions will be broadened to invite discussion of PII in criminal cases. The topic is a fast-moving one, with much academic material available, so good research will be rewarded if put to good use in an examination answer. The topic is likely to be examined in second/third year administrative law examinations rather than in first year constitutional law examinations, where the relevance of the Scott Report to the convention of Ministerial Responsibility is more likely to be emphasiesed.

5.5 Questions

QUESTON ONE

'In the cases where public interest immunity is claimed, the courts have to balance competing public interests to determine whether disclosure should be ordered.'

Discuss.

University of London LLB Examination
(for External Students) Administrative Law June 1992 Q5

General Comment

An answer to this question should show a thorough knowledge of the cases in which the courts have dealt with the issue of public interest immunity. When will a party to litigation be immune from disclosing documents? How do the courts decide whether or not a document should be immune? How have the courts justified their decisions? What are the competing public interests that must be balanced? Is public interest immunity justified?

Skeleton Solution

- Background.
- *Conway* v *Rimmer.*
- 'Class' claims.
- Inspection.
- Justification.

Suggested Solution

Public interest immunity involves the subordination of the interests of the individual in having all available evidence put before the court in a particular case, to a wider interest, claimed to be that of the public at large, in suppressing particular items of evidence. Since there is a very strong public interest in seeing that justice is done fairly, strong justification should be required before evidence is held immune from disclosure. In some circumstances the suppression of evidence may be justified, but the manner in which the doctrine presently operates places an unfair burden upon parties seeking disclosure of certain evidence.

Public interest immunity developed out of Crown privilege, which gave general and far-reaching immunity from legal action. The justification for automatic Crown privilege from disclosure of documents vanished when the Crown Proceedings Act 1947 did away with much of the previous immunity to litigation. The modern rules relating to non-disclosure do not apply solely to the Crown, but may be invoked by other individuals in certain circumstances. The starting point for the modern rules is the case of *Conway* v *Rimmer* (1968). This was the first case to introduce the balancing exercise at the heart of the decision to grant immunity. The House of Lords identified two interests that needed to be balanced. The first was the interest that harm should not be done to the nation or the public service through disclosure of particular documents. The second was that the public interest in the administration of justice should not suffer as a result of non-disclosure of evidence. It is not clear just how the respective interests would be seriously damaged, especially in view of the limited number of cases in which the claim to immunity is likely to be made. In view of the fact that this case was involved in limiting the extent of immunity, it may be surmised that claims by Ministers and government departments might become extensive if they had automatic immunity, leading to a stultifying of the judicial review process. However, the House of Lords held that it would balance the competing interests; if there was doubt in the matter the court should inspect the documents concerned to see which of the interests should prevail. Three difficulties emerge from this case. The first is the existence of 'class' claims. Secondly, when will inspection occur? Thirdly, when will non-disclosure be justified?

A 'class' claim is a claim that a particular document should not be revealed in a particular case not because it contains information which is sensitive but because it belongs to a class of documents that are inherently protected. Classes of documents falling into this category might include, for instance, Cabinet minutes, Foreign Office despatches and the like. After *Conway* v *Rimmer* it seemed that a claim of this kind made by a Minister would be accepted without challenge by the court. But it is particularly difficult to find justification for non-disclosure in court purely on the class basis. It used to be thought that their disclosure in court might hinder the candour of public servants, a claim that Lord Reid in *Conway* v *Rimmer* described as 'grotesque'. This is no longer credited, but Lord Reid's explanation that disclosure might lead to captious or ill-informed public criticism is hardly more creditable (and indeed Lord

Upjohn did not accept this explanation for immunity). The actions of the Government and the civil service are naturally the subject of a great deal of public interest and criticism in any democratic nation that respects freedom of speech. It is only in the most extreme of cases that the risk of public criticism can outweigh the merits of justice. It should be remembered that the court has the power to order that proceedings take place in camera. If necessary, disclosure could be made subject to strict undertakings on the part of the parties and could be limited to those parts of documents of strict relevance to the proceedings. It is perhaps in view of these arguments that Lord Fraser expressed the opinion in a later case that not even Cabinet minutes would be entirely immune from inspection by the court with a view to disclosure, although they would be entitled to a high degree of protection: *Air Canada* v *Secretary of State for Trade (No 2)* (1983). This is an indication that class claims are now less favourably regarded, although there is still room for arguments of national security, which the court is unlikely to challenge unless manifestly false: *Council of Civil Service Unions* v *Minister for the Civil Service* (1985).

The real difficulty for litigants is the question of when inspection will be ordered. *Conway* v *Rimmer* indicated that the court should inspect where there was doubt about which of the competing interests should be upheld. Subsequent House of Lords' authorities have laid down the principle that the court will not inspect documents unless the applicant shows that disclosure is necessary 'either for disposing fairly of the cause or matter or for saving costs': *Burmah Oil* v *Bank of England* (1980); *Air Canada* v *Secretary of State for Trade (No 2)*. This is derived from the normal rule preliminary to an order for discovery contained in O.24, r13(1), but the House of Lords have treated it as a preliminary to inspection, which itself is a preliminary to ordering discovery where a claim of public interest immunity is not upheld. It is submitted that this is an inappropriate point at which to apply the O.24 test; before inspection by the court takes place, an applicant's chances of demonstrating that the document is necessary for disposing fairly of the action or for saving costs are extremely slim, given the nature of the documents concerned. A more sensible result could perhaps be achieved by the court considering the issue of immunity first, and then, after inspection and if the immunity claim is not upheld, considering the issue under O.24. The fear of the courts that applicants will engage themselves in 'fishing expeditions' is, it is submitted, outweighed by the real risk an applicant may face of being stonewalled by administrative authorities who do not wish to be investigated.

The justification for non-disclosure may vary from case to case. National security has already been considered, and it is submitted will generally provide strong grounds for non-disclosure. The case of *D* v *NSPCC* (1978) illustrates the extension of immunity to a non-governmental organisation. This case is interesting for two further reasons. The first is that it involves the preservation of confidential relationships; confidentiality is not normally a sufficient ground for non-disclosure. Secondly, it lends support to the 'candour' justification in some circumstances. In reality *D* v *NSPCC* illustrates the point that public interest may be a matter for judgment in each case.

Public interest immunity is a necessary sacrifice of the interests of the individual to those of the public in particular circumstances, but strong justification should be required before a claim to immunity is successful. The strength of the case for immunity may need to be stronger where the litigant stands to lose more from the non-disclosure of evidence. However, public interest immunity should also be seen in perspective; it is claimed comparatively rarely and, subject to what has been argued above, the willingness of the courts to scrutinise such a claim means that there is unlikely to be a rash of cases in which justice fails to be done as a result of unjustified non-disclosure.

QUESTON TWO

'The courts should be more vigorous in challenging ministerial claims of public interest immunity.'

Discuss with reference to cases.

University of London LLB Examination
(for External Students) Administrative Law June 1989 Q3

General Comment

This question requires an outline of the current state of the law before the question as to whether or not the courts have gone far enough can be considered. Specific examples are required before it is possible to comment as to extent of vigour which has in fact been demonstrated by the courts.

Skeleton Solution

- Context and definition of public interest immunity claim.
- The original restrictive approach.
- Failure to challenge class claims.
- Effect of decision in *Conway* v *Rimmer.*
- Examples of rejection and acceptance of class claims.
- Different approach to high level documents.
- Effect of *Air Canada* case.

Suggested Solution

A claim for public interest immunity is a request that a court should not grant discovery of certain documents in the course of litigation because their disclosure would be contrary to the public interest. Most commonly a claim will be made by a minister who provides a certificate which sets out the reasons why the documents in question should not be revealed. A claim may be made either in the course of litigation between a private party and the state or where the state intervenes in litigation between the parties. Before addressing the question as to whether the courts should be more vigorous in challenging ministerial claims of immunity, it is necessary to consider briefly the important changes which have taken place in the attitudes of the courts in this area of law and, in particular, the effect of the decision in *Conway* v *Rimmer* (1968).

In *Duncan* v *Cammell Laird & Co Ltd* (1942), which was decided during the course of World War II, the House of Lords, in upholding a claim for immunity on national security grounds, stated that immunity could be claimed either because the contents of a particular document required secrecy or because a document belonged to a class which was required *as a class* to be treated as confidential. Furthermore, a validly taken objection by the responsible minister should be accepted as conclusive.

Following this decision there developed a practice, which was accepted by the courts, of withholding documents simply on the basis of an assertion by a minister that they belonged to a class which needed to be kept secret in order to protect the proper functioning of the public service (see, for example, *Ellis* v *Home Office* (1953)). As a result, a very wide range of documents was brought within the potential ambit of the privilege, irrespective of whether or not they in fact contained any material of a sensitive nature, simply on the basis that there was a need to secure freedom and candour within the public service. There was no attempt to look behind any claim which was expressed in the correct form nor was there any attempt to weigh up the rather vague interest in protecting candour within the government as against the important interest in the proper administration of justice.

Subsequently in *Conway* v *Rimmer* the House of Lords had an opportunity to reconsider its position. In particular, they held that the courts should have the final say in relation to any claim for privilege and that it was their function to hold a balance between the public interest as claimed by the minister and the public interest in ensuring the proper administration of justice.

Following *Conway* v *Rimmer* the courts have, on a number of occasions, rejected claims for exemption based on 'candour and frankness' arguments (see, for example, *Williams* v *Home Office (No 2)* (1982)), although they have been more ready to accept class claims in relation to documents connected with internal investigations and have gone so far as to accept that Cabinet papers should automatically be exempt (see *Attorney-General* v *Jonathan Cape Ltd* (1976)). They have also been prepared to accept class claims based on the need to protect confidential sources of information. For example, in *Rodgers* v *Home Secretary* (1973) the court upheld a claim for privilege in respect of information given by police informers on the grounds that its disclosure would lead to a 'drying up' of information thereby preventing the Board from effectively carrying out its functions.

It would appear therefore that the courts have been reasonably vigorous in challenging ministerial claims for exemption in the sense that they have been prepared to look behind them and to evaluate the competing interests and have reacted with appropriate suspicion to class claims based on vague candour-type arguments. In each case their comments in relation to Cabinet documents would, however, seem to suggest that they may be more ready to accept claims in respect of high level documents at face value. If this is the case then it is arguable that the courts should be more vigorous in their approach as there is no reason in principle why high level documents should be treated in a different manner.

Finally, it is necessary to consider the effect of the House of Lords' decision in *Air Canada* v *Secretary of State for Trade (No 2)* (1983) which is noteworthy for the fact that it appears to display a hardening of attitude in relation to applications for disclosure. That case has not directly affected the position as outlined above but it has made the position of applicants more difficult by requiring them to identify the specific documents sought and demonstrate that they are likely to be necessary for fairly disposing of the issues which are required to be determined by the court. The effect of placing this obstacle in the path of applicants who wish to obtain access to documents which are the subject of a ministerial claim for exemption is to make it less likely that the court will be in a position to challenge such a claim, whether vigorously or otherwise.

6 Tribunals and Inquiries

6.1 Introduction

A tribunal is a decision-making body which finds facts and applies law in resolving the issues before it. Its procedures are more informal than those of a court of law and as a result it is regarded as a cheaper, quicker, more accessible and non-technical alternative to litigation in many fields. A public inquiry is also a fact-finding body but, unlike a tribunal, will not make decisions. Instead it will make recommendations based on its findings of fact so that others, eg ministers, can take account of the views expressed at inquiries when formulating policy decisions. An inquiry tends to more inquisitorial in procedure than a court or a tribunal and in some contexts, eg planning, is mainly designed to provide a forum for the expression of local or regional views or sentiments. The Council on Tribunals, established by the Tribunals and Inquiries Act 1958, supervises the work of most kinds of tribunal and inquiry.

6.2 Key points

a) 'Tribunals are not ordinary courts, but neither are they appendages of Government departments ... tribunals should properly be regarded as machinery provided by Parliament for adjudication rather than as part of the machinery of administration': Franks Report (1957) Cm 218 at p9. This important finding means that, although tribunals are not expected to follow the high standards of procedure of a court of law, they must act fairly and not depart too far from the usual rules of evidence (though tribunals often allow the admission of hearsay evidence). Many tribunals, eg industrial tribunals, have legally qualified chairpersons and are regarded as independent judicial bodies, so that the distinction between such a tribunal and a court becomes a very fine one. Members of most kinds of tribunal are appointed from panels appointed by the Lord Chancellor's Department, with members coming from outside government service in order to ensure the appearance of impartiality and independence. A 'balanced tribunal' is favoured in some contexts, eg industrial tribunals, and consists of a legally qualified chairperson, one employer and one trade unionist. Appeals on points of law may be taken from all tribunals to the High Court unless appeal is expressly excluded by statute: Tribunals and Inquiries Act 1992, s11. Appeal tribunals also exist within the framework of many tribunal systems and the appeal tribunals can consider questions of ultra vires as well as appeals on the merits: *Chief Adjudication Officer* v *Foster* [1993] 1 All ER 705 (HL). The ultimate supervisory jurisdiction of the High Court on issues of ultra vires is unaffected by this position.

b) All tribunals listed in the Tribunals and Inquiries Act 1992 must on request give reasons (oral or in writing) for their decisions: 1992 Act, s10. Any reasons given must be adequate and intelligible: *Re Poyser and Mills Arbitration* [1964] 2 QB 467. The statutory list includes all the important public tribunals in such fields as property and land law, housing, rent, social security, employment, consumer credit, the National Health Service, taxation and rating, immigration and mental health. The list does not include the various kinds of domestic disciplinary tribunal found in trades and professions, but these will usually be regulated by contract which will have either express or implied terms ensuring a fair hearing and which may require the provision of reasons.

c) The Franks Report recommended that tribunal proceedings should be open, fair and impartial:

   '... openness appears to us to require the publicity of proceedings and knowledge of the essential reasoning underlying the decisions; fairness to require the adoption of a clear procedure which enables parties to know their rights, to present their case fully and to know the case which they have to meet; and impartiality to require the freedom of tribunals from the influence, real or apparent, of departments concerned with the subject-matter of their decisions'.

   The Tribunals and Inquiries Acts 1958, 1971 and 1992 reformed tribunal procedures to try to achieve these objectives: see (a) and (b) above. However, tribunals retain a generous discretion as to how to conduct their proceedings. Usually hearings are oral and some tribunals enjoy special powers to summon witnesses, order the production of documents and take evidence on oath, but usually proceedings are conducted informally without sworn evidence. There is no doctrine of binding precedent. Sometimes legal representation is refused on the ground that the presence of lawyers will slow down and formalise proceedings, thereby undermining the objectives of tribunals. However, legal representation is usually permitted where important rights of the individual are at stake. Legal advice and assistance are available, but not legal aid for representation and this may result in inequality where one side can afford a lawyer but the other side cannot. In the spring of 1995 Lord Mackay LC published a Green Paper on Legal Aid (1995) Cm 2854, in which he suggested, inter alia, that legal aid might be extended to tribunals in 'important' fields such as housing, immigration and mental health but this suggestion was dropped from the subsequent White Paper on Legal Aid (1996) Cm 3305. Lord Mackay also enjoys statutory power to permit tribunals to award costs to successful parties but he has not yet exercised this power. At present most tribunals have no power to award costs, which are therefore borne by the parties.

d) In some fields, eg social security and immigration, the final internal appeal tribunal may be the relevant Secretary of State, giving rise to the appearance of bias in the sense that a government minister responsible for policy is being entrusted with the task of adjudicating on a dispute between the citizen and the state on a matter determined by government policy. In France an independent tribunal of general jurisdiction, called the *Conseil d'Etat*, exists to reconsider in principle all discretionary administrative decisions. A similar body exists in Australia: the Administrative Review Commission. The introduction of such a body into England and Wales has been resisted on the ground that it would substitute an unaccountable policy-making tribunal for a minister who is directly accountable to Parliament.

e) The most typical kind of inquiry is the local planning inquiry, but statutory and ad hoc inquiries are also held into major disasters or other incidents attracting public disquiet, eg the King's Cross tube fire, the sinking of the Herald of Free Enterprise, the Cleveland child abuse allegations, the Matrix-Churchill inquiry into government policy on arms sales to Iraq and the Dunblane shootings. Company fraud allegations are investigated during inquiries conducted by inspectors appointed by the Department of Trade and Industry. The majority of 'routine' public inquiries, eg on planning, are conducted either by a Queen's Counsel or a lay person from the Planning Inspectorate, which is an independent executive agency responsible to the Department of Environment. (Prior to the setting up of this inspectorate civil servants from the Department were appointed to chair inquiries.) For the more important kinds of inquiry dealing with issues of public interest a senior judge may be appointed as chairperson.

f) The local public inquiry is at the heart of many planning, environmental and other land-use policy decisions. The purpose of this sort of inquiry is 'to ensure that the interests of citizens closely affected should be protected by the grant to them of a statutory right to be heard ... and to ensure that thereby the Minister should be better informed': per Viscount Dilhorne in *Bushell* v *Secretary of State for the Environment* [1980] 2 All ER 614 (HL). Such an inquiry is not designed to be a general political forum for debate on the substantive merits of proposals, such as the need for a new motorway. The merits are for government policy to assess and for Parliament to debate. The local inquiry should concentrate on the proposed implementation of the policy and the reactions of those affected, eg on the selection of routes which the new motorway might take. It is for the inquiry inspector to decide what is relevant, and to exclude matters which have no probative value or which trespass on issues of policy: *R* v *Secretary of State for Transport, ex parte Gwent County Council* [1987] 1 All ER 161 (though contrast the conduct of the Sizewell inquiry, below).

g) The planning inquiry inspector enjoys a generous discretion as to how to conduct the inquiry under the Town and Country Planning (Inquiry Procedure) Rules 1992, which were made under the Town and Country Planning Act 1990. Generally he should follow the recommendations of the Franks Report on the need for openness, fairness and impartiality. He may receive hearsay evidence and permit cross-examination of witnesses. All objectors should be given an opportunity to know the case they have to meet. He may order evidence to be given under oath and order the production of documents and witnesses (the latter power to send for witnesses indicates the inquisitorial aspects of proceedings which otherwise retain a strong adversarial character). Legal representation is usually allowed and costs can be awarded to successful objectors. Legal aid is not available. At the conclusion of the inquiry the inspector makes a report to the relevant minister and this report must be published.

h) Many planning inquiries involve expert scientific matters and on these the inspector may seek assistance from expert assessors, eg four assessors sat with Sir Frank Layfield when he conducted the major inquiry into the building of a nuclear reactor at Sizewell in Suffolk. In this kind of inquiry, involving controversial environment issues, the government may be willing to discuss policy issues and may, indeed, provide a witness to answer questions as to the merits of the policy behind the scheme. The Town and Country Planning Act 1968 (consolidated by the 1990 Act) provided for the setting up of special planning inquiry commissions to investigate the policy implications of major developments, such as the siting of nuclear reactors, but the need for such a commission disappears if the local public inquiry is encouraged to take on this task, as happened with the Sizewell inquiry: see further [1987] PL 162. To date no planning inquiry commissions have been set up.

i) After the inquiry the duty of the Secretary of State is to read and consider the inspector's report with an open mind. He should 'give such weight as he thinks fit to the recommendations of his inspector, but he is bound to form his own independent judgment': per Widgery J in *Nelsovil* v *MHLG* [1962] 1 WLR 404. The Secretary of State is entitled to consider new evidence arising after the close of the inquiry, but if he then disagrees with his inspector's recommendations on a finding of fact he must permit affected parties the right to make written representations to him or to ask for the re-opening of the inquiry in order to challenge the new evidence. The Secretary of State must give reasons for his decision: Tribunals and Inquiries Act 1992, s10. Any reasons given must be adequate and intelligible, though the courts have discouraged challenges based on excessively legalistic textual criticism of planning decision letters: *Save Britain's Heritage* v *Number 1 Poultry Ltd* [1991] 1 WLR 153 (HL).

j) *Tribunals of inquiry*

Such tribunals, often into the causes of major disasters, may be set up either on an ad hoc basis, eg the Scott inquiry into Matrix-Churchill and arms for Iraq, or under the provisions of the Tribunals of Inquiry (Evidence) Act 1921. In a recent article on such inquiries Sir Richard Scott has emphasised the inquisitorial character of their proceedings and has criticised the Salmon Report on Tribunals of Inquiry (1966) Cmnd 3121 for recommendations too heavily influenced by the adversarial system: Scott: 'Procedures at Inquiries: the Duty to be Fair' (1995) 111 LQR 596. The 1966 Report had identified 'six cardinal principles' which it recommended all tribunals of inquiry to follow:

1. Before any person becomes involved in an inquiry, the tribunal must be satisfied that there are circumstances which affect him and which the tribunal proposes to investigate.
2. Before any person who is involved in an inquiry is called as a witness he should be informed of any allegations which are made against him and the substance of the evidence in support of them.
3. a) He should be given an adequate opportunity of preparing his case and of being assisted by legal advisers;

   b) his legal expenses should normally be met out of public funds.
4. He should have the opportunity of being examined by his own solicitor or counsel and of stating his case in public at the hearing.
5. Any material witnesses he (ie the person to be called as a witness) wishes called at the inquiry should, if reasonably practicable, be heard.
6. He (ie the person to be called as a witness) should have the opportunity of testing by cross-examination conducted by his own solicitor or counsel any evidence which may affect him.

Sir Richard Scott contends that these principles, if slavishly adhered to, would undermine the inquisitorial character of such an inquiry.

It should be noted that Sir Richard Scott's conduct of the Matrix-Churchill inquiry attracted criticism from some politicians, notably Lord Howe, for departing from the Salmon principles and for risking the infliction of damage on the reputations of those called to give evidence. The risks to reputation (and the possibility of civil/criminal proceedings) which follow adverse findings in a report from a tribunal of inquiry might be said to justify the Salmon Report's six cardinal principles.

k) *Department of Trade and Industry investigations*

A useful guide to the approach to be adopted at such inquiries is to be found in the judgments in the Court of Appeal in *Re Pergamon Press Ltd* [1971] Ch 388. Lord Denning MR at p400 observed that whilst DTI inspectors must act fairly, they are masters of their own procedure. Buckley and Sachs LJJ also laid emphasis on the inquisitorial character of such inquiries and the need for the inspectors to enjoy sufficient flexibility in the conduct of them so as to be able to report with courage and frankness.

l) *The Council on Tribunals*

This was established by the Tribunals and Inquiries Act 1958 as an independent supervisory body over tribunals and inquiries. Its membership comprises a lay majority. It has the power to keep under review the constitution and working of almost all public tribunals and inquiries and to report on any matter concerning them referred to it by the Lord Chancellor. However, its influence and impact is limited by a largely part-time membership with limited government funding. There is a small secretariat with little capacity for research. Members of the Council visit tribunals and inquiries to monitor performance, but with only a maximum of 16 Council members the number of visits each year is obviously small. Yet despite these limitations it has built up a solid working relationship with government departments and is usually consulted about primary and delegated legislation affecting tribunal and inquiry procedures, though in its annual report for 1990 the Council complained of a less co-operative attitude by some departments on this matter. Ever since it issued a special report on its functions in 1980 the Council has been arguing for increased powers and resources but to no avail, probably because of lack of publicity for its work and weak political links (it has no select committee of MPs to assist it, unlike the case with the Parliamentary Commissioner). A notable failure came in 1986 when the Council was unable to persuade the Department of Health and Social Security of the case for retaining appeal rights upon the introduction of the Social Security Fund. However, the Council has had some successes, mainly in ensuring procedural consistency and fairness at tribunals and inquiries, and in persuading the government to appoint more legally qualified chairpersons for tribunals. It also succeeded in persuading the government to pay the costs of successful objectors at local planning inquiries out of central funds. It has yet to succeed in persuading government to extend legal aid to the tribunal system.

6.3 Recent articles

Foulkes, 'The Council on Tribunals: Visits, Policy and Practice' [1994] PL 564

Lord Howe 'Procedure at the Scott Inquiry' [1996] PL 445

Sir Richard Scott 'Procedure at Inquiries: the Duty to be Fair' (1995) 111 LQR 596

6.4 Analysis of questions

Tribunals and inquiries are not usually examined in first year constitutional law examination, but in second/third year administrative law examinations essay-type questions on the operation of tribunals and inquiries are common, requiring critical analysis. The operation of the Scott inquiry has renewed interest in tribunals of inquiry. Sometimes tribunals are examined with other remedies, eg Ombudsmen.

Note: some university syllabi do not directly examine tribunals and inquiries.

6.5 Questions

QUESTON ONE

What is the purpose of a local inquiry? What control do the courts exercise over the procedures of a local inquiry?

University of London LLB Examination
(for External Students) Administrative Law June 1992 Q3

General Comment

Inquiries are quite a complex matter – there are many types of local inquiry and they function in different ways. Further, the powers of the court to review the decisions and actions of local inquiries vary from inquiry to inquiry. It is important to show an awareness of the detail without getting bogged down in it. The real issue here is to what extent local inquiries are satisfactory. Do they really fulfil their function of public consultation? Is there sufficient judicial control over the operation of local inquiries?

Skeleton Solution

- Function of inquiries.
- Procedure.
- Duty of decision-maker.
- Judicial control.
- Substantive/procedural.
- Should courts intervene?

Suggested Solution

There are various types of local inquiry, and they are used to determine a wide range of issues of public concern ranging from where to build the Channel Tunnel rail link to whether or not to grant planning permission for a particular development. Some are more formal, and follow stricter procedures, than others and the degree of control exercised by the courts will also differ depending on the type of inquiry involved. Local inquiries are not free from controversy and their real function has always been open to question. The modern law must be seen in the light of post-war controversy surrounding the conduct of inquiries. This led to the publication of the report of the Franks Committee in 1957 and the reforms enacted by the Tribunals and Inquiries Act 1958 (now replaced by the Tribunals and Inquiries Act 1992).

Despite their variety there is a common theme behind local inquiries – public consultation. Inquiries are held to enable members of the public to participate in the decision-making process in cases where it is considered important that they should do so. They give objectors an opportunity to present their views and they allow a decision-maker, whether at local or at ministerial level, to sound out public opinion in relation to a proposed course of action. But this is a very superficial view and how far inquiries actually function in this way depends upon a number of factors which perhaps bear little relation to the underlying democratic theory of local inquiries.

The first, and most obvious of these factors is the amount of public interest in the matter being inquired into. This in itself bears some relation to the type of inquiry being held. For example, local inquiries are greatly used in determining whether or not to grant planning permission for a particular development. In this case it is not at all uncommon for the only parties at the inquiry to be the applicant and the local planning authority, and the inquiry itself is conducted in a similar fashion to a trial. Both parties call witnesses, and present their case and there is a right of appeal against the final decision, which is made by an inspector appointed by the Secretary of State. This stands in marked contrast to a preliminary inquiry into whether to build a motorway. In such a case there will frequently be a great number of objectors, some of whom will be called at the inspector's discretion. The inspector's role in this case is to conduct the inquiry and make a report to the Minister. Responsibility for the ultimate decision lies with the Minister and the findings of the local inquiry may be only one of several factors which are to be weighed in making the ultimate decision.

It is where the second type of local inquiry is concerned that its function is more open to question. In theory they provide for public consultation but they are often attacked as being little more than window dressing, or an opportunity for objectors to let off steam. Ultimate responsibility rests with the Minister and it may be impossible to deduce the degree to which he has taken into account public views or whether they have been ignored. For this reason it might be thought that there is a need for particularly vigilant supervision by the courts. The rights of members of the public are often in issue when important decisions are made, hence they are given the opportunity to present their views at an inquiry; and the courts should protect those rights. But before considering what controls the courts exercise in this sphere, it must be remembered that there are constitutional restraints upon the courts. The power to make a decision in a particular case is for the Minister concerned and not for the courts; constitutionally speaking the courts only have limited and defined ability to interfere with a decision made by the authority appointed by Parliament. That does not necessarily mean that the court's supervisory powers are inadequate.

The most significant powers of control exercised by the courts are thus procedural. The starting point is the Town and Country Planning Act 1990 which authorises the making of rules of procedure governing the conduct of statutory inquiries. Such procedures have been established in relation to a wide range of public inquiries, including the planning inquiries and inquiries into motorways and trunk roads discussed above. The most important procedures include the following: the preparation of a written statement of its case by the authority concerned, the right of representation, the right to call witnesses and cross-examine the witnesses called by the other parties, and the notification of the final decision with the reasons for it. Such rules are in effect a statutory crystallisation of the rules of natural justice, and a failure to observe correct procedure gives rise to an obvious right of challenge before the courts which, if successful, will lead to the decision being set aside. In relation to those inquiries where such procedures are mandatory, it is unrealistic to imagine that the inquiry is merely an opportunity to let off steam. The requirement to give reasons is particularly important since it will be apparent from the reasons whether the views of members of the public have been taken into account; and the reasons may reveal grounds of challenge on the basis of *Wednesbury* (1948) unreasonableness (relevance/irrelevance), thus giving the courts greater powers of control. However, it should be noted that the requirement to give reasons is not particularly onerous, and as long as a decision states words to the effect 'having considered all the circumstances of the case' it is likely that it will be difficult to challenge the decision for failing to take account of relevant factors.

Furthermore, notwithstanding these procedures, where a Minister orders an inquiry in order that the inspector may make a report, the Minister is not bound to follow the recommendations of the inspector. *Franklin* v *Minister of Town and Country Planning* (1948) was a case where it was alleged that the Minister had not fairly considered the inspector's report, because he had made up his mind in advance. The House of Lords held that the Minister could be as biased as he liked, his only duty was to follow statutory procedures. It is unlikely that this sweeping view still stands in the light of later authorities which support the view that the rules of natural justice apply to purely administrative decisions (cf *Bushell* v *Secretary of State for the Environment* (1981)), and to some extent the reforms enacted by the Tribunals and Inquiries Acts provide for a significant element of fairness in the process of decision-making by inquiry; but the court's control is largely purely procedural, in the absence of clear unreasonableness the courts will not examine the merits of a Minister's decision. It should be noted also that fairness has its limits; there is no duty to hear objections which are irrelevant or which repeat information already given, for instance: *Lovelock* v *Secretary of State for Transport* (1979).

Where inquiries are not subject to statutory rules of procedure, the courts will have more limited grounds of control, relying upon more generalised rules of natural justice. This is true in relatively few cases, and in those inquiries where certain procedures are not mandatory they are nonetheless applied by analogy, adding to the procedural fairness of the process. It is likely therefore that the courts will adopt a broad view of the requirements of natural justice in such cases.

Inquiries are by now a familiar technique of decision making, enabling the Minister concerned to make decisions based upon a knowledge of local or specialised criteria. But they are not courts of law, and it is thus not surprising that they do not function in the same way and that the grounds of intervention by the High Court are limited. Nonetheless, the courts have the usual powers of judicial review, and, as has been seen, the existence of well-established procedural rules provides a significant element of fairness and opportunities for control by the courts.

QUESTON TWO

Suppose that the government have decided to set up a scheme to provide compensation for deserving claimants who suffer injury in the course of medical treatment. Two schemes are being considered: the first would provide very detailed rules as to eligibility; the second would leave a very wide discretion; under the first decisions on individual claims would be made by an independent tribunal; under the second such decisions would be made by officials in the government department.

Explain the advantages and disadvantages of these rival schemes.

University of London LLB Examination
(for External Students) Administrative Law June 1991 Q4

General Comment

A complex question bringing together many diverse issues, such as the nature of ministerial responsibility, the nature of tribunals, the PCA, and the practical problems with judicial review. The question does not separate the issues of liability and compensation and this should be reflected in the answer. Also one should address the question of disadvantages and advantages from the position of both the claimant and government.

Skeleton Solution

- Rules-based system.
- Advantages to government and claimant.
- Disadvantages to government and claimant.
- Discretion-based system.
- Conclusion – issue of liability and quantum.

Suggested Solution

In assessing the two schemes proposed the issues of advantages and disadvantages will be assessed from the perspective of the claimant and the government.

Individual claims determined by an independent tribunal

a) *Advantages*

   i) *To the government*

   Setting up an independent tribunal to determine disputes between the individual and the state is a well tried method of providing a cheap and efficient system of justice whilst at the same time maintaining a degree of independence from ministerial control. The government will be able to take the credit for placing the decisions as to the level of benefit in the hands of independent arbitrators, whilst maintaining a degree of control presumably through its power of appointment (usually through the Lord Chancellor acting in conjunction with the Council on Tribunals). Tribunal members who consistently make decisions unpopular with the government may not be sacked as this would be too obvious a manifestation of government interference, but they may find that they are not re-appointed when their term of office expires.

   The awarding of compensation according to strict rules will help to prevent the growth of a body of precedent as decision makers have very little room to manoeuvre. It will also enable the government to budget more accurately in attempting to forecast likely levels of compensation. The rules will presumably have to be considered by Parliament at least in the form of delegated legislation, but their approval will in turn confer legitimacy upon them.

   ii) *To the individual claimant*

   Most claimants would feel happier with a decision making body that at least appears to be independent of ministerial control. Where a decision making body operates within the scope of fixed rules the claimant is less likely to suffer from arbitrary decision making. Like cases are more likely to be treated alike. The use of strict rules may make it easier to challenge the decisions of the tribunal by way of judicial review. The claimant may be able to indicate a failure to comply with mandatory express procedural requirements; a failure to take into account factors stipulated in the rules as being relevant; or an error of law in misinterpreting some provision in the rules. The rules themselves might even be challengeable on the basis that they are ultra vires the parent Act.

   If the tribunal is listed in the Tribunals and Inquiries Act 1992, the claimant will be able to challenge its decisions on the grounds that it has made a wrong decision in law eg *Woodhouse* v *Peter Brotherhood Ltd* (1972), or that it has not supplied adequate reasons for its decisions: see for example *Mountview Court Properties Ltd* v *Devlin* (1970).

b) *Disadvantages*

i) *To the government*

Entrusting the decision making to an independent decision maker does involve a loss of control, and opens up the decision making process to a wide range of legal challenges (as indicated at (a)(ii) above). If the rules adopted are found to be defective in some way, or are being applied in a manner considered to be too favourable to the claimant, the government will have to take the necessary steps to redraft them and seek the appropriate parliamentary approval. This may involve some political embarrassment. The use of ministerial circulars as guidance in the exercise of discretion is a technique frequently used by ministers. This may be seen to be inappropriate in a rules based system. The cost of providing an independent decision making process should not be overlooked. Issues that would have to be considered are the number of tribunals and any appeal structure that might be appropriate.

ii) *To the individual claimant*

The individual claimant may be treated unfairly if they decision maker has to follow strict rules. It may be difficult for the tribunal to make the decision that would be appropriate in his case. It is arguable that in dealing with a matter such as medical negligence claims each case needs to be looked at on its own merits. Having to prepare a case for a tribunal may in any event be beyond the capabilities of many claimants. How are they to marshal complex technical evidence without professional assistance? Legal aid is not widely available for tribunals, and without it many claimants are likely to be seriously disadvantaged.

Decisions made by officials of the relevant government departments

a) *Advantages*

i) *To the government*

Complete ministerial control over the decision making process. Policy as to the situations in which awards will be made, and the level of awards can be directly reflected in the decisions made by the civil servants administering the scheme. It is likely to be a much less costly system than that involving independent tribunals.

ii) *To the individual claimant*

Claimants would be spared the cost and difficulty of preparing a case for consideration by a tribunal. Individual cases could arguably be dealt with more fairly as each case would be considered on its own merits. Any errors in the decision-making process could be referred to the Ombudsman, providing the matter was not excluded from his jurisdiction by statute.

b) *Disadvantages*

i) *To the government*

The disadvantages here relate more to the allocation of functions than to the choice between rules and discretion. Allegations of political interference with the decision making process would obviously be more likely in a system administered from within a government department. Further, there is the prospect of the minister having to answer to Parliament for the administration of the scheme as it would be within the scope of ministerial responsibility. As indicated at (a)(ii) above, the department may find its decisions being investigated by the ombudsman if a claimant alleges that he has suffered injustice as a result of maladministration. A finding of maladministration can lead to the re-opening of many other similar cases.

ii) *To the individual claimant*

The individual claimant may find it more difficult to challenge a decision made by a minister exercising his discretion than by a statutory tribunal applying express provisions. There may be difficulties in obtaining evidence: see HIV Haemophiliac Litigation ([1990] NLJ 1349). The Ombudsman may refuse to investigate a complaint if he regards it as being a case where the claimant could apply to the court for judicial review. Legal aid may not be available for judicial review, the costs of which can escalate if the minister decides to appeal against a decision that goes against him at first instance.

In conclusion it is submitted that neither of the schemes proposed would be ideal for either side. At present such cases are dealt with by the courts because of the need for independence and the problem of dealing with complex factual issues. There is no evidence to suggests that these problems are solved by giving the decision to a tribunal or a minister. The solution may need to be more radical, such as the adoption of a no fault compensation scheme for victims of medical negligence. A tribunal might then be the appropriate body to determine levels of compensation.

QUESTION THREE

Evaluate the efficacy of institutions other than courts in ensuring that government bodies exercise their powers in conformity with legal principles.

University of London LLB Examination
(for External Students) Administrative Law June 1994 Q5

General Comment

This question is directed at the contrast between the approach of the courts, which are concerned with ultra vires and thus with legality in a pure sense, and with other 'institutions' which have different criteria for examining the manner in which powers have been exercised. There is a certain need for definition at the outset: what is meant by 'institutions other than courts', 'government bodies' and 'legal principles'?

Skeleton Solution

- The ambit of the question defined.
- Ministerial responsibility.
- The ombudsmen.
- Tribunals and inquiries.

Suggested Solution

If 'government bodies' is taken in the narrow sense of the organs of central government, then it may be seen that there are a number of institutions other than the courts which have a role to play in ensuring the legality of governmental actions. These include Parliament itself, and external institutions such as tribunals and inquiries and the ombudsmen. While the courts are concerned very narrowly and above all else with the legality of the actions of governmental bodies, which the courts police through the ultra vires doctrine, these other institutions invariably take a much broader approach. They thus contribute to the overall legality of the exercise of powers without necessarily focusing on legality as a ground of intervention.

The powers enjoyed by government bodies are normally conferred upon a particular minister although exercised by civil servants. This has the important consequence that the minister in question will be answerable to Parliament for the manner in which those powers are exercised. This doctrine of ministerial responsibility should thus provide an important check upon the way in which powers are exercised, whereby Parliament is itself able to police their exercise. But ministerial responsibility does not provide an effective check on the legality of governmental actions. This is for a number of reasons. The first is that Members of Parliament simply do not have time to consider the day-to-day running of the administration. Secondly, within the British system of democracy, the government will almost always have effective control of Parliament. The combination of these factors means that ministers will generally only be called into question where there is some political capital to be gained from a particular error of their department. Thus the vast majority of errors in the exercise of powers will not be accounted for. Where errors are questioned, the thrust of Parliament's investigation will be political rather than legal. A final consideration is that the normal parliamentary sanctions resulting from errors falling within a particular minister's jurisdiction is to call for that minister's resignation. That scarcely encourages openness of government. Parliament therefore provides an inefficient mechanism for policing the exercise of powers.

The ineffectiveness of ministerial responsibility as a method of detecting and eradicating illegality in the exercise of government powers highlights the need for an independent body which is able to devote its time to investigating the exercise of powers. Such institutions exist through the offices of the various ombudsmen. The ombudsman with general responsibility for the exercise of government powers is the Parliamentary Commissioner for Administration (PCA), introduced by the Parliamentary Commissioner Act 1967. The PCA's concern is not, strictly speaking, with legality. The PCA's role is to investigate complaints of 'maladministration'. This is a much broader concept, which covers a range of complaints including bias, neglect, delay, incompetence, arbitrariness and other forms of bad administration. Some of these may well be illegal in some contexts, but the PCA is expressly precluded from investigating a complaint where there is a remedy before the courts or a suitable tribunal, unless satisfied that it would not be reasonable to expect the complainant to pursue such remedies. This in effect means that the PCA's jurisdiction is specifically directed away from questions of illegality and towards the more general considerations set out above. Furthermore, the PCA has no power to reverse a decision or compel a government body to exercise its powers in a particular way. Thus, unlike the courts, the PCA cannot ensure that a government body acts legally.

Nonetheless, the PCA has an important contribution to make to the overall legality of governmental action. His presence and his ability to weed out maladministration means the PCA ensures that these bodies take care in the exercise of their powers. Furthermore, the

PCA is in some ways more penetrative than the courts, which are restricted to the ultra vires doctrine as a means of intervention. The PCA is able to intervene to correct all manner of abuse and unfairness. Furthermore, he is able to do so without the vast expense that is incurred by bringing matters before the courts. The PCA's role involves mediation and conciliation and thus may foster cooperation, as opposed to the antagonism that can result from court proceedings. In a very broad sense, therefore, the PCA and ombudsmen generally may be seen as encouraging and contributing to the overall legality of government actions, although admittedly this involves a certain flexibility in the definition of legality.

The institutions that are probably most effective in ensuring the legal exercise of governmental powers are, not surprisingly, those which function most like the courts. Within English administrative law there is a vast array of tribunals and inquiries, and some of these have a very important and effective role to play in applying legal principles to the exercise of powers. Most tribunals and some inquiries function in a manner similar to the courts. In the sphere of immigration law, the tribunal operates as a form of appeal against decisions of the Home Secretary. The tribunal of first instance hears all of the evidence and makes a determination which applies legal principles to its findings of fact, and the Immigration Appeal Tribunal hears appeals on questions of law from such determinations. Thus in this sphere, the tribunals contribute to the formation of legal principles which then shape the way in which the Home Office exercises its powers. Unlike the courts, however, such tribunals will be concerned with the merits of the cases before them, defined by reference to legal principles, rather than being concerned merely with questions of pure legality.

Tribunals that operate in this manner clearly have an effect on decision-making which is both ex post facto, in that the effect is an appeal from a particular decision, and which also operates as precedent which shapes the legality of future decision-making. Inquiries, on the other hand, may be either ex post facto, or they may operate as a means of making the decision itself. An inquiry may be called to examine some illegality or abuse of power after it has occurred; the Scott Inquiry into Arms Sales to Iraq is an example of such an ex post facto inquiry. These inquiries do not, as such, ensure that government bodies exercise their powers in conformity with legal principles save in the narrow sense that their findings should prevent such abuses occurring in the future. In contrast with this, the other type of inquiry, which forms part of the decision itself, is really an opportunity for public consultation; an example of this is a public inquiry into whether to build a motorway. Such an inquiry contributes to the legality of decision-making in the broadest sense: the chairman of the inquiry will make recommendations based upon the application of more or less predefined principles to the results of the consultation process. Some of these inquiries, particularly in the sphere of planning law, actually operate rather like courts of law, in the same way as the tribunals described above, and thus have a similar contribution to make.

It can be seen then that there are several different types of institutions which operate as checks upon the exercise of powers by government bodies. None of these institutions is truly effective in ensuring the legality of action as defined by reference to the ultra vires principle. Each of them does have its own contribution to make, however, although some are clearly more effective than others.

7 Statutory Corporations and Local Government

7.1 Introduction

A public corporation is a statutory body designed to administer public services in a manner largely independent of central government. All local authorities are public corporations, and are elected and accountable bodies. The few remaining nationalised industries are also run by public corporations, eg London Regional Transport. The Board administering a nationalised industry is accountable to an internal consumer council, which acts as a general watchdog on such matters as pricing policy. Board members are appointed and removable by the relevant Secretary of State and an annual report from the Board is laid before Parliament.

The policy of privatisation during the 1980s has switched the focus of attention in public law away from the traditional problems of control of the public corporations. However, local government remains an important area for the public lawyer, not only because of its constitutional significance in helping to separate and devolve power but also because of the special problems created in the field of legal controls, notably judicial review, and the policy/operation distinction created by the courts as a means of limiting the legal responsibility of public bodies for the negligent exercise of power. The rest of this chapter therefore concentrates on issues relating to local government.

The most interesting theme for students to develop is the impact of reforms during the past 16 years which have challenged and undermined local government autonomy. This has been done through privatisation of functions, the creation of new quangos to run local government services, and the centralisation of some functions. The financing of local government through central government grants and central government supervision through 'capping' of the community charge ('poll tax') and later the council tax is also a significant part of the story. It has been argued that local government has been reduced to the status of an agency responsible for ensuring the provision of a range of discrete services which the market cannot directly provide: see Loughlin's essay on central-local Government relationships in Jowell and Oliver's *The Changing Constitution* (3rd edn 1994).

7.2 Key points

a) *Structure*

Prior to 1 April 1986

i) London – London Government Act 1963

- Greater London Council (central coordinating body).
- 32 London Boroughs (and City of London Corporation).

ii) England and Wales – Local Government Act 1972

- England: six metropolitan county councils; 36 metropolitan districts; parish councils.
- 39 county councils; 296 district councils; parish councils.
- Wales: eight county councils; 37 district councils; community councils.
  – more centralised in the non-metropolitan countries.

b) *Subsequent reforms*

i) Local Government Act 1985

- Abolished central bodies – ie GLC and 6 metropolitan county councils.
- Functions of GLC and metropolitan county councils taken over initially by non-elected bodies – ultimately to be transferred to boroughs and districts.

ii) Reasons for reform

- Two-tier system not necessary – most functions already carried out at local level.
- Money saved.
- Political legislation to dispense with opposition.

iii) Further reforms have been implemented as from 1 April 1996. In Wales eight counties have been replaced by 22 new unitary districts. In England the reorganisation has involved the abolition of three county councils (Cleveland, Avon and Humberside) and the creation of 13 new unitary authorities. Further reorganisation is scheduled for 1 April 1997, though the county map will remain broadly intact. The reforms are partly the product of recommendations from the Local Government Commission.

c) *Internal organisation*

i) Members

- County council: 60–100; elected every four years.

  Metropolitan district council 50–80; 1/3 retire each year.

  Non-metropolitan district council: 30–60; one of above systems for election.

- London – elections every three years.

ii) Meetings

- Section 101 LGA 1972: widespread delegation to committees.
- Public Bodies (Admission to Meetings) Act 1960 – public and press entitled to be present at council and committee meetings unless authority passes resolution to exclude them in the public interest: *R* v *Brent Health Authority, ex parte Francis* [1985] QB 869.

d) *Sources of income*

i) Council tax

- Dwellings are allocated to one of eight valuation bands. The allocation is determined by the valuation office.
- Relief is available to sole occupants and those on low incomes.

ii) Grants from central government

- specific eg police, student grants, urbanisation.
- general 'revenue support grant'.

iii) Borrowing

iv) Charges for provision of services and facilities

e) *Powers of local authorities*

i) Dependent on Parliament (via statute) for their powers; subject to doctrine of ultra vires.

ii) Power involves exercise of discretion – must be exercised 'reasonably', 'bona fide'.

iii) Statutory corporations – can sue and be sued.

iv) Legislation

- Promote private bills.
- Bye-laws – subject to central government approval and the ultra vires rule: *Kruse* v *Johnson* [1898] 2 QB 91.

f) *Forms of control over local authorities*

i) By central government

- Enabling statutes.
- Bye-laws, borrowing, capital expenditure – subject to approval.
- Co-operation/consultation.
- Grants – general and specific – recently brought under great control.
- Default powers: minister may intervene where authority failing properly to exercise power.

ii) By extra-judicial authorities

- Local Commissioners hear complaints concerning maladministration by local authorities: see chapter 14.
- Local authority accounts audited annually by district auditors.

iii) By the courts

- Doctrine of ultra vires, eg local authority must not act 'unreasonably' – the '*Wednesbury* principle'.
- Civil liability – three torts may be relevant:

Negligence

The difficulty here is that there is a well-established distinction between negligence in policy-making (which attracts no liability in private law) and negligence in operation of policy (which does attract liability): *Anns* v *Merton LBC* [1978] AC 728, especially per Lord Wilberforce. This distinction is not an easy one to make in particular factual circumstances and was recently discarded in favour of a new approach: see *Stovin* v *Wise* (1996), section 7.3 below.

The general trend has been towards an ever greater unwillingness on the part of the courts to impose a common law duty of care on the exercise of statutory powers, so that even where the matter is justiciable (ie an operational decision) the plaintiff in a private law action must be able to prove foreseeability, proximity and that it is fair, just and reasonable for the common law duty of care to be imposed in the situation in question. The courts are especially reluctant to hold liable in negligence those who have been given special responsibilities of protecting society from the wrongdoing of others: *X* v *Bedfordshire County Council, M* v *Newham London Borough Council, E* v *Dorset County Council* [1995] 3 All ER 353, HL (child care responsibilities of local authorities).

Breach of statutory duty

Damages will be granted only if the particular statutory duty was designed to confer in private law rights of action for compensation for breaches of that duty. Since many statutory duties are designed for the benefit of the general public rather than for particular individuals, it may be difficult to establish this point. Further, even where the plaintiff can show that he is within the group of people intended to be given special protection by the statutory duty in question, he must go on to show that a duty of care at common law can be separately established on common law principles, since the statutory duty is not itself a sufficient basis for such a duty. Hence, as with the tort of negligence above, he must argue foreseeability, proximity and the fair, just and reasonable requirements, and once again the courts will be reluctant to find liability on the part of those given the task of protecting society from the wrong-doing of others: *X* v *Bedfordshire County Council; M* v *Newham London Borough Council; E* v *Dorset County Council*, above, especially per Lord Browne-Wilkinson. See also *Stovin* v *Wise* (1996), section 7.3 below.

The tort of misfeasance in a public office

This is a most unusual tort, being designed as a 'public law tort' and hence the only type of wrong-doing which is really suitable for an award of damages under RSC O.53 reviews. It is committed if the ultra vires act or decision was intended to injure the applicant or was taken in the knowledge that it was unlawful, ie taken in bad faith. This is difficult to prove and hence damages are rarely awarded under RSC O.53 reviews: *Dunlop* v *Woollahra Municipal Council* [1981] 1 All ER 1202. If the tort is proven it may be that vicarious liability for it can arise: *Racz* v *Home Office* [1994] 2 AC 45 (HL). The precise scope of the tort of misfeasance in public office was examined recently in *Three Rivers District Council* v *Bank of England (No 3)* (1996) see section 7.3 below.

7.3 Recent cases and articles

Stovin v *Wise (Norfolk County Council, Third Party)* [1996] 3 All ER 801 (HL) – the plaintiff had been injured in a collision at a road junction. The view of motorists was partly obscured by a high bank on private land adjoining the junction. The local authority, as highway authority, had statutory powers to require the removal of such a bank but, apart from contacting the landowner about paying for the removal of the bank, nothing had been done. The trial judge had held the local authority partly to blame for the plaintiff's injuries. The House of Lords *held*, by a majority of three to two, Lords Slynn and Nicholls dissenting, that the local authority was not liable.

The decision is of great importance in the field of tortious liability of public authorities because the majority of the Law Lords appeared to discard previous tests for the establishment of liability for negligence and breach of statutory duty. In particular the majority judgements make it clear that the '*Anns*' distinction between policy and operations is an inadequate tool with which to determine the existence of a duty. The issue of whether a statutory duty can give rise to a common law cause of action in respect of a failure to act must be determined by reference to:

i) the question of whether it would in All the circumstances have been irrational not to have exercised the power, (so that there was in effect a public law duty to act); and

ii) the question of whether there were exceptional grounds for holding that the policy of the statute required compensation to be paid to persons who suffered loss because the power had not been exercised: per Lord Hoffmann at pp827g–828e.

On the facts it was found that it was not irrational for the local authority to have decided not to remove the bank, but that, even if it ought to have done so, there were no grounds upon which it could be said that the public law duty gave rise to a liability to compensate persons who suffered loss because it was not performed; there had been no question of general reliance on the local authority to improve the junction. Further the majority had in mind the broader consequences of imposing a duty of care, notably that local authorities might increase expenditure on highways to avoid large claims for damage at the expense of education and social service budgets; the courts ought not to develop policies on the imposition of liability that would cause such budgetary distortions. *Comment*: The majority decision indicates a new approach to liability for the negligent exercise or non-exercise of statutory powers and the effect may be to rehabilitate a decision long thought to be discredited: *East Suffolk Rivers Catchment Board* v *Kent* [1941] AC 74. *Stovin* v *Wise* is consistent with the views of the Privy Council in *Rowling* v *Takaro Properties Ltd* [1988] AC 473 in showing distaste for the policy/operational test used in *Anns*. On the other hand the policy/operational test was used by the Law Lords in *X* v *Bedfordshire County Council* in which it was indicated that an ultra vires exercise of power at the operational level could give rise to a private law duty of case if this was appropriate. The uncertainty that has been created in this field of law is probably the result of the influence of policy factors on the minds of the judges. The authorities could be said to illustrate Dicey's warnings against the creation of special rules or immunities for public bodies based on subjective judicial assessments of what the 'public interest' may require.

Three Rivers District Council v *Bank of England (No 3)* [1996] 3 All ER 558 (QBD) – the plaintiff local authority had brought an action against the defendant (the Bank of England) as a result of having lost money deposited with the Bank of Credit and Commerce International at the time of its collapse. The essence of the claim was misfeasance in the licensing of BCCI. As a preliminary issue the court was asked to rule as to the scope of the tort of misfeasance in a public office. It was held that:

i) the tort would be committed where either

- the defendant intended to injure the plaintiff or a person in a class of which the plaintiff was a member; or

- the defendant knew that he had no power to do the act complained of and that the act would probably injure the plaintiff;

ii) that for the purposes of proving intention it was sufficient that the defendant had actual knowledge that the act was unlawful or, in circumstances, in which he believed or suspected that the act was beyond his power, that he did not ascertain whether or not that was so or failed to take such steps as would be taken by an honest and reasonable man to ascertain the true position; and

iii) that if as a result the plaintiff had suffered loss or damage, that the plaintiff had a sufficient right or interest to maintain an action of misfeasance in a public office.

Applying those principles to the facts, the judge provisionally ruled that, firstly, the plaintiff local authority, as depositor or potential depositor, had sufficient interest to sue for misfeasance; but that, secondly, the defendant Bank of England was not capable of being liable to the plaintiff for the tort of misfeasance in public office; and thirdly, that no causal link could be established between the losses of the plaintiff local authority and the acts and omissions of the defendant Bank of England.

Comment: This is an important clarification of the scope of liability for what may be properly described as the only 'public law tort' – the tort of misfeasance in a public office. Although it has similarities with private law torts which require proof of an intention to injure, the tort of misfeasance in a public office is primarily concerned with public officials who deliberately and dishonestly abuse their powers. Malice, in the sense of an intent to injure, and knowledge that a certain activity is ultra vires, are alternative, not cumulative, bases for an allegation of misfeasance.

Butler and Wood, 'Negligence in Residential Care: *X* v *Bedfordshire CC*' [1995] NLJ 1826

Cane, 'Suing Public Authorities in Tort' (1996) 112 Law Quarterly Review 13

Carnwath, Sir Robert, 'The Reasonable Limits of Local Authority Powers' [1996] PL 244

Hopkins, 'East Suffolk Rehabilitated in South Norfolk' [1996] CLJ 425

7.4 Analysis of questions

For first year constitutional law some syllabuses examine the topic of local government, eg London LLB (External). The emphasis is usually on the relationship with central government within the general context of the separation of powers. However, some syllabuses, eg Wolverhampton LLB, do not directly examine the topic of local government structure and finance. For second/third year administrative law the emphasis is usually on judicial review of local authority powers rather than on the structure and finance of local government. London LLB (External) examination papers have also favoured examination of the policy/operation dichotomy within the context of problem-type questions on local government exercise of powers and this may become a regular topic for examination in the light of recent re-evaluation of principles in such cases as *X* v *Bedfordshire County Council* (1995) and *Stovin* v *Wise* (1996).

7.5 Questions

QUESTION ONE

'One result of the legal reforms over the past fifteen years is that local government, once the most responsive form of democracy, is being relegated to the position of manager of local services with little or no residual autonomy.'

Critically assess this statement.

University of London LLB Examination
(for External Students) Constitutional Law June 1994 Q8

General Comment

As with all questions on the constitutional role and position of local government, a good answer requires a fairly detailed knowledge of rather a technical area. However, if the candidate has such knowledge, it should be possible to produce just such a good answer. But, as ever, the most important thing to do is to answer the question: by discussing the statement quoted.

Skeleton Solution

- Historical development.
- Local government: representative role.
- Financial control.
- Functional control: education; housing; police.

Suggested Solution

It is hard to deny that the past 15 years have seen considerable legislative activity by Parliament in the sphere of central-local government relations. No doubt, such is inevitable where the political complexion of central government has remained unchanged during that period, so that the almost inevitable tension between central and local government, where the two are of different political persuasions, has been exacerbated. However, the question in essence rests upon two assumptions: first, that local government was 'once the most responsive form of democracy' and, second, that the result of the recent reforms has been to relegate local government to the position of a 'manager of local services with little or no residual autonomy'. In discussing the quote, it is necessary to consider whether these are valid assumptions.

English law has long recognised a functional division of powers between local and central government, moreover, it is clear that a considerable degree of local autonomy was enjoyed by local officials such as sheriffs and constables before the fourteenth century. By the seventeenth century, however, central control was much reduced. 'For the next 200 years', as Hood Phillips notes, 'local government was, subject to the legislative power of Parliament, almost autonomous' (O Hood Phillips and P Jackson, *Constitutional and Administrative Law* (7th edn, 1987), p583). Since the main reforms of the nineteenth century, establishing the modern framework of local government, the central-local relationship has been well-recognised as an essential part of the constitutional system in England.

It was in these nineteenth century reforms that local government first acquired its representative function. Several Acts were enacted to provide for locally elected councils. Loughlin has pointed out that, at least until the advent of direct elections to the European Parliament, 'Local councils are the only governmental institutions outside of Parliament which are subject to direct periodic election' (M Loughlin, 'The Restructuring of Central-Local Government Relations' in J Jowell and D Oliver, *The Changing Constitution* (3rd edn, 1994), 261, at p264). The basic legal framework of local government elections is now contained in the Representation of the People Act 1983. As elected bodies, they thus enjoy a democratic legitimacy unmatched by any other institution of the constitution, save the House of Commons itself.

Indeed, it may be argued that in some respects local government enjoys more legitimacy than its central counterpart. Thus, unlike a prospective Westminister candidate, an intending councillor, to qualify as a candidate, must have some connection with the area in which the election is fought, either as an elector for the area, or as having resided, worked or occupied land there during the previous year; similarly, a local authority's term of office is fixed by statute (the main statutory provisions, in the Local Government Act 1972, are rather complex; see, generally, Wade and Forsyth: *Administrative Law* (7th edn, 1994), p122 et seq). In these senses, then, it is possible to argue that local authorities are a highly responsive form of democracy, where the links between represented and representative are much closer than at the national level. However, it should be pointed out that the turn-out of voters at local elections is generally far poorer than that for general elections, which tends to undermine their legitimacy and, hence, the claim that they are the 'most' responsive form of democracy.

Nevertheless, it might seem, given that they enjoy considerable democratic legitimacy, to be appropriate that they enjoy a degree of local autonomy in the conduct of those aspects of the executive function that may properly be carried out at local level. It is somewhat ironic, no doubt, that the current government should put such faith in the principle of subsidiarity as the 'local' authority vis-à-vis the 'central' European Community, and yet be unwilling to concede a similar sphere of competence to local authorities in England. Yet it seems true that reforms in the last 15 years have tended to reduce local government to the status of a 'manager of local services with little or no residual autonomy'.

Central government has always exercised ultimate control over the structure of local government, culminating in the enactment of the 1972 Act. This process is certain to continue under the Local Government Act 1992 with the establishment of the Local Government Commission empowered to make recommendations to the Secretary of State for structural, boundary or electoral changes in local government (Local Government Act 1992, s13). In terms of finance, central government exerts the power of the purse-string, since local government relies primarily on government grants for the revenue to carry out its tasks: it may not therefore be too surprising that central government might wish to exercise greater control over how this money is spent, but it is certainly arguable that party political considerations have been to the fore of late. Further, although the alterations in the system empowering local authorities to tax – the community charge and its replacement the council tax – were intended to make local government more responsive to its electors, they have instead proved highly controversial and led to considerable friction over the issue of central governmental controls 'capping' local expenditure. As Wade says, 'the Local Government Finance Acts 1982–92 have given the central government a stranglehold on local authority revenue and expenditure' (see Wade and Forsyth (above) at p139).

The period since 1979 has also seen considerable legislative action by central government encroaching on the functions of local government. In matters such as education and housing, for example, historically typical areas of local control, recent changes have seen further centralisation.

In conclusion, there is much force in the assertion in the quote that local government, a responsive form of democracy, has been reduced to the status of agent of central government, deprived of much of the autonomy that it enjoyed in practice, if not strict law, in earlier years.

QUESTION TWO

Local councils are empowered by the (fictitious) Caravan Sites Inspection Act 1990 to issue bye-laws regulating health and safety on caravan sites and to prosecute site owners who fail to respect any bye-laws that the council might produce.

In May 1992 Seaside Council passes bye-laws requiring site owners to provide a fire extinguisher for every caravan on the site, to institute a system for ensuring that no threat to health or safety was posed by waste, vermin or vegetation, and to place no more than 12 caravans on each acre of the site. Seaside decided that it would inspect each site only once every three years. In May 1994, the council stopped all inspections, claiming it could no longer afford the service. The council had learned in March 1994 that one of its inspectors had dishonestly reported that he had inspected sites which he had not in fact visited, but took no action in response to this.

In late May 1994, the unusually hot summer lead to a series of fires at the adjacent 'Happy Holiday' and 'Retirement World' caravan sites in Seaside. As a result of the site owners' failure to clear debris from the ground and the siting of more than 12 caravans on each acre, the damage wrought by the fire was substantial. Fire brigade officers reported that few of the fire extinguishers provided by the owners were in working order. 'Happy Holiday' was due for inspection the week after Seaside cancelled the service. 'Retirement World' was one of the sites falsely reported as inspected.

Basil had a caravan on 'Happy Holiday' which was destroyed by the fire. Sybil's caravan on 'Happy Holiday' remained intact, but repair costs are estimated at £2,000. Polly owned a caravan in 'Retirement World'. Her caravan escaped unscathed, but because of the devastation wreaked on the site she is no longer able to lease it to holidaymakers over the summer. This will cost her some £2,000 in lost income.

Advise Basil, Sybil and Polly if they could successfully establish claims for liability in negligence or for breach of statutory duty against Seaside Council or the site owners.

University of London LLB Examination
(for External Students) Administrative Law June 1994 Q9

General Comment

Where a statute confers powers upon an authority rather than creating duties, difficult questions can arise about the point at which the council's actions give rise to a liability in tort. Does a duty of care arise when the council considers whether or not to exercise its powers, or only when it actually exercises them? Other issues raised by this question are vicarious liability, liability for economic loss and the extent to which bye-laws may create actionable statutory duties on the part of the persons whom they bind.

Skeleton Solution

- General considerations: the policy/operation test and recent case law.
- Basil and Sybil:
  - the council;
  - the site owners.
- Polly's economic loss generally irrecoverable.

- Negligent mis-statement by the council: whether fair, just and reasonable to impose a duty of care.
- Fraud.

Suggested Solution

Whether or not any of these caravan owners can establish a claim in negligence or for breach of statutory duty against either the council or the site owners may depend upon certain factors which we are not told about. In particular, it will depend upon whether the owners placed their caravans on the sites before or after the breaches took place, how much control the caravan owners had over the conditions of the site, and how much they collaborated with the site owners in breaching the bye-laws. It is not at all clear how far the caravan owners can be said to have relied upon the council or upon the site owners to ensure compliance with the bye-laws. Since the relevant regulations are contained in bye-laws, the caravan owners may be presumed as a matter of law to know about their contents, since everybody is presumed to know the law. If the caravan owners collaborated in their breach then they may have difficulty in establishing liability, or may be held to have been contributorily negligent. These are considerations of general application which must be taken into account in advising the caravan owners.

Basil and Sybil's prospects may be considered together as they have both suffered physical damage to their caravans, and their caravans were on the same site. It seems unlikely that they will be able to establish claims against Seaside Council. There is no basis for a claim of breach of statutory duty; the Act confers a power on the council and not a duty. It is doubtful that they will be able to establish claims in negligence. The only actions of the council that can be impugned are its decisions to inspect each caravan site only once every three years, and then to withdraw the service altogether; the effect of these decisions being that 'Happy Holiday' was never inspected. Such decisions on the allocation of resources are generally beyond the scope of negligence unless they are ultra vires (*Rowling* v *Takaro Properties Ltd* (1988)). There is no apparent ultra vires here. This opinion is confirmed by recent case law which requires that the exercise (or non-exercise) of statutory power must be 'irrational' before the question of liability can arise: *Stovin* v *Wise* (1996) (HL).

There may, however, be a slim chance of demonstrating negligence on the part of the council. In *Anns* v *Merton London Borough Council* (1978) the House of Lords held that an authority with such a discretionary power had a duty to consider properly whether or not to use that power. *Murphy* v *Brentwood District Council* (1990) overruled *Anns* but did not consider this specific issue. It is unclear therefore whether authorities are still subject to such a duty. If they are, Basil and Sybil may be able to show that the council did not consider properly whether or not to exercise its power and thus was negligent. There may be grounds for concluding that this was the case if the report of the fire officers was made to the council; it may be argued that this would have put the council on notice that there was a potential breach of the bye-laws and should have caused them to order inspection of the sites.

As against the site owners, Basil and Sybil may have stronger claims depending upon the general considerations set out above. Unlike the council, the site owners may be considered to be under a statutory duty resulting from the bye-laws made pursuant to the hypothetical Caravan Sites Inspection Act 1990, although this may depend upon the provisions of the Act itself. Statutory duties giving rights of action do sometimes arise from regulations made pursuant to a statute (for instance, under the Health and Safety at Work Act 1974). Even if an actionable statutory duty does not arise, it may be difficult for the site owners to defend claims of negligence in view of the breach of the bye-laws, and in view of the fact that fire officers have reported that few of the fire extinguishers were in working order.

In *X* v *Bedfordshire County Council* (1995) a unanimous House of Lords held that it must be fair, just and reasonable to impose the common law duty of a care in a case involving the breach of a statutory duty. On the facts of the present case there would appear to be no public policy reasons for exempting the site owners from such a duty of care.

Polly's loss is economic in nature. As a general rule, such loss is not recoverable in an action for negligence unless it arises from reliance upon negligent advice in accordance with *Hedley Byrne & Co Ltd* v *Heller & Partners Ltd* (1964). Unless Polly has received such advice and relied upon it, she will not be able to pursue Seaside council or the site owners for negligence. As has been explained above, an action for breach of statutory duty will not lie against the council because the Act conferred a power and not a duty. Given that this statute appears to be concerned with health and safety, and not with the protection of caravan owners' economic interests, Polly may also be unable to pursue an action for breach of statutory duty against the site owners, assuming that such an action would be available in any event (see *Peabody Donation Fund Governors* v *Sir Lindsay Parkinson & Co Ltd* (1985)).

If statutory powers are exercised, they must be exercised with reasonable care. When the council learnt that one of its inspectors had dishonestly reported inspecting 'Retirement World', it may be argued that it should have ordered a proper inspection of the site, an argument that is stronger if the limb of *Anns* v *Merton* referred to above is still good law. The council's failure to order a proper inspection means that it did not take reasonable care in the exercise of its powers. It might further be argued that the council's failure to warn Polly that the inspector had reported dishonestly amounted to a negligent representation that the site complied with the bye-laws and was thus safe. Thus it might be argued that the council comes within the *Hedley Byrne* class of negligent advice. Whether this is so will depend upon the extent to which Polly relied upon this representation so that it constituted negligent advice within that doctrine. There is little evidence to suggest that that was the case.

However, unlike the site owners, the council may be able to argue that it would not be fair, just and reasonable to impose upon it a common law duty of care for the exercise of its statutory powers, having regard to its general responsibilites to protect sections of the community and its limited financial resources: *X* v *Bedfordshire County Council, Stovin* v *Wise*, above.

Polly may have a claim in tort based upon the inspector's dishonest report. This may amount to a tortious fraud. As the council is vicariously liable for the torts of its employees acting in the course of their employment, and as the inspector appears to have been employed by the council, Polly might be able to recover damages from the council for this tort. But, once again, the substantial problem is in showing that she relied upon the inspector's false report in such a way that she can be said to have suffered loss as a result of it.

8 Introduction to Judicial Review: Procedural Issues

8.1 Introduction

The procedure for obtaining judicial review is by way of an application for judicial review under RSC O.53, which has been partially enacted by s31 Supreme Court Act (SCA) 1981. The procedure raises a number of complex issues which have given rise to much case law. The issues may be broken down into the following categories:

a) the scope of judicial review: nowadays this will depend mainly on the subject-matter of the power or duty being challenged rather than the source of that power or duty;

b) the reservation of judicial review for public law issues involving public bodies: nowadays this is known as the exclusivity principle of *O'Reilly* v *Mackman* [1983] 2 AC 237 (HL);

c) the legal standing (locus standi) requirement under O.53, r3(7) and s31(3) SCA 1981;

d) the effect of alternative remedies upon an application for judicial review; and

e) the effect of undue delay upon an application for judicial review.

The issues arising from these categories may be resolved at the leave stage before a single judge, but sometimes it is necessary for them to be resolved at the full hearing before three judges of the Divisional Court of the Queen's Bench Division. The recommendations of the Law Commission Report No 226 (1994) are significant and are noted, where relevant, as each category is discussed in the key points below.

8.2 Key points

a) *The scope of judicial review*

Order 53 requires that the application for judicial review must relate to a decision of 'an inferior court, tribunal or other body of persons charged with the performance of public acts and duties'. At one time the source of the inferior body's powers was the essential test for this purpose: the source had to be statutory so that, traditionally, the ultra vires rules has been regarded as a check on the exercise of statutory powers, duties and discretions. However, in modern times the source of power has become less relevant and instead the focus has switched to the functions being exercised, so that judicial review has expanded in order to recognise the realities of executive power. This process began when a body created by the royal prerogative was held to be subject to review because of the public character of its functions: *R* v *Criminal Injuries Compensation Board, ex parte Lain* [1967] 2 All ER 770. Twenty years later this expansion of judicial review received a dramatic boost when it was held that review was in principle available over decisions of the City of London's Panel on Take-overs and Mergers: *R* v *Panel on Take-overs and Mergers, ex parte Datafin* [1987] 2 WLR 699 (CA). The Panel has no statutory or prerogative pedigree; it is essentially a voluntary, self-regulatory body set up by the City financial markets. There is no appeal from its decisions and no contractual relationship between it and the members it governs. Hence, without judicial review its decisions would be unchallengeable and the Panel would be 'above the law'. The decision to subject it to judicial review as a matter of principle was therefore another landmark decision marking the expansion of judicial review over non-statutory action: see Forsyth, 'Of Fig Leaves and Fairy Tales' [1996] CLJ 122 at 124–126. However, the *Datafin* principle has not been extended to the many kinds of disciplinary, self-regulatory bodies operating within trades, professions, sport, etc, because in these areas the powers are not regarded as being sufficiently 'governmental' in character to attract the description of 'public', and also because the existence of a contractual relationship ensures the matter can be adequately dealt with by private law. See further Black 'Constituting Self-regulation' (1996) 59 MLR 24 at 32–43 especially.

It follows that the *Datafin* principle does not apply to:

i) ordinary employment relationships, even if the employer is a public institution, unless there is a special public law status about the employment evidenced by statutory rules which 'underpin' the office in question, because then ultra vires is applicable to any excess of statutory power: *R* v *Secretary of State for the Home Department, ex parte Benwell* [1984] 3 All ER 854;

ii) the exercise of discipline or general regulation within various occupations, including sport: *R* v *Disciplinary Committee of the Jockey Club, ex parte Aga Khan* [1993] 2 All ER 853 and *R* v *Football Association, ex parte Football League* [1993] 2 All ER 833, in which Rose LJ (at pp848–849) observed that 'it would take a quantum leap in thinking to describe a typical governing body in sport as a public institution'. See also on religious discipline: *R* v *Chief Rabbi, ex parte Wachman* [1993] 2 All ER 249;

iii) the exercise of disciplinary and regulatory powers by private (independent), fee-paying schools or colleges; it is different in regard to universities or schools in the public (state) sector because of the statutory basis on which they rest or, in the case of the older universities, the prerogative basis of royal charters under which disciplinary power is exercised by a Visitor: here judicial review is in principle available: *R* v *Lord President of the Privy Council, ex parte Page* [1992] 3 WLR 1112 (HL). See further chapter 9 on jurisdiction.

b) *The exclusivity principle of* O'Reilly *v* Mackman

Even though the respondent may be a public body exercising governmental functions, the applicant for review must also show that the issues in the case are ones of public law. This reservation of review for public law cases means that it will be an abuse of process to try to use private law proceedings by way of writ or originating summons to challenge the vires of the exercise of public powers or duties. This rigid distinction between public and private law in regard to the forms of action has generated much litigation on procedural points because the definitions of the terms public law and private law are not clear cut, especially in the interpretation of statutory discretions in particular contexts. To add to the complexity there is a series of exceptions to the general exclusivity rule created by *O'Reilly* v *Mackman*.

i) If both sides consent to the use of private law processes

This is rare since it is usually to the advantage of the public body being challenged to insist on review because of the safeguards contained in O.53 to protect public bodies from groundless or tardy applications, eg, inter alia, the leave requirement, the need to prove standing, the need for a prompt application within three months of the taking of the decision being challenged. It follows that the public body will only consent to a private law action if such procedure will cause it no administrative inconvenience: *Gillick* v *West Norfolk and Wisbech Area Health Authority* [1986] AC 112 (HL).

ii) Where the public law issue of ultra vires is collateral to private law issues in the case

In this case it follows that if the public law issue is the dominant issue, the exclusivity principle will apply even though private law rights are involved in the case: this is known as the 'narrow' approach to the principle set out in Lord Diplock's judgment in *O'Reilly* v *Mackman*. Adherence to the collateral issue rule proved particularly difficult for judges faced with the task of disentangling public and private law elements contained in various statutory powers and duties: see *Cocks* v *Thanet District Council* [1983] 2 AC 286 (HL); *Doyle* v *Northumbria Probation Committee* [1991] 4 All ER 294. It was not surprising that judges began to express their frustration at the amount of time and money spent on litigation of such technical procedural issues. An argument began to develop that it was possible to put a broader interpretation on the Diplock judgment in *O'Reilly* v *Mackman*, to the effect that the exclusivity principle should operate only where no private law rights were involved, and this broad approach received a favourable response from Lord Lowry in *Roy* v *Kensington and Chelsea and Westminster Family Practitioner Committee* [1992] 1 All ER 705 (HL). However, the collateral issue exception was not formally abandoned in this case and it may be that some judges who favour the public/private divide will continue to use the narrow approach: see recent case law in section 8.3 below.

iii) Where the public law issue of ultra vires is raised in proceedings other than judicial review, ie in collateral proceedings before either a civil court or tribunal or in a criminal court: *Wandsworth London Borough Council* v *Winder* [1985] 1 AC 461 (HL), *Avon County Council* v *Buscott* [1988] 1 All ER 841.

This exception is based on the view that the collateral proceedings should not be stayed to allow an application for judicial review to be brought if the court or tribunal is competent to resolve the public law issues, ie it is in the public interest to permit 'one-stop litigation'. Much will depend on whether the particular court or tribunal has the necessary skills and enforcement powers to deal adequately with the particular issue of vires raised before it, eg it was held that a social security tribunal can determine the vires of statutory regulations where the challenge is based on pure statutory construction: *Chief Adjudication Officer* v *Foster* [1993] AC 754 (HL). It was also held that a Crown Court judge can determine the vires of bye-laws in criminal proceedings: *R* v *Reading Crown Court, ex parte Hutchinson* [1988] 1 QB 384. However, in *Bugg* v *DPP*; *DPP* v *Percy* [1993] 2 All ER 815 (QBD) Woolf LJ (as he then was) opined that *substantive* ultra vires involving excess or abuse of power or irrationality could be raised in collateral proceedings in criminal courts (magistrates' courts as well as Crown

Courts), but that *procedural* ultra vires involving challenges to the process leading up to the making of the bye-laws could only be challenged under O.53 procedures, since only the Divisional Court had the necessary skills and tools (remedies) for dealing with this kind of vires issue. This distinction further complicates the collateral proceedings exception to the general exclusivity principle of *O'Reilly* v *Mackman*: see also *Boddington* v *British Transport Police*, section 8.3 below.

c) *The recommendations of the Law Commission Report No 226 (1994) on* O'Reilly *v* Mackman *and related procedural issues*

The Report recommends the retention of the exclusivity principle despite the strong criticisms voiced of it by, inter alia, Wade and Forsyth (*Administrative Law* (7th edn, 1994), pp680–695 especially). However, the Commission recommends that the exclusivity principle should be operated in the 'broad' way as expounded by Lord Lowry in *Roy* v *Kensington and Chelsea and Westminster Family Practitioner Committee*, above. The Report also recommends a new mechanism to facilitate the transfer of proceedings in or out of O.53 (at present O.53 allows only for judicial review proceedings to be switched to private law proceedings whilst staying in the Divisional Court if the public law proceedings result in a private law claim, eg where an ultra vires decision involved the commission of a tort for which the applicant demands compensation: *R* v *Secretary of State for the Home Department, ex parte Dew* [1987] 2 All ER 1049 at pp1061–1063 especially). The Commission rejected, however, a reference mechanism for cases where ultra vires is pleaded in collateral proceedings. For critical reaction to these recommendations: see Hare (1995) 54 CLJ 268 at p273 especially and Emery [1995] PL 450 at pp458–461 especially. See also Bamforth (1995) 58 MLR 722 and Fredman (1995) 111 LQR 591.

d) *Locus standi*

Order 53, r3(7) and s31(3) SCA 1981 provide that no leave shall be granted to proceed with an application for judicial review unless the applicant has 'sufficient interest in the matter to which the application relates'. The commentary to O.53 states that this issue is a mixed question of fact and law, that it is a question of fact and degree, and will depend on the relationship between the applicant and the matter to which the application relates, having regard to all the circumstances of the case. Consequently it will be necessary for the single judge at the leave stage to take a 'bird's eye view' of the merits of the application in order to decide the issue of standing. He should approach the issue of locus standi by simply deciding whether the applicant has no interest whatsoever, ie is the applicant no more than a meddlesome busybody? If the application appears to be arguable and there is no other discretionary bar, such as undue delay, then leave to apply should be granted, with the issue of locus standi to be reconsidered at the full hearing and decided as a matter of discretion, the strength of the applicant's interest being only one of several factors to be weighed in the balance: *IRC* v *National Federation of Self-Employed and Small Businesses* [1982] AC 617 (HL); [1981] 2 WLR 722 (HL).

Prior to the decision in *IRC* (above) the old law on standing had been generally restrictive in terms of access to the courts, with different tests of standing being used for different remedies: see further on the old law, Wade and Forsyth, *Administrative Law* (7th edn, 1994) at pp696–708. The landmark decision of *IRC* introduced a new law on standing which switched the emphasis to allowing access to the courts in order to ensure that ultra vires action did not go unchecked:

'It would be a grave lacuna in our system of public law if a pressure group ... or even a single public spirited taxpayer were prevented by outdated technical rules of locus standi from bringing the matter to the attention of the courts to vindicate the rule of law and to get the unlawful conduct stopped': per Lord Diplock in *IRC* v *National Federation of Self-Employed and Small Businesses* [1981] 2 WLR 722 at p740.

Lord Diplock therefore welcomed the concept of an *actio popularis* (ie a citizen action with no formal test of standing) to challenge apparent flagrant and serious breaches of the law, or exceptionally grave or widespread illegality. In such cases any individual citizen with a sincere concern in the constitutional issues arising from such a state of affairs should be granted leave to bring an application for judicial review: *R* v *HM Treasury, ex parte Smedley* [1985] 2 WLR 576; *R* v *Felixstowe Justices, ex parte Leigh* [1987] QB 582; *R* v *Secretary of State for Foreign and Commonwealth Affairs, ex parte Rees-Mogg* [1994] 2 WLR 115. The new, relaxed test of standing has also worked in favour of established pressure groups (special interest groups), especially as such a group may be able to mount a more focused and well-argued challenge than an individual supporter of that group's aims: *R* v *Secretary of State for Social Services, ex parte Child Poverty Action Group* [1989] 1 All ER 1047; *R* v *Secretary of State for Employment, ex parte Equal Opportunities Commission* [1994] 1 All ER 910 (HL); *R* v *Inspectorate of Pollution, ex parte Greenpeace Ltd (No 2)* [1994] 4 All ER 329 (QBD); *R* v *Secretary of State for Foreign and Commonwealth Affairs, ex parte World Development Movement Ltd* [1995] 1 All ER 611. The only case out of step with this line of authority on public interest standing is *R* v *Secretary of State for Environment, ex parte Rose Theatre Trust Co* [1990] 1 All ER 754 (QBD) in which it was held that the ministerial discretion of whether or not to list a site as a protected ancient monument was one of those rare public decisions in respect of which the ordinary citizen or group of such citizens did not have sufficient interest to challenge. The decision was not followed in *ex parte Greenpeace (No 2)*, above, although it was not expressly disapproved.

It may be that the *Rose Theatre* case can be explained in terms of the character of the Trust Company which was seeking leave, ie a body which had been formed solely to mount such a challenge and therefore lacking the established reputation and skill of the other special interest groups which had been granted standing in the other cases listed above. The decision in *Rose Theatre* is also consistent with the decision in *IRC* (above) which had denied the concept of 'associational standing', ie the lack of standing of an individual member of the public on a particular issue of public interest cannot be overcome by a number of such individuals combining and claiming to represent all like-minded individuals on the matter in question. There is a similar rule that the lack of capacity of an unincorporated association to seek judicial review on any matter cannot be overcome by the simple device of incorporation, since leave should be granted or refused according to the general tests of locus standi.

Finally it should be noted that the Law Commission in its 1994 Report (No 226) welcomed the recent trends towards a more liberal and relaxed test of locus standi in regard to public interest standing. In order to facilitate challenges by special interest groups the Commission recommended a two-track system of locus standi: the first track would cover those persons who have been personally adversely affected ('personal standing cases'), and the second track would be discretionary to cover public interest challenges mounted by special interest groups, or, possibly, by individual citizens ('public interest standing'). The Commission also recommended that unincorporated associations should be recognised as having capacity to seek judicial review, though they would still have to satisfy the general tests of locus standi, ie 'associational standing' by itself would still not be recognised.

Note: This chapter is concerned with application for judicial review proceedings. In ordinary civil proceedings by writ for injunctions to restrain actions which threaten the public interest the role of the Attorney-General becomes relevant: under the royal prerogative he alone can claim to represent the general public interest, and therefore an applicant who is unable to establish sufficient personal interest must apply to the Attorney-General either to take over the challenge or to lend his name to the application (a relator action) so as to give the applicant necessary standing. The Attorney-General's prerogative discretion whether to take either of these courses is unreviewable by the courts: *Gouriet* v *Union of Post Office Workers* [1978] AC 435. As a Member of Parliament and a member of the government the Attorney-General is naturally reluctant to take action against a government department or other institution which supports his party, and Lord Woolf has suggested that for this reason the office of Attorney-General should be abolished and replaced by a 'Director of Civil Proceedings' who, like the Director of Public Prosecutions, would be seen to be independent of government and of party political influence: Woolf [1986] PL 220 at pp236–237 especially.

d) *Alternative remedies*

The judge at the leave stage may refuse leave to apply for review if an alternative remedy is available to the applicant. This principle is based on the concept of judicial review as a 'residual' jurisdiction. The rule also ensures that the judicial review case-load does not overburden the judges. At one time the discretion was exercised generously in favour of applicants so that leave would be granted if the alternative remedy, such as a right of statutory appeal, would not be as cheap or as speedy as judicial review: *R* v *Paddington Valuation Officer, ex parte Peachey Property Corporation* [1966] 1 QB 380; *R* v *Hillingdon London Borough Council, ex parte Royco Homes Ltd* [1974] 2 All ER 643; *R* v *Chief Immigration Officer, Gatwick Airport, ex parte Kharrazi* [1980] 3 All ER 373. However, this attitude changed, probably due to the explosion in numbers of applications for review, particularly in the fields of housing and immigration, during the 1980s. It became the rule that the existence of any alternative remedy excluded judicial review, even where that remedy was slow, expensive and more inconvenient to the applicant than an application for judicial review: *R* v *Civil Service Appeal Board, ex parte Bruce* [1989] 2 All ER 907 (CA). However, the judicial attitude to alternative remedies has not proven consistent and there are departures from this general trend: see *R* v *Deputy Governor of Parkhurst Prison, ex parte Leech* [1988] 1 All ER 485 at p496 especially, where Lord Bridge explained that a prisoner's right of petition to the Home Secretary against the deputy governor's decision should be no bar to judicial review; and *R* v *Devon County Council, ex parte Baker* [1995] 1 All ER 73 at pp86j–87c and 92f–h especially, per Dillon and Simon Brown LJJ explaining that a statutory right of appeal to a minister over the closure of an old people's home should be no bar to judicial review.

In its Report (No 226 of 1994) the Law Commission recommends that an applicant should normally have exhausted alternative legal remedies before applying for judicial review, and that the principle of exhaustion should be applied strictly in cases where the alternative remedy is an appeal to a court, tribunal or minister.

e) *Undue delay*

Order 53 requires that an application for judicial review should be made 'promptly' and within three months of the decision which is being challenged. Failure to do so must be classified as 'undue delay' and becomes a discretionary ground for refusing leave to apply for review. The process is broken down into three stages: Stage 1 – the judge must rule on whether there has been undue delay; Stage 2 – if there has been undue delay, the judge must decide whether to grant leave out of time because there may be good reasons for the undue delay, eg the need to exhaust alternative remedies; Stage 3 (which may be taken at the leave stage or at the full hearing before three judges of the Divisional Court) – the judge(s) may refuse leave or refuse to grant relief if it would cause hardship to the other side or prejudice good administration to grant leave or relief because of the undue delay, notwithstanding that at the full hearing the applicant may have established a clear case of ultra vires decision-making: *R* v *Dairy Produce Quota Tribunal, ex parte Caswell* [1990] 2 All ER 434 (HL); *R* v *Secretary of State for Health, ex parte Furneaux* [1994] 2 All ER 652 (CA).

In its report (No 226 of 1994) the Law Commission seems to favour this approach by proposing a unified provision of a three-month time limit which may be extended or reduced by reference to the presence or absence of any likely substantial hardship or prejudice to the rights of others or detriment to good administration. See further Lindsay [1995] PL 417.

8.3 Recent cases and articles

The exclusivity principle of O'Reilly *v* Mackman

Mercury Communications Ltd v *Director-General of Telecommunications* [1996] 1 WLR 48; [1996] 1 All ER 575 (HL) – held that dispute over true construction of a licence granted to British Telecommunications plc by the Minister could properly be raised by way of an originating summons for a declaration: the challenge was not restricted to an application for judicial review under O.53. Lord Slynn emphasised the need to retain some flexibility in regard to choice of proceedings, particularly as the precise limits of 'public law' and 'private law' were by no means worked out. The overriding question should be whether the proceedings that had been instituted constituted an abuse of the process of the court, and since the present dispute was essentially concerned with the true construction of a contract the procedure by way of originating summons in the Commercial Court was at least as well suited as, and might be better than, the determination of the issues by way of judicial review.

Comment: The decision is another example of the modern trend away from the rigid public/private divide created by *O'Reilly* v *Mackman* and 'may well herald a new and yet more liberal test for deciding when an applicant can pursue a claim by way of ordinary action than previously existed': Craig (1996) 112 LQR at p531. See also McHarg [1995] PL 539 at p550 especially.

R v *Legal Aid Board, ex parte Donn and Co (A Firm)* [1996] 3 All ER 1 – the issues were whether the franchising decisions of a legal aid committee were subject to judicial review and, if so, whether the particular decision being challenged was invalid for procedural impropriety. It was *held* that the matter was reviewable because the selection process was more 'governmental' in character than commercial, not least because the Legal Aid Board was dispensing large sums of public money and acted as the final arbiter of the issue before it. There was also a vital public interest in the system of franchising of legal aid. For the resolution of the procedural impropriety issue see chapter 10, section 10.3 below.

Great House at Sonning Ltd v *Berkshire County Council* (1996) The Times 25 March (CA) – the defendant highway authority had used its statutory powers to order the temporary closure of a highway. The plaintiffs (owners of a hotel) sued by writ seeking an injunction and damages for nuisance caused by wrongful obstruction of the highway. It was held (Saville LJ dissenting) that the only claim was by way of judicial review since the plaintiffs had to establish the invalidity of the order before a private right of action in nuisance arose. The statutory order prevented any obstruction caused by the road closure from being a nuisance until such time as the order was shown to be invalid. Saville LJ, dissented on the ground that the plaintiffs should have been permitted to proceed on the basis of the 'broad' approach propounded by Lord Lowry in *Roy*'s case [1992] 1 AC 624.

British Steel plc v *Customs and Excise Commissioners* [1996] 1 All ER 1002 – the plaintiff company argued that it was entitled to statutory relief from the payment of excise duty on the use of hydrocarbon oil and in an action by writ sought restitution for the repayment of alleged overpayments of excise duty. A preliminary issue was tried as to whether the action could proceed or the plaintiff company should have proceeded by judicial review. It was held that the decision as to whether a taxpayer was entitled to the relevant statutory relief was a matter of statutory discretion entrusted to the defendants and was entirely a matter within the field of public law. A private right of action could arise only after it had been established by judicial review that the plaintiff company was entitled to the statutory relief. The action was accordingly struck out: *Cocks* v *Thanet District Council* [1982] 2 AC 286 applied.

Comment: the judgment of Laws J (especially at pp1012a–1013j) contains a comprehensive and detailed analysis of the authorities from *O'Reilly* v *Mackman* [1983] 2 AC 237 to *Mercury Communications Ltd* v *D-G of Telecommunications* [1996] 1 All ER 575 (HL). It is clear from the judgment that the decision in *Cocks* v *Thanet District Council* is still good law despite the doubt thrown on it in the view of some commentators by the more flexible approaches to the issue of form of proceedings adopted in cases such as *Roy* and *Mercury*:

'Where statute confers what is plainly a private right, if on the Act's true construction the right enures only after and in consequence of a purely public law decision in favour of the claimant, any complaint directed to the public decision-making stage must be brought by O.53 ... this is by no means surprising: the public policy which requires that purely administrative decisions be subject only to the supervisory jurisdiction of the High Court in O.53 proceedings is in no sense weakened by the circumstance that the out-turn of a favourable decision may be to confer a private right' (per Laws J at p1013f–g).

Boddington v *British Transport Police* (1996) The Times 23 July – the appellant had been convicted of contravening a bye-law prohibiting smoking in certain trains. On his appeal by way of case stated from the magistrates' court he challenged the policy of imposing a total prohibition on smoking on those trains, arguing that it was totally unreasonable and ultra vires. It was *held* that such a challenge could only be made by means of an application for judicial review. The court took the view that the no-smoking policy and the bye-law which enforced it were not 'bad on their faces', ie there was no obvious case of ultra vires. If ultra vires were to be proved it would require evidence and such evidence was best examined in an O.53 review. It would create chaos if criminal courts embarked on wide-ranging examinations of administrative decisions were not invalid on their face.

Comment: The decision emphasises the narrow character of the 'collateral proceedings' exception to *O'Reilly* v *Mackman*, above. In *Bugg* v *DPP*, above, it had been said that 'substantive ultra vires' could be raised as a defence in criminal proceedings whereas 'procedural ultra vires' could only be raised in O.53 proceedings. In *Boddington* counsel for the appellant had framed the challenge in terms of substantive ultra vires so as to benefit from this distinction. This was not successful because the no-smoking policy was not so patently unreasonable as to be invalid on its face. Evidence would be needed to persuade the court of the irrationality of the policy. The court in *Boddington* went further than the judges in *Bugg* v *DPP* by restricting collateral challenges to cases where the instrument or policy was 'bad on its face'. By contrast Woolf LJ (as he then was) in *Bugg* v *DPP* was prepared to allow collateral challenges based on *evidence* of irrationality, abuse of power or 'mala fides' (bad faith): All matters described as 'substantive ultra vires'. The collateral proceedings exception seems to have a more generous interpretation in civil proceedings: *Wandsworth London Borough Council* v *Winder*, above (though Lord Woolf has criticised this decision extra-judicially: [1986] PL 220 at 228, and 234–235).

Locus standi

R v *Secretary of State for Foreign and Commonwealth Affairs, ex parte Rees-Mogg* [1994] 2 WLR 115 (QBD) – applicant granted leave to challenge legality of the signing of the Treaty of Maastricht because he had a 'sincere concern for constitutional issues' and the issue at stake was a grave one: *R* v *HM Treasury, ex parte Smedley* [1985] 2 WLR 576 applied.

R v *Secretary of State for Employment, ex parte Equal Opportunities Commission* [1994] 2 WLR 409; [1994] 1 All ER 910 (HL) – held the Commission, having a statutory duty to promote equal opportunities, should be recognised as having standing in judicial review proceedings challenging views or decisions on interpretation of sex discrimination laws, particularly as such questions were ones of public importance and affected a large section of the public. The case is discussed by Gordon [1994] PL 217 and Villiers and White (1995) 58 MLR 560.

R v *Inspectorate of Pollution, ex parte Greenpeace Ltd (No 2)* [1994] 4 All ER 329 (QBD) – Greenpeace given leave to challenge legality of nuclear waste disposal in Cumbria because it was a respectable and responsible special interest group with a genuine concern for the issue and with many supporters living in the region affected by the waste disposal who might not, as individuals, be able to bring the matter to the court as effectively as Greenpeace, which, with its experience and expertise, would be able to mount a carefully selected, focused, relevant and well-argued challenge on this serious environmental issue. Greenpeace's challenge would therefore spare scarce judicial resources, ensure a speedy hearing and an early result: per Otton J at pp350c–351d.

R v *Secretary of State for Foreign and Commonwealth Affairs, ex parte World Development Movement Ltd* [1995] 1 All ER 611 (QBD) – the Movement was given leave to challenge the legality of a foreign aid and trade grant for the construction of the Pergau Dam in Malaysia because it was a well-established, reputable and expert international body with a sincere concern for promoting and protecting aid to underdeveloped nations. The issue was a serious one and, since it was unlikely that there would be any other responsible challenger, it was important to grant the Movement standing in order to vindicate the rule of law and review possible excess of power. The decision is discussed by Hare (1995) 54 CLJ 227.

The above decisions illustrate the modern trend to relaxing the locus standi text in judicial review applications under O.53. Indeed, in *ex parte World Development Movement* (above), Rose LJ approved the view expressed in Wade and Forsyth (7th edn, 1994 at p712) that 'the real question is whether the applicant can show some substantial default or abuse, and not whether his personal rights or interests are involved'.

Other articles: Cane [1995] PL 276; Gordon [1995] NLJ 116; Hare (1995) 54 CLJ 268; Bamforth (1995) 58 MLR 722.

Effect of alternative remedies on an application for judicial review under O.53

R v *Devon County Council, ex parte Baker* [1995] 1 All ER 73 (CA) – held statutory appeal to a minister over closure of old peoples' home no bar to judicial review: Simon Brown LJ at p92f–h opined that the decision to grant leave should depend on which avenue of redress is the more convenient, expeditious and effective. Issues of law were best left to courts rather than ministers, though ministers were better if given default powers as then a factual inquiry could be conducted with all the expertise of a government department.

Harley Development Inc v *IRC* [1996] 2 WLR 474 (PC) – a taxpayer applied for judicial review of an assessor's decisions. It was *held* that a comprehensive appeal procedure existed designed to consider issues of merits and vires, and that therefore this alternative means of challenge must be used. Judicial review proceedings would be appropriate in such a case only in exceptional circumstances, eg where a serious abuse of power was alleged.

Effect of delay on an application for judicial review under O.53

Ex parte World Development Movement Ltd (above) – leave was granted out of time because of the gravity of the issue raised.

R v *Secretary of State for Health, ex parte Furneaux* [1994] 2 All ER 652 (CA) – leave refused when undue delay would cause detriment to good administration if remedy were to be granted after such delay: *R* v *Dairy Produce Quota Tribunal, ex parte Caswell* [1990] 2 All ER 434 (HL) applied: see further Lindsay [1995] PL 417.

The Law Commission Report (No 226 of 1994) contains recommendations covering all the above procedural issues: see further Gordon [1995] PL 111, Hare [1995] CLJ 268, Emery [1995] PL 450 and Fredman (1995) 111 LQR 591.

Craig, 'Proceeding Outside Order 53: a Modified Test? *Mercury Ltd* v *D-G of Telecommunications*' (1996) 112 LQR 531

Schiemann LJ, 'Interventions in Public Interest Cases' [1996] PL 240

8.4 Analysis of questions

For first year constitutional law students it is unlikely that questions would be set exclusively on the complex issues covered in this chapter, but a knowledge of the relevant procedural principles is required when answering general problem-type questions on judicial review of administrative action: see chapter 15.

For second/third year administrative law students the public/private divide is probably the most controversial feature of modern administrative law and therefore questions are set regularly on the exclusivity principle of *O'Reilly* v *Mackman*. A detailed knowledge of the case law subsequent to *O'Reilly* v *Mackman* is essential, particularly a sensitive appreciation to the gradual movement away from a rigid public/private divide to a broader, more flexible interpretation and application of the judgments in *O'Reilly* v *Mackman* [1983] 2 AC 237 in such cases as *Roy* v *Kensington and Chelsea and Westminster Family Practitioner Committee* [1992] 2 WLR 239 above and, more recently, *Mercury Communications Ltd* v *Director-General of Telecommunications* [1996] 1 All ER 575, above and *British Steel plc* v *Customs and Excise Commissioners* [1996] 1 All ER 1002, above.

The *Datafin* principle, which switched the emphasis away from source of power to functions, is also regularly examined, though often as part of a general problem-type question on judicial review. Occasionally there have been essay-type questions on the 'sources v functions' debate.

The locus standi issue has become so important in recent years that it is likely to deserve regular individual examination: in judicial review applications the recent trend toward relaxing the test for special interest groups and even individuals has come close to creating an 'actio popularis' in English administrative law, so it is a subject worthy of critical analysis. In ordinary civil proceedings the role of the Attorney-General and the relator action becomes relevant, and it may be that some questions will invite a critical examination of the Attorney-General's role.

It is unlikely that the topics of alternative remedies and undue delay will be examined individually, but they will be relevant in many general problem-type questions on judicial review.

8.5 Questions

QUESTION ONE

Anna believes that she has been unfairly and unreasonably treated by a number of bodies. She seeks your advice as to whether she would be successful, if the claims of unfairness or unreasonableness could be substantiated, in applications for judicial review against these bodies, namely:

a) The British Broadcasting Corporation

b) Panel on Take-overs and Mergers

c) University of London

d) The Arts Council

e) The Welsh Rugby Football Union

Advise Anna.

University of London LLB Examination
(for External Students) Administrative Law June 1989 Q10

General Comment

A question requiring consideration of the scope of judicial review. It is suggested that the answer does not require a detailed investigation of the background of each of the organisations listed, since the principle in the *Datafin* case is applicable to all. Care should still be taken in assessing the range of remedies that might be available as the question gives no details as to the nature of Anna's dispute with the various organisations.

Skeleton Solution

- Source of power no longer the significant criterion.
- *Datafin* case.
- Whether a public law issue.
- How the courts will review actions.
- Remedies available.

Suggested Solution

It is submitted that, in relation to each of the organisations listed, three questions need to be considered. First, is the organisation amenable to judicial review? If this is answered in the affirmative, the second question that arises is as to how the court should approach the task of reviewing its actions. Thirdly there is the problem of which remedy, if any, is going to be available.

Before 1977, judicial review would only have been suitable where an applicant sought to review the actions of a statutory body, or one created under the royal prerogative (see *R* v *Criminal Injuries Compensation Board, ex parte Lain* (1967)). Since 1977, it has been possible to apply for judicial review of a wider range of organisations, since the range of remedies available on an application for review has been extended to include declarations, injunctions, and damages. The determinant of whether or not an organisation is amenable to judicial review is no longer the source of its power, but the significance of its decisions as regards the public. This breakthrough was the result of the Court of Appeal's decision in *R* v *Panel on Take-overs and Mergers, ex parte Datafin plc* (1987). The applicants had complained to the Panel about the conduct of certain other companies during the course of a contested takeover bid. The Panel had rejected the complaint. The applicants then applied for judicial review of the Panel's decision, but this was rejected at first instance on the basis that, as the Panel was neither exercising statutory nor prerogative powers, its decisions were not amenable to judicial review. The Court of Appeal held that, despite the fact that the Panel was an unincorporated association and was not exercising statutory or prerogative powers, its decisions were amenable to judicial review. The Panel was performing a public duty when administering the Code on Take-overs and Mergers, and as there was no other means readily available by which the legality of its actions might be tested, judicial review would lie in respect of its decisions.

On this basis it is submitted that, in theory, any of the organisations referred to in the question could be amenable to judicial review. The fact that an organisation may be a company registered under the companies' legislation will not prevent its decisions from being reviewed in an appropriate case.

If judicial review is possible, is it appropriate? Much may depend upon the nature of Anna's dispute with the organisation concerned. On the basis of decisions such as *R* v *BBC, ex parte Lavelle* (1983), and *R* v *East Berkshire Health Authority, ex parte Walsh* (1984), it is submitted that Anna may not be allowed to proceed by way of judicial review if her complaint is essentially based upon an allegation of breach of contract. Where no contractual remedy is available, however, the courts may be willing to bring the applicant's claim within the scope of public law so as to ensure that the applicant has some means by which he might be able to challenge the decision (see *R* v *Secretary of State for the Home Department, ex parte Benwell* (1985)) and dicta of Sir Thomas Bingham MR in *R* v *Disciplinary Committee of the Jockey Club, ex parte Aga Khan* (1993).

Assuming that judicial review of the bodies mentioned in the question is, in theory, possible, how should the courts approach the task? How should the courts review the actions of a body which has drawn up its own rules, or one that may have no written rules whatsoever? Some guidelines were provided by Lord Donaldson MR in *R* v *Panel on Take-overs and Mergers, ex parte Guinness plc* (1989). Taken individually, his Lordship felt that the established grounds of challenge, irrationality, illegality, and procedural impropriety, were difficult to apply to bodies such as the Panel. As regards illegality, because it acted as both legislator and interpreter of its rules; as regards irrationality, because it was itself charged with determining what were, and were not, relevant considerations; as regards procedural unfairness, because what was fair would depend upon underlying value judgments made by the Panel as to what was appropriate in a given case. Since the constitution, functions, and powers of the Panel were, to a large extent, sui generis, it was better to adopt a broad view of its actions, without resorting to formal classifications of illegality. The question in the instant case, that of whether or not proceedings should have been adjourned was, par excellence, one for the Panel to make itself and it could not be said that in refusing to adjourn it had acted unlawfully.

It is submitted, therefore, that the courts may not be willing to intervene to quash the decisions of the bodies listed in the question on the grounds of unreasonableness and unfairness as those terms have been developed to date. In particular, University Visitors, although reviewable for jurisdictional errors resulting from procedural impropriety or irrationality, are not reviewable for non-jurisdictional errors: *R* v *Lord President of the Privy Council, ex parte Page* (1992).

If an application for judicial review succeeds, will any remedy be available? In respect of those bodies which derive their powers from statute or the prerogative the prerogative orders would be available, but only if the issue is one of public law. Disputes based on alleged breaches of contract can only be dealt with by remedies such as a declaration, or injunction. The conventional wisdom is that decisions such as *R* v *Aston University Senate, ex parte Roffey* (1969), which suggest that the prerogative remedies would be available in such a situation, are wrongly decided. Where the allegation is not based on contract, perhaps because as in the Panel case there is no contractual relationship, certiorari might be available, but again the court will have to consider whether any other remedy is available to the applicant. In respect of the Arts Council it should be noted that Anna could make a complaint of maladministration to the Ombudsman, which may be a more effective and efficient route to a remedy.

QUESTION TWO

Does the decision of the House in Lords in *Roy* v *Kensington and Chelsea and Westminister FPC* ([1992] 1 All ER 705) represent a welcome departure from the principles espoused in *O'Reilly* v *Mackman* concerning the distinction between private law and public law questions?

University of London LLB Examination
(for External Students) Administrative Law June 1994 Q3

General Comment

This question is much more difficult than it looks. In the heat of an exam it would be all too easy to launch into a thorough exposition of the cases decided since *O'Reilly* v *Mackman* which illustrate the difficulty of the distinction between public law and private law issues, and then to realise that there is not enough time to deal with the specific question raised. On the other hand it is clearly necessary to demonstrate a thorough understanding of the difficulties caused by *O'Reilly*. It is very difficult to find the correct balance between these two alternatives. This question shows very clearly the importance of taking the time to think about the question and to isolate the issues identified by it before starting to write the answer. How far does *Roy* v *Kensington* actually attempt to define the distinction between public and private law? Is that distinction the only, or even the principal, difficulty caused by *O'Reilly*? Isn't *Roy* v *Kensington* more concerned with the situation where questions of both public law and of private law arise?

Skeleton Solution

- *O'Reilly* summarised.
- Brief critique of the post-*O'Reilly* case law:
  - the problem of distinguishing public and private law;
  - the problem of collateral questions.

- *Roy* v *Kensington* – a flexible approach with limitations.
- Conclusion – post-*Roy* v *Kensington* case law.

Suggested Solution

The decision of the House of Lords in *O'Reilly* v *Mackman* (1983) has been controversial from the outset. While some commentators have favoured a division between public and private law procedures, most agree that the rigid dichotomy between procedures introduced by *O'Reilly* is one that is unworkable in the context of English administrative law. The decision in *Roy* v *Kensington and Chelsea and Westminster Family Practitioner Committee* (1992) was a welcome departure in that it suggested a more flexible approach to these procedural requirements in cases where public law and private law issues are both involved but it did not go far enough in providing guidance for future litigants. As a result of this, there is a danger that subsequent decisions will revert to the rigidity of *O'Reilly*.

Prior to *O'Reilly* a litigant wishing to challenge a decision of a public body had a choice of procedures with which to do so. It was possible to bring an action by way of judicial review, seeking one of the prerogative remedies. Alternatively, an action could be brought by way of writ claiming the 'private law' remedies of declaration and injunction. The latter had become well established in administrative law so that, when the O.53 procedure was revised, the remedies of declaration and injunction were included as possible outcomes of an application for judicial review. The difficulty faced by the House of Lords in *O'Reilly* was that O.53 contained certain procedural constraints; notably a requirement to obtain leave, and a three-month limitation period. To allow litigants to continue to use the private procedure to claim declarations and injunctions was seen as subverting the intentions of the revised O.53 procedure because in writ procedure there is no requirement to obtain leave, and the time limits are much longer. The House of Lords felt that all litigants seeking to challenge the decisions or actions of public bodies should be subject to the same procedural constraints. On the other hand, public bodies should enjoy the same procedural protection regardless of the remedies sought. It was on these two bases that the House of Lords decided that it was an abuse of process to bring an action by writ where the issue was one of public law. It was equally an abuse of process to proceed by way of judicial review where the issue was one of private law, but in this case an applicant could be saved by the provision enabling the court to effectively transfer the matter by allowing it to continue as if begun by writ.

Thus *O'Reilly* introduced a rigid dichotomy between public law and private law issues. There are at least two difficulties with this approach. The first of these is that it has never been clear how this dichotomy could be worked out in a legal system that does not traditionally distinguish between public and private law. It is a constitutional fundamental of English law that public bodies and their officers are subject to the same courts of law as ordinary individuals, and this tradition means that there is no clear basis for drawing a distinction between public and private law. The second, and arguably more difficult problem arising out of *O'Reilly* and subsequent cases, is the implication that public law issues may not be raised at all in private law actions, even where the public law issues are collateral. This may be seen clearly in the case *Cocks* v *Thanet District Council* (1983). In this case the claimant brought an action by writ to enforce the council's (private law) obligation to provide him with accommodation under the Housing (Homeless Persons) Act 1977. In order to further his case, the claimant had to challenge the preliminary decision of the council that he did not satisfy the Act's criteria. His action was struck out as an abuse of process as this issue was one which arose in public law. This reasoning has been carried on into other cases where litigants have sought to enforce private law rights, but have had to raise issues of public law. For instance, where a claimant's employment conditions were contained in a statutory code, it was held that judicial review was the appropriate procedure for claiming a breach of those conditions (*R* v *Secretary of State for the Home Department, ex parte Benwell* (1985)). It is not clear why this should be so, since employment rights are essentially a matter of private law.

Roy v *Kensington and Chelsea and Westminster Family Practitioner Committee* did little to assist lawyers with the first difficulty, that of distinguishing between public and private law issues. It did, however, introduce some welcome flexibility to the second difficulty, that of collateral public law issues raised in private law proceedings. The case bears some resemblance to *Cocks* v *Thanet District Council* in that the claimant was seeking to enforce a private law right (to be paid monies due to him) that was based upon statutory criteria. Thus the claimant had to challenge the application of those criteria in order to further his claim. The House of Lords held that this case was an exception to the rule in *O'Reilly*. There were a number of reasons for this, which emerge in the leading speech of Lord Lowry. It was accepted that Dr Roy had a private law right to the monies claimed. This private law right dominated the proceedings. The claim might involve disputes of fact, and was therefore unsuitable for judicial review where, in any event, payment of the monies could not be enforced. There was no need for a requirement of leave or a special time limit to be applied when individual rights were at stake. The action should be allowed to proceed unless it was plainly an abuse of process.

In the context of collateral public law issues, *Roy* v *Kensington* appeared to provide some welcome relief from the rigours of *O'Reilly*. In particular, the decision suggests that the question of which procedure should be adopted may be judged by reference to which procedure is suitable; this would be a useful pragmatic approach to a difficult conceptual problem. But in a number of respects the decision did not go far enough. First, as has been stated, *Roy* v *Kensington* did not really provide any assistance in drawing the difficult distinction between public law and private law questions. It was decided on the footing that both types of question arose in the case. Secondly, the reasoning in *O'Reilly* was expressly upheld, although Lord Lowry's speech gives the impression that he upheld it reluctantly. The facts in *Roy* v *Kensington* were seen as exceptional, which will make it all too easy for future judges to dismiss *Roy* v *Kensington* as a case decided on its own facts (albeit decided by the House of Lords), rather than one of general application. Nor did the decision go far enough in identifying the circumstances in which it would be proper to raise public law issues in private law cases. Lord Lowry outlined two approaches to this question. The broad approach would permit all public law issues arising as a part of the private law claim to be raised in proceedings begun by writ. The narrow approach only permits collateral public law issues to be raised where the private law rights dominate the proceedings. It is submitted that the broad approach is to be preferred, since it is difficult to see either how procedural constraints are necessary where essentially private rights are being asserted or that there is any justification for requiring a division of procedure where it is private rights that are ultimately to be enforced. While stating that he preferred the broad approach, Lord Lowry expressly based his decision upon the narrow one.

That this is a serious defect in *Roy* v *Kensington* is illustrated by the case law decided since then. *Ali* v *Tower Hamlets London Borough Council* (1993) is another case factually similar to *Cocks* v *Thanet District Council*, involving an attempt by the claimant to enforce his right to housing in private law proceedings. Once again, the writ proceedings were struck out because the claimant needed to challenge preliminary decisions based upon statutory criteria. Far from victoriously routing the rigidity of *O'Reilly*, *Roy* v *Kensington* has simply not done enough to end the tyranny of the inflexible approach to public law and private law procedures. Although welcome in the approach it offers to cases where private law rights dominate the proceedings, it is likely that meritorious claimants will continue to stumble over procedural hurdles that remain ill-defined.

For example, the rule in *Cocks* v *Thanet District Council* clearly survives *Roy*'s case and has been applied to justify the striking out of writs in cases where public law issues were preconditions to the emergence of private law rights: *Great House at Sonning Ltd* v *Berkshire County Council* (1996) and *British Steel plc* v *Customs and Excise Commissioners* (1996). By contrast an even more flexible test than the one laid down in *Roy* is the 'abuse of power' test laid down in *Mercury Communications Ltd* v *D-G of Telecommunications* (1996). It is not surprising that this area of law has been described as a procedural landmine for litigants.

QUESTION THREE

How might section 31 of the Supreme Court Act 1981 be reformed in order to reduce the amount of litigation generated since *O'Reilly* v *Mackman* on the question of which procedural route an applicant should follow when seeking to challenge 'public law' decisions?

University of London LLB Examination
(for External Students) Administrative Law June 1995 Q5

General Comment

This is a very difficult question. It requires far more than an ability to discuss the public law/private law distinction introduced by *O'Reilly* v *Mackman*. Because this is a complex subject, with a lot of case law, and time is very limited in the exam room, it is very important to identify precisely what the problems are and how they might be dealt with. Be sure to answer the question. What reforms would you propose?

Skeleton Solution

- Summary of the principal effect of *O'Reilly*.
- Emergence of the public law/private law distinction.
- Three problems caused by *O'Reilly*:
  - exclusivity of procedure;
  - distinction between public and private law;
  - mixed cases.
- Reform by allowing mixed cases to proceed by writ.

Suggested Solution

The chief damage done by the decision in *O'Reilly* v *Mackman* (1983) was the ruling that s31 of the Supreme Court Act 1981 and O.53 of the Rules of the Supreme Court 1977 had created an exclusive procedure for challenging certain actions and decisions of government bodies, and that it was prima facie an abuse of process to proceed by any other means. To do so would lead to a claim being struck out. The principal justification for this approach was that the new O.53 had consolidated the various prerogative remedies with the equitable remedies of declaration and injunction, and had moulded them into a new single procedure which included a requirement that leave of the court be obtained before proceeding, and a three-month time limit for making applications for judicial review. The House of Lords felt that this new single procedure conferred benefits on litigants and protection upon government bodies. It would be an abuse for litigants to evade this protection by resorting to writ procedure which formerly was the means of obtaining declarations and injunctions.

It is unfortunate that the House of Lords decided so firmly that O.53 was an exclusive procedure. It appears that this was not Parliament's intention. An early proposal of the Law Commission that the new procedure should be exclusive was dropped following consultation. Both the final report of the Commission and the Rules Committee of Parliament avoided making any recommendation of exclusivity. But if it was not Parliament's intention to create an exclusive procedure, then s31 is rather poorly drafted since it states that an application for one of the above remedies 'shall be made ... by a procedure to be known as an application for judicial review'. The use of the word 'shall' in this context does give weight to the view that O.53 should be the exclusive procedure for seeking those remedies.

While the prerogative remedies are of application only in cases involving government bodies and tribunals, the remedies of declaration and injunction are of more universal application, and have their origins in the enforcement of obligations owed between private individuals. Clearly there are circumstances where government bodies behave in the same way and are subject to the same laws as private individuals; for instance, they enter into contracts. It is therefore necessary to define the circumstances in which judicial review will be the appropriate procedure rather than an ordinary action by way of writ. In *O'Reilly* v *Mackman* the House of Lords attempted to distinguish between public law rights and private law rights. If a litigant was asserting the former, he should proceed by way of judicial review; if the latter, then by way of writ. But public law and private law are not concepts inherent in English law, where constitutional law has always dictated that government bodies and officials should be subject to the ordinary law and courts, and not a distinct regime. So English law lacks a traditional basis for distinguishing between public and private law.

Any reform of s31 must tackle three problems that have arisen since *O'Reilly* v *Mackman*. First, it must make it clear whether O.53 should indeed be an exclusive procedure. Were the legislature to replace the word 'shall' with the word 'may' in s31(1) much of the difficulty would evaporate. The difficulty with that approach, however, is that it may make O.53 unworkable in practice. Litigants who failed to proceed within the three-month time limit, or who thought that they might not get leave, would simply issue writs. Even if Parliament did not intend O.53 to be an exclusive procedure; it must have intended it to be the normal route for challenge of government actions.

The other two problems that have flowed from *O'Reilly* are related to one another and are more mischievous than the decision that O.53 should be an exclusive procedure. That might be justifiable if the circumstances in which judicial review should be brought were certain. But since *O'Reilly* it has been apparent that the distinction between public and private law cannot be drawn with certainty, and that particular difficulty arises where both types of law arise in the same proceedings. It is natural that 'mixed cases' should be the source of such particular difficulty, bearing in mind that the choice of procedure will be less uncertain where only one remedy is sought. This difficulty is amply illustrated by the case of *Cocks* v *Thanet District Council* (1983), decided by the House of Lords on the same day as *O'Reilly*. In this case the plaintiff brought an action by writ seeking to enforce the Council's obligations to him pursuant to the housing the homeless legislation. The House of Lords attempted to distinguish between two duties under that legislation. On the one hand, there was the preliminary duty to decide whether the plaintiff fulfilled the statutory criteria, and on the other the duty to provide him with housing if he did so. The former duty was a matter of public law, but the duty to provide housing was enforceable as a private law right. Since the plaintiff was attacking the first duty, his claim was struck out as an abuse of process. This decision illustrates both the artificiality of the distinction between public law and private law, and the difficulty in dealing with government actions that involve both elements.

Most of the cases that the courts have had to decide have had a mixture of public and private claims. The way in which the courts have dealt with such cases has been somewhat inconsistent, and the distinction between public and private law is still without a coherent legal basis. It has been accepted that public law matters may be raised as a defence to ordinary actions where they are a genuine legal defence to the claim being made. Thus, if an authority does not have the power to raise the rents it charges, that will be a genuine defence to a claim for arrears of rent, because it amounts to an allegation that there was no obligation to pay the higher rent; this allegation may be raised as a defence in the 'private' proceedings: *Wandsworth London Borough Council* v *Winder* (1985). But the failure of an authority to provide a caravan site for gypsies is not a defence to an action for possession based on trespass, because it does not make the trespass lawful. It may not, therefore, be raised without recourse to judicial review: *Avon County Council* v *Buscott* (1988).

While there has been this sensible recognition that 'public law' issues may be brought into ordinary proceedings where they amount to a defence, the position is less certain where they are part of a claim. In *Davy* v *Spelthorne Borough Council* (1984) the plaintiff brought such a mixed claim by way of writ. His 'private law' negligence claim was allowed to stand, but his 'public law' claims for an injunction and certiorari were struck out as being an abuse of process. It is submitted that this approach lacks sense: it cannot be right to require a litigant affected by negligent advice to maintain two separate claims in order to deal with all the issues that arise out of that negligence. To do so leads to greater expense, inefficiency and arguable injustice. The situation has been mitigated to some extent by the decision in *Roy* v *Kensington and Chelsea and Westminster Family Practitioner Committee* (1992). In this case it has been held that public law issues might be raised in private claims where such issues were collateral to the claim. This will be the case where it is clear that the action is brought to enforce private law rights (in this case a contractual right to be paid), that such rights dominate the proceedings, and that writ procedure is a more suitable way of dealing with the dispute. This is a useful pragmatic approach, but unfortunately it was put on the footing that the case was an exception to the rule in *O'Reilly*. Since *Roy* v *Kensington* is seen as exceptional, it is unlikely to be extended very greatly. This view is confirmed by *British Steel plc* v *Customs and Excise Commissioners* (1996), another mixed case which upheld the general trend set by *O'Reilly* and *Cocks* v *Thanet*. By contrast a more relaxed view was taken by the House of Lords in *Mercury Communications Ltd* v *D-G of Telecommunications* (1996) where a mixed issues case was allowed to proceed by originating summons in the Commercial Court since that was an appropriate forum and using it would not be an 'abuse of process'. If judges were to follow this more flexible approach to the public/private dichotomy statutory reform of s31 of the Supreme Court Act 1981 would be unnecessary, but it is far from certain that this will happen.

It is clear that s31 is in need of some reform to deal with these difficulties. What is needed is some way of distinguishing between cases that must proceed by way of judicial review, and those that must proceed by way of writ. This problem is not particularly difficult where an applicant raises a claim for damages in O.53 proceedings, since s31 specifically permits such a claim to be made and the claim may be allowed to continue as if begun by writ. The real difficulty is deciding how to proceed when claims have a private aspect, but the remedies of declaration and injunction are sought. This difficulty is particularly acute where cases involve a mixture of 'public law' and 'private law' rights. Section 31 needs to address this situation in particular. Perhaps the best way in which it may do so is to include a sub-section stating that the need to use O.53 procedure is without prejudice to the right to attack a government decision in writ proceedings where that is necessary and/or ancillary to a claim for one of the normal remedies available on a writ action. Such an amendment would make it clear that there is no objection to the raising of public law issues in such cases and this would enable substantial justice to be done in every case. If it became clear that the 'private law' remedies were not being genuinely sought, then the action might still be struck out as an abuse of process. But where such remedies genuinely form the substance of a claim, it is only proper that the court should be able to consider ancillary public law questions without the need for separate proceedings. Furthermore, the proposed amendment would substantially do away with the need to define public and private law – which is most prevalent in mixed cases. The task of providing such a definition is one which the legislature would do well to avoid in the light of the inconsistent results achieved by the courts.

QUESTION FOUR

The Law Reform Commission of the newly independent nation of Caraba has been instructed by its government to produce proposals concerning the law of locus standi in Caraban administrative law. As a general rule, the Caraban Supreme Court attaches considerable importance to English law as a source of persuasive authority.

At present, locus standi in Caraba is granted to any citizen 'who objects to a governmental decision'. The government is much concerned that the litigious predisposition of the Caraban people is leading to an overloading of the courts and a paralysis of the government process. The government has instructed the Law Reform Commission to fashion a much more restrictive law of standing which could plausibly be defended against accusations from opposition parties that the government is seeking to undermine the rule of law.

You have been retained by the Law Reform Commission to produce an opinion outlining the extent to which English law might provide a model through which the Caraban government could achieve its objectives.

What would you propose?

University of London LLB Examination
(for External Students) Administrative Law June 1994 Q7

General Comment

This question requires an evaluation of the English rules of standing against two criteria, their effectiveness in restricting access to the courts and their compatibility with the rule of law. Are the English rules good enough to export?

Skeleton Solution

- Difficulties presented by rules of standing.
- The test of 'sufficient interest':
  - the first stage;
  - the second stage.

- Public interest cases:
  - – the relator action;
  - – judicial review.

Suggested Solution

The difficulty in drawing up rules of standing is in striking the balance between restricting access to the courts on the one hand and allowing an effective means of challenge on the other. If the criteria of standing are too narrow then it may be difficult to subject governmental bodies to the rule of law simply because there is too small a class of people who have standing to bring ultra vires decision-making before the courts. There must also be an effective mode of challenge in matters of public interest if the rule of law is not to be undermined.

The English model of standing attempts to solve these difficulties by making standing a matter of discretion for the courts. Within the English system of administrative law the leave of the court is required before judicial review proceedings may be brought. The present rule of standing is contained in O.53, r3(7) of the Rules of the Supreme Court and states that leave shall not be granted unless the court considers that the applicant has a 'sufficient interest' in the matter to which the application relates. This is clearly a deliberately vague concept designed to maximise the court's control over entry into judicial review proceedings. In order to evaluate the efficacy of this model of standing, and its ability to be imported into Caraban administrative law, one must therefore look at the way in which it has been interpreted by the English courts.

Order 53, r3(7) clearly requires the 'sufficient interest' test to be applied on the application for leave. It has been held by the House of Lords that, at this stage, the test should be applied in such a way as to filter out those claims which are frivolous and vexatious, or where the applicant has no genuine interest in the matter (*IRC* v *National Federation of Self-Employed and Small Businesses* (1982)). Thus the test is interpreted at the application for leave as a simple threshold or filter which will dispose of those objections to decisions that are not based upon some concrete grounds of challenge, or interest in the outcome of the matter. This is certainly preferable to the test granting locus standi to any citizen 'who objects to a governmental decision' since objections may be made on a number of bases, some of which may be entirely frivolous, but which may be of nuisance value to the objector in slowing down the decision-making process. It should be noted also that the English model of standing does not confine standing to citizens; and indeed some important decisions in English administrative law have concerned non-citizens. This, it is submitted, is itself more conducive to the rule of law since non-citizens, such as immigrants, should have an opportunity to challenge ultra vires decisions affecting them. If they do not have this opportunity, the effect may be that certain government agencies are immune from challenge, which is unlikely to be healthy.

It should be noted, however, that in *ex parte National Federation of Self-Employed and Small Businesses* the House of Lords held that the test of standing should also be applied after the application for leave and at the substantive hearing itself. At this second stage in the test, standing should be determined by reference to the legal and factual context of the case, judged in relation to the applicant's concern in it. It is extremely odd that the test of standing should be applied at this stage. Order 53, r3(7) only applies the test to the application for leave to move for judicial review. Logically, there is some difficulty in applying a test restricting access to the courts at the stage where that access has already been acquired. For that reason, by the time that the substantive hearing has been reached, locus standi has ceased to be a method of restricting access to the court, and has become a ground for refusing relief in the court's discretion.

Since Caraba is seeking a rule restricting access, the second stage of the test may be irrelevant to its purposes. But applying the test in two stages can be beneficial in certain respects. At the second stage the court has the opportunity to look at the merits of the case, and to some extent at the motives of the applicant and the benefit to him or her, in some detail. By using locus standi to extend its discretion, the court ensures that at the substantive hearing relief will not be granted to those who will not benefit from it, or where there are more appropriate methods of challenge. An example of the latter type of case is *R* v *Boundary Commission for England, ex parte Foot* (1983), where it was held that the applicant did not have standing to challenge a review of parliamentary constituency boundary lines. The matter was one of public importance but the applicant's challenge was in essence a political one. The concern of the court is with law and not with politics. This should be borne in mind with reference to Caraba's present rule, which would appear to allow challenges to be brought before the courts on purely political grounds.

This case does illustrate a difficulty that can arise in introducing a restrictive rule of standing; such a rule may make it practically impossible to bring matters of public importance before the courts. There may be very few people with standing to challenge a particular decision, or those who do have standing may be unable to do so for a variety of reasons. Legal proceedings are complex and costly. One way to overcome this difficulty is to introduce a specific mode of challenge in public interest cases. The English system has such a mode of challenge, known as the relator action. This permits the Attorney-General to bring civil proceedings in matters of public importance. If such an action is adopted in Caraba, it needs to be introduced in such a way that it is effective. One of the difficulties with the English relator action is that the Attorney-General has seemingly unchallengeable discretion whether or not to bring relator proceedings. This means that there is no guarantee that a case brought to his attention will ever reach the courts (*Gouriet* v *Union of Post Office Workers* (1978)).

The court has itself overcome this difficulty in judicial cases by applying the rules of standing with some flexibility. The court has permitted individuals or public interest groups to bring actions in suitable cases of wider public interest. Thus in *R* v *Secretary of State for Social Services, ex parte Child Poverty Action Group and Greater London Council* (1985) the court had to consider whether two interest groups had standing to challenge a decision by the Social Services Secretary. The court held that the GLC did not have standing, because it had an insufficient interest in the outcome of the case. But the Child Poverty Action Group represented the interests of individuals who were directly affected by the decision in question, and thus was held to have standing. By opening up the gateways of standing to suitable interest groups, the English court has to some extent provided relief from the difficulties of obtaining judicial review in matters of public importance.

The English model of standing is thus highly flexible, giving a large range of flexibility to the judiciary to determine who should have access to the judicial review remedies. For this reason, it could hardly be said to undermine the rule of law. From the point of view of restricting access to the courts, the English model is preferable to the existing Caraban test in that it requires an applicant at least to have some tangible interest in the outcome of the case, as opposed to an objection based on any grounds, however insubstantial or non-legal.

9 Jurisdiction and Parliamentary Attempts to Exclude Judicial Review

9.1 Introduction

'Jurisdiction' in a broad sense means power and in a narrower sense means the power to decide. The development of judicial review was inhibited by early attempts to distinguish between jurisdictional errors (reviewable) and non-jurisdictional errors (non-reviewable, but able to be appealed against provided a statutory right of appeal existed which had not been limited or excluded on the matter being challenged). The distinction became a source of concern to some judges and led to the revival of an ancient doctrine called 'error of law on the face of the record', which permitted review of non-jurisdictional ('intra vires') errors of law provided they appeared on the face of the record of the inferior body, ie the doctrine could only operate in regard to courts of record. This anomalous and artificial doctrine impeded a rational categorisation of ultra vires until the landmark decision in *Anisminic Ltd* v *Foreign Compensation Commission* [1969] 1 All ER 208 (HL) effectively discarded the distinction between jurisdictional and non-jurisdictional error for the purposes of review of the errors of administrative tribunals.

Parliamentary attempts to limit or exclude judicial review have been crucially affected by the story of jurisdictional error and so, for the purposes of convenient exposition, exclusion and limitation clauses are dealt with in this chapter in this context, rather than in the later chapter on remedies.

9.2 Key points

a) *Errors of fact*

In general errors resulting from evaluation of relevant facts (including mixed law and fact, ie questions of judgment) are not challengeable by way of judicial review but only by an appeal, if one is provided by statute. It has been suggested that the distinction drawn between questions of law and of judgment reflects a desire on the part of the judges not to interfere with the interpretation of regulatory provisions rather than being a sustainable conceptual distinction: McHarg [1995] PL 539 at p549. However, the distinction between error of fact and error of law is often a fine one and in some areas, eg procedural ultra vires, an error of fact may have led to the error of law which constitutes the ground for review. This is why, infrequently, oral cross-examination may be permitted under O.53 as the best way to settle disputes over facts in a case involving alleged breaches of natural justice.

Further, an 'error of jurisdictional fact' (sometimes called error of collateral fact) is reviewable because it is in reality an error of law as it occurs when the inferior body completely misunderstands the task it has to do and instead performs a different task, thereby committing a jurisdictional error and rendering all its subsequent decisions void: *R* v *Fulham, Hammersmith and Kensington Rent Tribunal, ex parte Zerek* [1951] 2 KB 1. Finally, findings of fact for which there is no sufficient or reasonable evidence, and misdirections of fact, such as illogical findings, may be treated as affecting jurisdiction since they amount to errors of law under the categories of illegality/irrationality: see, eg, Lord Diplock in *Mahon* v *Air New Zealand Ltd* [1984] 1 AC 808 at p832g, discussing a finding of fact involving an 'evident illogical fallacy'.

b) *Jurisdictional errors of law*

Strictly speaking, these occur when the inferior body, having correctly identified its jurisdiction as a question of fact, then does something or fails to do something which is of such a nature as to render its decision a nullity, ie by committing an excess or abuse of its jurisdiction in any of the ways identified by the ultra vires doctrine (procedural impropriety, illegality or irrationality): per Lord Diplock in the GCHQ case (*Council of Civil Service Unions* v *Minister for the Civil Service* [1984] 3 All ER 935 (HL)).

c) *Non-jurisdictional errors of law*

These may occur where the inferior body exercises its correct jurisdiction and applies the relevant law to the case before it but then makes a mistake in the interpretation of that law so that it makes the 'wrong' decision as a result of its error of law. Until the *Anisminic* decision, such an error was treated as if it involved no ultra vires and could only be reviewed if it appeared on the face of the record of the inferior body (see (d) below). Alternatively, it could be appealed. But in the absence of a statutory right of appeal and in the absence of a record such an error would be unchallengeable; hence the effective abolition of the distinction between jurisdictional and non-jurisdictional error in the *Anisminic* case was crucial in preventing further injustice in individual cases.

d) *Error of law on the face of the record*

The need to find some way of reviewing non-jurisdictional errors of law in the years prior to the *Anisminic* ruling had become urgent due to the growth of the Welfare State after World War II and the mushrooming of administrative tribunals to administer it, because these tribunals (often composed of non-lawyers applying complex pieces of legislation) were especially prone to making non-jurisdictional errors of law. The danger of injustice being committed in individual cases became even greater as Parliament, for reasons of expedience, excluded or limited rights of appeal from such tribunal decisions. Lord Denning MR found the 'solution' by reviving the ancient doctrine of error of law on the face of the record, under which intra vires errors of law could be quashed in order to correct the record of the inferior body: *R* v *Northumberland Compensation Appeal Tribunal, ex parte Shaw* [1952] 1 KB 338. The doctrine was given a new, wider interpretation in order to reflect modern realities of administrative decision-making so that the concept of the 'record' was broadened to include a wide range of documents used in the case, thereby enabling the review court to examine the reasons for the decision as part of the 'record': *R* v *Knightsbridge Crown Court, ex parte International Sporting Club Ltd* [1981] 3 WLR 640. The doctrine of error of law on the face of the record became obsolete after *Anisminic* effectively declared all errors of law to be jurisdictional errors, provided the error is relevant

Relevant

and affects the decision. The abandonment of the doctrine of error of law on the face of the record has been confirmed in *R* v *Lord President of the Privy Council, ex parte Page* [1992] 3 WLR 1112 (HL).

e) *Parliament's attempts to exclude or limit challenges*

The *Anisminic* decision needs to be set in the context of parliamentary attempts to exclude or limit challenges in the courts. Some decisions are protected by 'ouster clauses', eg 'this decision shall not be questioned in any legal proceedings whatsoever' or 'this decision is final'. Others may be protected by time limits for challenge, eg 'this decision shall not be questioned in any legal proceedings whatsoever more than six weeks after the decision has been taken'. Logically, an ultra vires decision is null and void, and there will be nothing left capable of protection by a finality or a time limit clause. This would mean that such clauses could only operate in regard to non-jurisdictional errors of fact, ie excluding an appeal on the merits, but not capable of excluding review for ultra vires. Such an interpretation has found favour with some judges as a means of bolstering the rule of law over administrative decision-making, as well as being justified in terms of conceptual logic: see per Lord Denning MR in *R* v *Medical Appeal Tribunal, ex parte Gilmore* [1957] 1 QB 574 and in *Pearlman* v *Keepers and Governors of Harrow School* [1979] QB 56; per Lord Reid in *Anisminic*; and per Lord Diplock in *Anisminic, Re Racal Communications Ltd* [1981] AC 374 and *O'Reilly* v *Mackman* [1983] 2 AC 237.

However, other judges were concerned at such neutering of parliamentary exclusion clauses and took the view that Parliament must have intended to exclude judicial review as well as appeal at least in regard to non-jurisdictional errors committed by inferior regular courts of law: see per Geoffrey Lane LJ (dissenting) in *Pearlman*, whose judgment received the approval of the Judicial Committee of the Privy Council in *South East Asia Fire Bricks Sdn Bhd* v *Non-Metallic Mineral Products Manufacturing Employees Union* [1981] AC 363. *Pearlman* concerned the decision of a county court judge, whilst the *Fire Bricks* case concerned the decision of the Industrial Court of Malaysia. Presumably this approach is based on the view that, by putting in an exclusion clause, Parliament intends to run the relatively low risk of non-jurisdictional errors of law being committed by judges. Such an intention is not to be inferred in regard to purely administrative tribunals, not composed of lawyers or judges, so that an ouster clause would not protect such errors by such a body: *Anisminic*. If this view is correct (and it was confirmed in *ex parte Page,* above), it perpetuates the distinction between jurisdictional and non-jurisdictional error in some contexts and creates a further difficult distinction between regular and 'irregular' courts and tribunals. As Wade and Forsyth comment (7th edn at p306): 'To that extent the old rule may still have life in it.'

f) *Review is context-based*

It appears, therefore, that review may be context-based: an exclusion clause using the words 'the decision shall not be appealable' in regard to the decisions of a High Court judge makes his decisions on the matters covered by the exclusion clause unchallengeable because, as a superior judge, he is not subject to the supervisory jurisdiction of the Divisional Court of the Queen's Bench Division of the High Court: *Re Racal*, above. It also follows that when High Court judges exercise their visitorial jurisdiction of the Inns of Court their decisions are also unreviewable: *R* v *Visitors to Lincoln's Inn, ex parte Calder and Persuad* [1992] 3 WLR 994. Less satisfactory is the position of University Visitors, who, despite probably not being High Court judges or even judges at all, enjoy for historical reasons exclusivity of decision-making on questions of law and fact within their jurisdiction: *ex parte Page*, above.

Hence the demands of a pragmatic, contextual approach may prevail over strict legal logic. See further Wade: 'Visitors and Errors of Law' (1993) 109 LQR 155.

g) *Interpretation of time limits*

The contextual approach also explains the interpretation given to time limits which have been held effective to protect ultra vires determinations after the relevant time has expired even though logically there is no 'decision' capable of setting the time limit into motion. The effectiveness of time limits in such cases can only be explained in terms of the need for finality for certain kinds of decision-making, eg planning decisions relating to the building of housing, motorways, etc, and the presumed intention of Parliament to exclude the possibility of any challenge in the courts once the relevant time limit has expired. Any persons aggrieved would be left with extra-judicial remedies, eg a possible complaint to the Ombudsman (Parliamentary or Local) for maladministration: *Smith* v *East Elloe Rural District Council* [1956] AC 736 (HL); *R* v *Secretary of State for the Environment, ex parte Ostler* [1977] QB 122 (CA); *R* v *Cornwall County Council, ex parte Huntingdon* [1994] 1 All ER 694 (CA).

9.3 Recent cases

R v *Secretary of State for the Home Department, ex parte Fayed* [1997] 1 All ER 228 (CA) – the applicants had applied unsuccessfully for naturalisation so as to become British citizens. The Home Secretary had rejected their application on the ground that they were not of 'good character', but declined to give reasons for this conclusion. Under s44(2) of the British Nationality Act 1981 the Home Secretary is exempted from a requirement to provide reasons for such a decision, which is also declared by s44(2) not to be subject to appeal or review in any court. The Court of Appeal (Kennedy LJ dissenting) *held* that the Home Secretary's decision was reviewable. The ouster clause did not prevent review in cases of procedural unfairness, because the Home Secretary only had jurisdiction to make decisions consequent upon a fair process: *Anisminic* (1969), applied. For the issue of the procedural fairness in this case see chapter 10, section 10.3.

9.4 Analysis of questions

First year constitutional law students are referred to the advice given in chapter 15. Students of administrative law usually find the topic of jurisdictional error to be among the most difficult in their syllabus, mainly because of the conceptual analysis and because of the confusing twists and turns in its development. Yet careful study is worthwhile because exam questions on the topic (and on the related area of exclusion/limitation clauses) occur regularly and usually in the form of straightforward essay-type questions. Sometimes a problem-type question will contain reference to an ouster/limitation clause so that part of the answer will be on the effect of such a clause in the general context of judicial review of administrative action.

9.5 Questions

QUESTION ONE

'Ouster clauses are a necessary ingredient of the government process in a complex, modern society. Judicial attempts to circumvent them are thus not only incompatible with the principle of parliamentary sovereignty, but are also inimical to efficient government decision-making.'

Discuss.

University of London LLB Examination
(for External Students) Administrative Law June 1995 Q2

General Comment

This question involves considerations of constitutional theory and day-to-day governmental practice, as well as the principles of administrative law. It is important to understand thoroughly the doctrine of ultra vires, since it is this which has enabled the court to evade the provisions of ouster clauses. It is a question of individual judgment whether the interests of efficient government decision-making are more important than those of the citizens affected by the decisions!

Skeleton Solution

- Ouster clauses defined.
- The ultra vires doctrine as justification for ignoring ouster clauses.
- The modern interpretation of ultra vires and its effects.
- Clearly worded ouster clauses.
- Conditional ouster clauses.

Suggested Solution

There are many different ways in which Parliament places limits on the power of the courts to interfere in the decision-making powers of administrative bodies. True ouster clauses are those which purport to exclude judicial challenge altogether. The use of such clauses is an indication that Parliament wishes the body in question to have complete and final jurisdiction to exercise its powers and to make decisions, and that those decisions should not be questioned by the courts. The courts have adopted liberal interpretations of ouster clauses that have enabled them to subject decisions to judicial review despite the apparent intentions of Parliament. It might be thought that this endangers the principle of parliamentary sovereignty, since the courts appear to be deliberately ignoring the express intentions of Parliament. In the modern complex state that we live in, however, it is vital that the courts are bold and prepared to intervene to check illegality and abuse in the decision-making process, and it is arguable that in doing so they are actually assisting Parliament to carry out its intentions.

The foundation for the present judicial approach to ouster clauses is the House of Lords' case *Anisminic Ltd* v *Foreign Compensation Commission* (1969). In this case the Commission was given power to make determinations, subject to a clause which stated that those determinations should 'not be called into question in any court of law'. It is quite apparent from this wording that Parliament meant to exclude judicial review. As mentioned above, the administrative justification for such a clause is that it provides an element of finality and certainty to the decision-making process. Yet the House of Lords held unanimously that the clause would not bar judicial review where the Commission made a determination that lay outside its jurisdiction. The justification for the court's approach was founded on the doctrine of parliamentary sovereignty itself. Parliament had conferred a certain jurisdiction on the Commission. It was not Parliament's intention that the Commission should make determinations that lay outside that jurisdiction. Since the Commission did not have power to make such extra-jurisdictional determinations, they were ultra vires and would be quashed by an order of certiorari on judicial review.

This approach, in which the court claims to be merely policing the borders of jurisdiction granted by Parliament, and thus enforcing parliamentary intention, seems to have found favour with Parliament itself, for two years later Parliament enacted legislation which abolished any so-called 'no certiorari' clauses applied to tribunals enacted before 1958: see Tribunals and Inquiries Act 1971, s14. The apparently simple nature of this approach belies the subtlety and complexity of the results that have flowed from *Anisminic*. It is all very well to ensure that bodies keep within the jurisdiction conferred upon them, but how is that jurisdiction to be defined? In particular, what happens if the decision-maker proceeds upon an error of law? At the time when *Anisminic* was decided the courts used to distinguish between errors of law that took a tribunal outside its jurisdiction, and those which it had jurisdiction to make. An example of the former error might be where a tribunal decides that it has some power that it has not been granted by Parliament. The latter type of error might arise where the tribunal makes a minor error of interpretation in the course of its decision. Where a tribunal has made the first kind of error, there is clear justification for intervention by the courts, but such justification might not exist in the second case. It seems likely that the House of Lords in *Anisminic* had this distinction in mind and intended to preserve it (cf *South East Asia Fire Bricks Sdn Bhd* v *Non-Metallic Mineral Products Manufactuing Employees Union* (1981)). If this is correct, then *Anisminic* probably presented no real threat to the doctrine of parliamentary sovereignty, nor indeed to the efficient workings of administrative bodies, as long as they kept to the jurisdiction assigned to them.

The real difficulty arises from the fact that subsequent judicial decisions have used *Anisminic* as a springboard from which to launch an entirely new concept of ultra vires. Thus it has been held that *Anisminic* in fact abolished the distinction between the two types of error of law identified above. According to Lord Diplock in *Re Racal Communications Ltd* (1981) and *O'Reilly* v *Mackman* (1983), any error of law in the decision-making process will make the decision ultra vires and thus enable the court to exercise its powers of judicial review. This view has been confirmed by the House of Lords in *R* v *Lord President of the Privy Council, ex parte Page* (1992) on the ground that any error of law which was relevant in the making of the decision is jurisdictional. If this view is followed through to its logical extent, then ouster clauses become generally meaningless in the context of judicial review. Of course, such clauses will still make it clear that no appeal is possible, and therefore no judicial consideration of the merits of the decision is possible, but since judicial review is concerned with the legality of decisions and not with their merits, it appears that ouster clauses cannot exclude judicial review. This interpretation of *Anisminic* does present a threat to parliamentary sovereignty since it is clear that Parliament does intend that decision-makers should benefit from some degree of finality and certainty, so long as they remain within their jurisdiction. It does also undermine the efficiency of the decision-making process since tribunals may find themselves subject to the scrutiny of the court even where they have made comparatively minor errors of interpretation. Of course, this may not be a bad thing. It has been said that citizens affected by the decisions of tribunals are entitled to expect that those decisions will be lawful, and that the court will correct them if they are not (per Griffiths LJ in *R* v *Knightsbridge Crown Court, ex parte International Sporting Club Ltd* (1981)).

Perhaps in reaction to the more extreme possibilities of the 'new' ultra vires doctrine described above, it has been held that it will be open to the legislature to exclude judicial review by using very clear language in the legislation in question. It may, in any event, have been unlikely that the court would dare to intervene where Parliament expressly stated that under no circumstances would judicial review of a decision be permitted. A more subtle approach, and one which takes the courts at their word, is simply to confer a sufficiently broad jurisdiction on the tribunal in question. Thus, where a tribunal was given power to decide 'all ancillary questions', this was interpreted to include questions of law, and thus to give the tribunal the jurisdiction to make errors of law, effectively excluding judicial review except, possibly, in cases where the tribunal gives itself a power not conferred on it by Parliament: *R* v *Registrar of Companies, ex parte Central Bank of India* (1986).

A word must be said about ouster clauses that appear in conditional form. Such clauses are usually expressed to give a limited period of time during which a challenge may be made, and following which a decision may not be challenged in any legal proceedings whatsoever. Such clauses are normally upheld. Although expressed as conditional ouster clauses they are in fact interpreted as limitation clauses: *R* v *Secretary of State for the Environment, ex parte Ostler* (1977). If the logic of *Anisminic* is applied strictly to these clauses, then there is no reason why they should be upheld where errors of law have occurred. It is perhaps curious that a person affected by an unlawful decision may be better off when faced with an absolute form of ouster clause, than when provided with a limited period for challenge which has expired. The practical reality is that the courts are far more willing to accept that there should be some time limit placed upon a challenge by way of judicial review than they are to accept that such a challenge should be excluded altogether.

It is clear from the above discussion that the courts have somewhat jealously guarded their powers of judicial review, and that in some circumstances this may encroach upon parliamentary sovereignty and hinder the efficient exercise of government powers. This is not necessarily a bad thing. The very complexity of modern society means that individual citizens are constantly subject to administrative interference. Given that the English constitutional system has no formal separation of powers or system of checks and balances, it is incumbent upon the courts to protect these citizens from abuse of those powers and unlawful decisions made by inferior tribunals. What they need to do is to strike the balance between giving adequate protection on the one hand, and allowing Parliament to be sovereign and government agencies to carry out their executive tasks on the other. So far there is no evidence to suggest that, in practice, the courts have got the balance wrong.

QUESTION TWO

Section 312(5)(g) of the (fictitious) Local Government Revenue Act (LGRA) 1992 requires local authorities to exempt from the new council tax 'any house which by reason of its current state of disrepair cannot be occupied in the present financial year'. Section 319 provides that the council's decision 'shall be final'.

Section 3 of the (fictitious) Unfit Premises Restoration Act 1991 obliges councils to grant £5,000 towards the cost of renovating 'unfit houses'. Section 7 entrusts the question of determining unfitness to the council. Section 8 provides that the council decision is 'final'. Section 8(1) further provides that s8's reference to 'final' 'shall preclude initiation of proceedings for judicial review'.

Barry Smith has recently acquired two bungalows in identical states of disrepair in the area of Eastham Borough Council, 70 and 72 Acacia Avenue. Smith seeks council tax exemption and improvement grants for both dwellings.

The following decisions are made during May (in chronological order):

1) The Council approves a grant for 72 Acacia Avenue, noting it has rarely seen so unfit a dwelling.
2) The Council refuses to exempt 70 Acacia Avenue on the grounds that 'a bungalow is, by definition, not a house, and therefore not covered by s312(5)(g)'.
3) The Council refuses to exempt 72 Acacia Avenue, on the grounds that 'despite being in severe disrepair, this dwelling could reasonably be expected to be occupied within six months'.
4) The Council, noting decision number 2, refuses to approve a grant for 70 Acacia Avenue. The Council accepts that the bungalow is uninhabitable, but that since it is a 'bungalow' and not a 'house' it is not eligible for a grant.

Advise Smith if he might successfully challenge any of these decisions by judicial review.

University of London LLB Examination
(for External Students) Administrative Law June 1993 Q8

General Comment

This question requires a consideration of a number of points, some of them quite subtle. How will the court approach the different kinds of ouster clause? Is the definition of a commonplace word in a statute a matter of fact or of law? Can an apparent finding of fact be challenged? Consider what relief will be available to Smith if he is successful.

Skeleton Solution

- The obligations imposed by the statutes.
- Decision 2:
  - effect of 'shall be final';
  - review on basis of error of law;
  - relief available.
- Decision 4:
  - effect of ouster clause;
  - review on basis of error of law;
  - possibility of a legitimate expectation;
  - relief available.
- Decision 3:
  - question of fact?
  - *Wednesbury* unreasonableness;
  - no evidence;
  - relief available.

Suggested Solution

Smith may be able to bring judicial review against each of these decisions, although presumably he has no complaint about decision 1. It may be observed that both s312(5)(g) of the LGRA (1992) and s3 of the Unfit Premises Restoration Act (UPRA) 1991 impose obligations upon the Council; performance of these obligations may be enforced by order of mandamus.

In the case of decision 2, although s312(5)(g) states that the Council's decision 'shall be final', this wording has never precluded proceedings for judicial review (see *R* v *Medical Appeal Tribunal, ex parte Gilmore* (1957)). Judicial review may be brought on the ground of error of law. The definition of the word 'house' is clearly fundamental to the Council's duty, and thus is a matter that the court should investigate (*White and Collins* v *Minister of Health* (1939)). If the court finds that, in the absence of a statutory definition, the word 'house' is broad enough to include a bungalow, then the appropriate relief will be an order of certiorari to quash decision number 2. An order of mandamus can only compel the Council at this stage to consider whether or not the house can be occupied within the present financial year, since that consideration is preliminary to making the exemption.

The position with regard to decision 4 is more difficult, since the UPRA contains the clearest wording ousting the jurisdiction of the court to review the Council's decision judicially. It is not clear from the way in which s8 is cited whether the provision that the Council's decision is final applies only to the determination of unfitness, or whether it applies also to the decision whether to make a grant. If the former is true, then the Council's decision may be judicially reviewed on the basis of its definition of 'house'. If the provision in s8 applies to the whole of the Council's decision, then it may none the less be possible to obtain judicial review. It has been held by the Court of Appeal that a statute can exclude the jurisdiction of the court by using a 'conclusive evidence' clause (*R* v *Registrar of Companies, ex parte Central Bank of India* (1986)), but this must be set against the decision of the House of Lords in *Anisminic Ltd* v *Foreign Compensation Commission* (1969) which considered different wording ('shall not be called into question in any court of law'), and held that this could not exclude judicial review proceedings where the decision-maker made an error going to its jurisdiction. It is submitted that the rationale of *Anisminic* should apply to decision 4, since the definition of 'house' is fundamental, and since the UPRA imposes an obligation upon the Council which must be enforceable. Parliament cannot have intended the Council to evade its obligations by deciding for itself when they arise. Although the Council has in decision 1 treated 'house' as meaning 'dwelling', it is submitted that this can have no effect on the correct definition of the word, since that will be a matter for the court. However, it provides further ammunition for Smith, since the Council has clearly acted inconsistently. If Smith can show that the former definition was a matter of policy, then he may have a legitimate expectation that the policy will not be changed without giving him an opportunity to make representations (*R* v *Secretary of State for the Home Department, ex parte Khan* (1985)). There seems to be little evidence of a policy in this case, however. If Smith is able successfully to challenge decision 4, the appropriate relief will be an order of certiorari to quash the decision and an order of mandamus to compel the Council to make the grant.

Decision 3 may be rather difficult to review, since it seems to be founded on a straightforward question of fact (whether the house could be inhabited in the present financial year). However, it may be possible to challenge the decision on the basis that the Council has asked itself the wrong question, and thus taken into account an irrelevant consideration (*Associated Picture Houses Ltd* v *Wednesbury Corporation* (1948)). Section 312(5)(g) is concerned with whether a house cannot be occupied, not with whether it can reasonably be expected to be occupied. It may also be argued that the Council should have taken into account its earlier decision that it had rarely seen so unfit a dwelling. If Smith is unable to challenge decision 3 on these grounds, then he may be able to do so on the basis that the Council had no evidence on which to base its finding that the dwelling could reasonably be expected to be occupied within six months (*R* v *Secretary of State for the Home Department, ex parte Zamir* (1980)). If Smith is successful, then he should be able to obtain an order of certiorari to quash decision 3, combined with an order of mandamus to compel the Council to make the exemption. This may be contrasted with the position as to decision 2.

Smith has grounds on which he might be able to challenge each of the unfavourable decisions in this case, although his success in some of them may depend upon his being able to persuade the court to adopt a robust approach to these decisions.

QUESTION THREE

'Administrative lawyers still await a set of logical principles with which one can distinguish questions of law from questions of fact.'

Discuss.

University of London LLB Examination
(for External Students) Administrative Law June 1994 Q2

General Comment

This is quite a difficult question. It is implicit in the quotation that some importance is attached to the distinction between questions of law and questions of fact. Is the distinction important? If so, why? What are the consequences of classifying a particular question in one way or the other? Does the court always approach similar questions in a similar way? Is a question of fact always and only a question of fact, or may it also be a question of law? Regardless of the label attached to different questions, the real issue for the administrative lawyer is whether the court will intervene or not on an application for judicial review.

Skeleton Solution

- The court concerned with legality.
- Jurisdictional or 'collateral' facts.
- Reclassification by the court.
- A pragmatic approach to the distinction.
- The 'no evidence' rule – fact or law?
- Material mistake of fact.

Suggested Solution

It is axiomatic to administrative lawyers that judicial review is concerned principally with the legality of a particular decision and not with its merits. The role of the court is to police the borders of a particular authority's jurisdiction, not to invade that authority's territory. Prior to *Anisminic Ltd* v *Foreign Compensation Commission* (1969) the court would only consider questions of law or questions of fact if they went to an authority's jurisdiction. It is now clear that questions of law are always jurisdictional, and therefore the court will always be able to consider them. The same is not true of questions of fact: they should still only be considered if they go to a body's jurisdiction. It is necessary, therefore, to distinguish between questions of law and questions of fact for the purposes of judicial review. As will be seen, the court has allowed itself a wide margin in determining the borderline between questions of law and questions of fact and this is responsible for the lack of clarity in the distinction between the two types of question.

It is clear that there may be certain facts that are crucial to an authority's jurisdiction. The principle of ultra vires means that an authority should not be permitted to give itself powers that Parliament never intended it to have. Thus, where a statute provides certain objective criteria which are preconditions of an authority's decision-making powers, the court will always be astute to ensure that the authority applies those criteria correctly and thus remains intra vires. So, for instance, a rent authority may have the power to reduce the rent on a dwelling house; if it mistakenly defines business premises as a dwelling house, then its decision to reduce the rent will be ultra vires. While the question whether the premises are a dwelling house is a question of fact, it is plainly one which goes to the jurisdiction of the authority.

While the court is clearly justified in intervening in such jurisdictional or 'collateral' questions confusion arises because such questions are often treated as questions of law. Thus in *R* v *Secretary of State for the Home Department, ex parte Khawaja* (1984) the jurisdictional question whether the plaintiff was an illegal entrant was treated as a question of law for the court to decide, although it was a question which depended upon issues of fact. In one sense jurisdictional questions of fact *are* also questions of law, because they are related to the ultimate legality of the decision that is challenged. Thus a question may be one of both fact and law. It is submitted, however, that this is a conceptual distinction which is not necessary. The court probably defines particular questions as ones of law in order to give its intervention in a decision the hallmark of propriety; it does not need to do so where a question of fact is plainly fundamental to the exercise of power, for in these circumstances the court is quite justified in intervening to uphold the ultra vires doctrine.

This redefinition of questions of fact as questions of law in some circumstances is largely responsible for any confusion that exists between the two. The real issue here is probably not whether an issue is one of law or fact, but whether the court will intervene or not. The court is itself able to capitalise upon the blurred line between fact and law to justify its own conclusions as to whether it should disturb a particular decision or not. While this usually operates to bring questions of fact into the range of the court's powers of review, it sometimes works in reverse as well. Where an authority had a statutory duty to provide accommodation, the House of Lords held that whether the applicant had 'accommodation' within the meaning of the statute was a question of fact for the authority to determine, and that the court would only intervene if the authority had obviously acted perversely (*R* v *Hillingdon London Borough Council, ex parte Puhlhofer* (1986). The interpretation of a statute is almost invariably a question of law. In this case the court was confronted with a statutory duty, the fulfilment of which must be peculiarly sensitive to local factors. By redefining the question as one of fact the court was able to adopt a 'hands off' approach, recognising that the authority was in the best position to allocate its resources.

This suggests that lawyers need to move away from the purely conceptual approach to defining fact and law, and to ask the more pragmatic question whether the court will consider the question or not. If the court will consider it, the question can probably be defined in terms of legality since the vires of a decision will be in issue. If the court will not consider the question then it should be seen as one of fact for the authority concerned to determine. Such an approach may not help in determining the conceptual line between fact and law, but it is commended by the approach the court itself appears to have taken. It should be clear that there are some issues of fact which are 'central', rather than 'collateral', and lie entirely within an authority's jurisdiction, and the court should not disturb such findings of fact. But even where questions appear to be purely factual in this sense, the court may redefine them as questions of law so as to justify setting a decision aside.

A good example of this approach is the 'no evidence' rule. This rule relates specifically to findings of fact and it may seem plain that, where a body finds facts which are not supported by evidence, then it has made an error of fact. In such circumstances the court's intervention is only justified if the error of fact is jurisdictional. This, indeed, was the rationale underlying the decision in *R* v *Nat Bell Liquors Ltd* (1922), which held that such an error was immune from challenge. It is now clear that such an error may be challenged, but it is treated as an error of law. The 'no evidence' rule does not refer merely to the absence of evidence; to find facts without an evidential basis is an error of law, and all errors of law are open to challenge. The concept of 'evidential basis' is a broad one which has come to mean that, as a matter of natural justice, there must be evidence of probative value supporting a finding of fact (*R* v *Deputy Industrial Injuries Commissioner, ex parte Moore* (1965)). This poses an immediate problem, since a tribunal that deals with the evidence first-hand must be in a better position to assess its probative value than the court on an application for judicial review, which, though empowered to order cross-examination of witnesses, generally deals with evidence only on affidavit.

By using the sleight of hand of redefining questions of fact as questions of law, the court has even extended its powers of review to cases where the authority concerned acts upon an incorrect basis of fact. In *Secretary of State for Education and Science* v *Tameside Metropolitan Borough Council* (1977) Lord Scarman referred to 'misunderstanding or ignorance of an established and relevant fact'. Where an authority proceeds on the wrong factual basis, that may cause as much injustice as where it proceeds on the wrong legal basis. By redefining such questions as ones of law, the court is upholding the ultra vires doctrine and using that doctrine to expand its powers of review. If such expansion continues it may be that the issue whether a question is one of fact or of law will become irrelevant; it will be swallowed up in the more pragmatic consideration of whether justice has been done. If that happens, then the court may in reality be in danger of trespassing in the factual territory of the authority concerned, instead of keeping to its constitutional function of policing the legality of administrative decision-making.

10 Procedural Impropriety

10.1 Introduction

Procedural impropriety is a category or head of ultra vires which may occur through a failure to observe mandatory statutory requirements as to the exercise of a duty or a power, or through breach of common law requirements as to natural justice or fairness in the exercise of power. 'Procedural impropriety' is the umbrella term given to this very extensive basis for review: see per Lord Diplock in the GCHQ case (*Council of Civil Service Unions* v *Minister for the Civil Service*) [1984] 3 All ER 935 (HL).

10.2 Key points

a) *Mandatory and directory requirements*

It is a matter of statutory construction and will depend on the context of each case as to whether a specified procedural step is mandatory or directory. Breach of a mandatory requirement will be subject to review, but breach of a directory requirement will not. There will be no breach if the body on which the mandatory procedural requirement was imposed has substantially complied with it: *Coney* v *Choyce* [1975] 1 All ER 979. As a general rule, requirements designed to protect citizens' rights are usually classified as mandatory, eg duty to consult interested parties before a decision is taken, whereas requirements put in for administrative convenience only will be interpreted as directory, eg time limits for taking certain kinds of decision.

b) *Effect of* Ridge *v* Baldwin *on applicability of rules of natural justice*

Following the landmark decision of *Ridge* v *Baldwin* [1964] AC 40 (HL), the application of natural justice or fairness will depend on the context of each case. As a general rule, the closer the proceedings come to a judicial process involving the adjudication of a dispute, the settlement of rights and the imposition of penalties, the higher the standard of fairness required from such proceedings. If the proceedings are of a purely administrative character only minimal standards of fair procedures may be required. In some contexts there may be no duty to act fairly because of overriding considerations of public policy, eg national security or a national emergency requiring urgent executive response: the GCHQ case, above. The exact standard of fairness required in each case will therefore vary according to the 'character of the decision-making body, the kind of decision it has to make and the statutory or other framework in which it operates': per Lord Bridge in *Lloyd* v *McMahon* [1987] 1 All ER 1118 at p1161 (HL). The concept of 'fair play in action' has also been used in this context.

c) *Legitimate expectation*

'Legitimate expectation' has become the modern concept for determining whether an applicant is entitled to a fair hearing. It was defined by Lord Diplock in the GCHQ case ([1985] AC 374 at p408 (HL)) as some kind of established right or benefit of which it would be unfair to deprive the holder without first giving the holder a fair hearing. This reflected the distinction drawn in cases such as *McInnes* v *Onslow-Fane* [1978] 3 All ER 211 between legitimate expectations and mere hopes of a future benefit, the latter not attracting the requirement of fairness of determination except in a very minimal way such as a right to an unbiased determination and disclosure to the applicant of information unfavourable to his case: *R* v *Gaming Board for Great Britain, ex parte Benaim and Khaida* [1970] 2 QB 417. Many administrative decisions involve the allocation of scarce resources, such as council homes, university places, licences for various activities, etc, and the bare applicant for such a resource should therefore not expect a fair hearing of the sort granted to someone about to be deprived of such a resource.

However, the doctrine of legitimate expectation has proved to be an expansionist one in extending the scope of judicial review so as to protect citizens' interests, and it may be that administrative convenience will no longer be permitted to stand in the way of ensuring a fair hearing even to a bare applicant. Recent dicta have cast doubt on the rigid conceptual distinction between expectations and hopes:

'The concept of legitimate expectation ... seems to me no more than a recognition and embodiment of the unsurprising principle that the demands of fairness are likely to be somewhat higher when an authority contemplates depriving someone of an existing benefit or advantage than when the claimant is a bare applicant for a future benefit. That is not to say that a bare applicant will himself be without any entitlement to fair play. On the contrary, the developing jurisprudence suggests that he too must be fairly dealt with, not least in the field of licensing': per Simon Brown LJ in *R* v *Devon County Council, ex parte Baker* [1995] 1 All ER 73 at pp90j–91b. In this case the closure of an old peoples' home was held to have been made in breach of natural justice because the residents had a legitimate expectation of consultation.

Legitimate expectations may arise in two other situations: first, where there has been an established regular practice of consultation of certain parties before decisions are taken, those parties have a legitimate expectation that such consultation will continue on those matters: obiter in the GCHQ case (above); second, where the administration has announced a policy rule, or made some other kind of public statement or promise giving rise to the reasonable belief on the part of those affected that the rule or statement will not be changed unless those affected are first given a fair hearing (this is described as a procedural legitimate expectation): *Attorney-General of Hong Kong* v *Ng Yuen Shiu* [1983] 2 AC 629.

d) *'Substantive' legitimate expectation*

There are some authorities which suggest that legitimate expectation may be substantive as well as procedural, ie that the public statement has been relied on to such an extent that, as a matter of fairness, it cannot be revoked or modified unless an overriding matter of public interest requires it. This position applies only where the public statement committed the public body to an 'intra vires' course of action, since it is well established that a public body cannot extend its jurisdiction or otherwise act ultra vires through the operation of any kind of estoppel (see chapter 12). Authorities which suggest that a doctrine of substantive legitimate expectation could operate in respect of some kinds of intra vires promise are: dicta in *R* v *Secretary of State for the Home Department, ex parte Khan* [1984] 1 WLR 1337; *R* v *Secretary of State for the Home Department, ex parte Ruddock* [1987] 2 All ER 518; *R* v *Secretary of State for Health, ex parte US Tobacco Inc* [1991] 3 WLR 529; [1992] 1 All ER 212; and, more recently, in *R* v *Devon County Council, ex parte Baker* [1995] 1 All ER 73 at p88e–88g per Simon Brown LJ:

'Sometimes the phrase [legitimate expectation] is used to denote a substantive right: an entitlement that the claimant asserts cannot be denied him ... the claimant's right will only be found established when there is a clear and unambiguous representation upon which it was reasonable to rely. Then the administrator or other public body will be held bound in fairness by the representation made unless only its promise or undertaking as to how its power would be exercised is inconsistent with the statutory duties imposed upon it. The doctrine employed in this sense is akin to an estoppel.'

However, there are also many authorities which deny the concept of substantive legitimate expectation on the ground that to permit a form of promissory estoppel in public law would be inconsistent with the rule that public bodies have no power to fetter the exercise of their discretionary powers. These authorities therefore recognise only the concept of procedural legitimate expectation, ie that the public statement may be revoked or modified but only after those affected have been given an opportunity to make representations arguing against change. The relevant authorities are reviewed and interpreted in this way by Laws J in *R* v *Secretary of State for Transport, ex parte Richmond-upon-Thames London Borough Council (No 1)* [1994] 1 WLR 74.

The controversy over the character and effect of the doctrine of legitimate expectation has been given an added dimension by a recent judgment which tries to avoid the difficulties of estoppel in public law by formulating a substantive doctrine purely in the context of fairness: see per Sedley J in *R* v *Ministry of Agriculture, Fisheries and Food, ex parte Hamble* [1995] 2 All ER 714 especially at pp723c–724e, 725h–j and 730j–732e. In this case it was held not unfair for the government to change its announced policy on fishing licences even though the applicant had taken out a provisional licence and would be adversely affected by the change. Sedley J, then ventured to make the followings observations:

i) It is precisely because public authorities have public duties to perform that they can no more be estopped from performing them than they can contract out of them. This is why the decision-maker's knowledge or ignorance of the extent of reliance placed by the applicant upon the factors upon which the expectation is founded has no bearing upon the existence or legitimacy of the expectation. It is upon the practices or promises of the public authority that any such expectation will be built.

ii) It is difficult to see why it is any less unfair to frustrate a legitimate expectation that something will or will not be done by the decision-maker than it is to frustrate a legitimate expectation that the applicant will be listened to before the decision-maker decides whether to take a particular step. Such a doctrine (of substantive or reasonable legitimate expectation) does not risk fettering a public body in the discharge of public duties because no individual can legitimately expect the discharge of public duties to stand still or be distorted because of that individual's peculiar position.

iii) Legitimacy is itself a relative concept, to be gauged proportionately to the legal and policy implications of the expectation. This, no doubt, is why it has proved easier to establish a legitimate expectation that the applicant will be listened to than that a particular outcome will be arrived at by the decision-maker. But the same principles of fairness govern both situations.

iv) It is the court's task to recognise the constitutional importance of a public authority's freedom to formulate and to reformulate policy; but it is equally the court's duty to protect the interests of those individuals whose expectation of different treatment has a legitimacy which in fairness out-tops the policy choice which threatens to frustrate it. This may mean that the policy statement should not be changed so as to override the individual's prior expectation, unless there is an overriding public interest requiring such change. This is as near as public law is able to approach an estoppel.

v) The doctrine of legitimate expectation cannot be used to defeat a duty which public law imposes on a body, nor to extend the power of a public body beyond that which legislation has prescribed, but it can be used to ensure that an act which is intra vires is performed if the public body has given rise to a legitimate expectation that it will be.

However, these propositions proved to be short-lived and were overruled by the Court of Appeal in *R* v *Secretary of State for the Home Department, ex parte Hargreaves* [1997] 1 All ER 397; see section 10.3 below.

e) *Content of a fair hearing*

Assuming that natural justice or the duty to be fair applies to a particular decision-making process, the determination of the precise content of the fair hearing will depend on the context, but as a general principle it may be said that fairness will very often require that a person who may be adversely affected by the decision should have an opportunity to make representations, and for this purpose will need to know the factors which may weigh against his interests, so that he is informed of the gist of the case which he has to answer. This is the modern formulation of the ancient maxim 'audi alteram partem' (hear the other side): see per Lord Mustill in *R* v *Secretary of State for the Home Department, ex parte Doody* [1993] 3 All ER 92 at p106e–h (HL). Subject to context, a fair hearing may require a reasonable opportunity to correct or contradict opposing evidence, to make representations orally or in writing, to be represented by a lawyer or other person, and to receive reasons for a decision, though on reasons see (f) below.

f) *Is there a duty to give reasons?*

It had been thought that in the absence of a statutory duty to give reasons for a particular decision, common law would not impose such a requirement as part of the general rules on fairness of decision-making or as part of the rules on lawful and rational decision-making. The absence of a general duty to provide reasons for an administrative decision has for long been subject to criticism as a grave defect of English administrative law, but it may be that the expansion of the doctrine of legitimate expectation and the trend toward more openness of decision-making has resulted in a duty to give reasons being imposed in many more specific situations than previously: per Lord Mustill in *ex parte Doody* (above) at p111f. In *R* v *Higher Education Funding Council, ex parte Institute of Dental Surgery* [1994] 1 All ER 651 at p666b–c, Sedley J observed that each case will come to rest between two poles or possibly at one of them: the decision which cries out for reasons and the decision for which reasons are entirely inapposite. Only pragmatic case-by-case development will indicate where the dividing line comes between the two poles separating those cases where reasons should be given from those cases where they need not to be given. He then went on to sum up the present state of the law (at pp671j–672a):

'i) there is no general duty to give reasons for a decision, but there are classes of case where there is such a duty;

ii) one such class is where the subject-matter is an interest so highly regarded by the law, eg personal liberty, that fairness requires that reasons, at least for particular decisions, be given as of right; and

iii) another such class is where the decision appears aberrant. Here fairness may require reasons so that the recipient may know whether the aberration is in the legal sense real (and so challengeable) or apparent; and it follows that this class does not include decisions which are themselves challengeable by reference only to the reasons for them. A pure exercise of academic judgment is such a decision' (so that in the present case the Council was not obliged to supply the Institute with reasons for the grades it had awarded for the purpose of grant funding of clinical dental research).

See further *R* v *Secretary of State for the Home Department, ex parte Fayed*: section 10.3 below.

Where either statute or common law requires the provision of reasons those reasons must be adequate and intelligible so as to show the basis of the decision: see further *R* v *Criminal Injuries Compensation Board, ex parte Cook*: section 10.3 below.

On the duty to give reasons: see Allan [1994] CLJ 207, Barlow and Craig [1993] NLJ 1005, Campbell [1994] PL 184, Craig and Ashtiagbor [1994] NLJ 291, Craig [1994] CLJ 282 and (1994) 110 LQR 12 and Lindsay (1994) 57 MLR 954.

g) *The useless formality principle*

As a general principle the procedure by which a decision is taken is distinct from the merits of that decision, so that an unfair decision in the context of procedural impropriety should be set aside as an ultra vires decision even if the reviewing court is of opinion that to require a rehearing would be a 'useless formality' because the outcome would be the same on the merits. The weight of authority supports this proposition, though there are exceptions, eg *Cinnamond* v *British Airports Authority* [1980] 1 WLR 582. The relevant authorities are reviewed by Bingham [1991] PL 64 at pp72–73.

h) *Bias*

It is well established that a fair hearing requires an unbiased decision: 'nemo iudex in causa sua' (no man should be judge in his own cause). Actual bias is very rare, but where established invalidates the decision. The typical case involves apparent bias. In approaching allegations of apparent bias, common law has drawn a distinction between direct financial interest in the outcome of a case and non-financial interest. An apparent direct financial interest, no matter how small, will invalidate the decision, no matter how high the standing or reputation of the decision-maker: *Dimes* v *Grand Junction Canal Proprietors Ltd* (1852) 3 HL Cas 759. However, the principle is subject to the doctrine of necessity, which allows a financially interested adjudicator to hear and dispose of the case if no other financially unbiased adjudicator is available.

In regard to non-financial bias, the test is whether there is a real danger of bias in the sense that an impartial observer could reasonably suspect a real danger that the decision-maker might unfairly regard with favour or disfavour one party's case. This test for apparent non-financial bias applies to all types of adjudication: *R* v *Gough* [1993] 2 All ER

724 (HL). In *R* v *Inner West London Coroner, ex parte Dallaglio* [1994] 4 All ER 139 at pp151f–152d Simon Brown LJ observed that 'a real danger clearly involves more than a minimal risk, less than a probability. One could, I think, as well speak of a real risk or a real possibility'. He confirmed that proof of a real danger of bias is enough to vitiate the proceedings and that it is irrelevant whether a different decision on the merits would have been reached by an unbiased tribunal. In this case it was held that a coroner's descriptions of relatives of victims of a Thames boating disaster as 'unhinged' and 'mentally unwell' indicated a real danger that he had unfairly regarded their views at the inquest with disfavour.

The real danger of bias test replaces two tests previously established at common law: the 'reasonable suspicion of bias' test and the 'real likelihood of bias' test. The former set a low threshold of proof and was therefore favourable to the citizen making the challenge (a 'red light' test); the latter set a much higher threshold by appearing to require proof of a probability of bias and was therefore more favourable to the body being challenged (a 'green light' test). The real danger of bias test sets a standard of proof somewhere between these poles.

It had been thought that a different test for bias applied in the field of administrative decision-making, such as local authority planning decisions. Here it had been held that even a financial interest in land development might not disqualify the local planning authority from making a planning decision in regard to such land; the test was whether the particular financial (or other) interest unlawfully fettered the exercise of discretion on the matter: *Steeples* v *Derbyshire County Council* [1984] 3 All ER 468. But, after *R* v *Gough*, above, it seems that the 'real danger of bias' test is applicable even to this kind of administrative decision-making: see *R* v *Secretary of State for the Environment, ex parte Kirkstall Valley Campaign Ltd* [1996] 3 All ER 304, section 10.3 below.

i) *Effect of breach of natural justice: void or voidable?*

Where a decision has been taken in breach of the rules of natural justice or fairness it will usually be classified as an ultra vires and void decision, void in the sense of void ab initio, never having had legal effect. However, the granting of relief under O.53 is discretionary and may take into account the public interest, which may require the granting of prospective rather than retrospective relief in a particular context. This pragmatic approach to the granting of relief has led to a dilution of the concept of total invalidity so as to produce what Professor Wade has described as a concept of 'limited interim validity', ie a decision enjoys a presumption of validity until rebutted by a challenger with sufficient legal standing through the correct form of proceedings: Wade (1974) 90 LQR 436. It then follows from this modified concept that a breach of natural justice or fairness is capable of being 'cured' by a further full and fair hearing 'de novo' through the particular domestic procedures in question: *R* v *Governors of St Gregory's Roman Catholic Aided High School, ex parte Roberts* (1995) The Times 27 January (QBD) – an exclusion hearing before school governors had been flawed because of breaches of natural justice, but the procedure adopted at a subsequent hearing by an appeals committee was fair and was therefore sufficient to allow the court to hold that their decision was valid. See also *Calvin* v *Carr* [1979] 2 All ER 440, although Lord Wilberforce at pp447–449 warned that there may be cases where the breach is so flagrant and the consequences are so severe, that the most perfect of appeals and rehearings will not be sufficient to produce a just result. It is also possible that the right to object may be lost as a result of waiver. See further *Percy* v *Hall* (1996), section 10.3 below.

The gradual erosion of the concept of absolute nullity in this context is controversial because it leaves considerable uncertainty as to the legal nature of an act done without power or in excess or abuse of power: see especially the pungent criticism of Sedley in [1989] PL 32 at pp33 and 38 especially. The problem of the status of an ultra vires decision arises also in regard to the other categories of review considered in chapters 9, 11 and 12.

10.3 Recent cases and articles

Legitimate expectation

R v *Secretary of State for the Home Department, ex parte Fire Brigades Union* [1995] 2 All ER 244 (HL) – for facts and detailed analysis of this case, see chapter 3, section 3.3. On the issue of legitimate expectation Lord Keith observed, at p248:

'... the doctrine of legitimate expectation cannot reasonably be extended to the public at large, as opposed to particular individuals or bodies who are directly affected by certain executive action.'

'Substantive' legitimate expectation

R v *Secretary of State for the Home Department, ex parte Hargreaves* [1997] 1 All ER 397 (CA) – the applicants were prisoners who, upon commencing their sentences, were informed that it was Home Office policy for prisoners in their category to become eligible to apply for home leave after serving one-third of their sentences. Later the Home Office changed this policy, requiring half of the sentence to be served before such eligibility could arise. The applicants sought judicial review, contending that the change of policy was ultra vires in depriving them of their legitimate expectation that home leave might be available upon completion of one-third of their sentences. It was *held* that the change of policy was lawful and that the legitimate expectation of a prisoner related only to the proper consideration of an application for home leave under the terms of whatever regime existed at the time of the application, not at the time of commencement of sentence: *Findlay* v *Secretary of State for the Home Department* [1985] AC 318; [1984] 3 All ER 801 (HL) applied. The Court of Appeal made it clear that since the deferment of eligibility for home leave was a matter of substance and not of procedure, the court was not required to conduct a balancing exercise based on fairness and proportionality when deciding the legality of the change of policy; rather, the correct test was whether the change of policy was unreasonable in the *Wednesbury* sense. To the extent that Sedley J's judgement in *R* v *MAFF, ex parte Hamble*, above, had suggested that such a balancing exercise could be undertaken as a matter of 'substantive fairness', it should be regarded as overruled by this decision. Hirst LJ, observed (at p412j):

'Mr Beloff characterised Sedley J's approach as heresy, and in my judgment he was right to do so. On matters of substance (as contrasted with procedure) *Wednesbury* provides the correct test. It follows that while Sedley J's actual decision in the *Hamble* case stands, his ratio in so far as he propounds a balancing exercise to be undertaken by the court should in my judgement be overruled.'

Comment: The decision in *ex parte Hargreaves* is a set back for the 'red light' approach of Sedley J in *ex parte Hamble*, which some commentators had welcomed as embracing a doctrine of 'substantive' or 'reasonable' expectation. The Court of Appeal made it clear that the statutory discretion of the Home Secretary to change parole policy could not be restricted by the application of such a doctrine. To that extent the decision could be classified as a 'green light' one for the executive in a sensitive area of public policy.

Content of a fair hearing

R v *Parole Board, ex parte Mansell* (1996) The Times 21 March – the applicant had been sentenced to five years' imprisonment for indecent assault. The Parole Board Rules made provision for an oral hearing of a parole application only in the case of a discretionary life sentence and made no such provision in the case of an applicant serving a determinate sentence. Accordingly, the Parole Board decided the application for parole on the basis of papers only. The applicant then sought judicial review on the basis that natural justice required an oral hearing of his parole application. It was *held* that a fair hearing of the application could take place without an oral hearing being granted. Whilst the court could impose on the Parole Board greater procedural safeguards than those imposed by statute, it was not an appropriate case in which to do so, because the applicant's case could not be equated with that of a prisoner serving a discretionery life sentence.

R v *Legal Aid Board, ex parte Donn and Co (A Firm)* [1996] 3 All ER 1 – for facts see chapter 8, section 8.3. Having *held* that the franchising decisions of the Board were a matter of public law and subject to judicial review, the court turned to the issue of fairness and found that there had been a procedural impropriety because the adjudicating committee had not met as a whole when hearing the tender application. Ognall J, at p13h quoted the principle stated by Taylor LJ, in *R* v *Army Board of the Defence Council, ex parte Anderson* [1991] 3 All ER 375 at 387:

'There must be a proper hearing ... in the sense that the board must consider, as a single adjudicating body, All the relevant evidence and contentions before reaching its conclusion. This means, in my view, that the members of the board must meet. It is unsatisfactory that the members should consider the papers and reach their individual conclusions in isolation and, perhaps, as here, having received the concluded views of another member.'

R v *Secretary of State for the Home Department, ex parte Fayed* [1997] 1 All ER 228 (CA): for the facts see chapter 9, section 9.3. Having determined that the ouster clause did not preclude judicial review, the Court of Appeal turned to the issue of whether the Home Secretary had acted unfairly. It was *held* (Kennedy LJ dissenting) that, although the statute excused the Home Secretary from the duty to provide reasons for his decision, he was not relieved of the common law obligation to be fair in arriving at his decision. For this purpose, in the present context, the Home Secretary was required to give the applicants sufficient information as to the subject matter of his concern as to their suitability for naturalisation. Such information must be given in such a way as to enable the applicants to make adequate representations. If there was information which the Home Secretary felt he could not disclose in the public interest he was obliged to indicate this conclusion to the applicants so that they could challenge the justification for the refusal in the courts. Since the Home Secretary had failed to observe these aspects of his common law obligation to be fair it followed that his decisions regarding the applications must be quashed so that they could be retaken in a fair manner.

Comment: This is a remarkable decision, and can be classified as another example of judicial activism in trying to restrain the exercise of public power. The majority of the Court of Appeal (Lord Woolf MR, and Phillips LJ) were influenced by the substantial benefits at stake, and the imputations upon the reputations of the applicants (the Fayed brothers, owners of Harrods) if their applications were unsuccessful other than on technical grounds. The majority judgements are therefore 'red light' in character in ensuring that judicial review protects individual human rights from abuse of power. The majority judgements have been criticised for undermining Parliamentary sovereignty, because the statute, in very clear and unambiguous language, appeared to exempt the Home Secretary from the duty to justify his decision.

Further the majority judgements appear to create a new common law right (for an applicant to be informed *before any decision is taken*, why he might be turned down). It may be that the majority felt it was necessary to create such a right in the absence of a general common law duty to provide reasons for administration decisions, but such judicial activision provoked the following condemnation in a *Times* editorial (14 November 1996):

'With his judgement yesterday, Lord Woolf was not only creating a new right but one in defiance of Parliament's express intentions.'

It should be noted that Kennedy LJ, dissenting, did so because he was persuaded by the language of the statute that the Home Secretary was to be relieved not only of the obligation to give reasons for his decision but also of any duty to indicate at any earlier stage why he might refuse (at p246j).

The duty to give reasons

R v *Criminal Injuries Compensation Board, ex parte Cook* [1996] 2 All ER 144 (CA) – the applicant had applied to the Board for a payment following the death of her husband, who had been murdered after escaping from prison where he had been serving a sentence for armed robbery. The application was refused on the ground that, in view of the husband's bad character, it would be inappropriate to make an award to his widow. The decision made no reference to the good character of the applicant. The applicant sought judicial review, contending, inter alia, that inadequate reasons had been provided for the decision. It was *held* that the decision was lawful. The Board was only required to give sufficient detail to enable the applicant to know what conclusion it had reached on the main issues; it was not required to deal with every material consideration to which it had had regard: per Aldous LJ, at p150d. Hobhouse LJ, agreeing, added that although the reasons provided were brief they were adequate for the purpose of making clear the basis of the decision, but that he would prefer in future to see rather fuller reasons in cases such as the present one: 'it is usually a better practice to make explicit what is otherwise only implicit.' (at p160c).

Bias

R v *Secretary of State for the Environment, ex parte Kirkstall Valley Campaign Ltd* [1996] 3 All ER 304 – an urban development corporation had granted planning permission for a supermarket complex on a site belonging to a rugby club. The applicants challenged the decision on the ground of bias, contending that the chairman of the corporation owned land to which the rugby club was interested in moving if the development took place, and that other members of the corporation had personal associations with the rugby club. It was *held* the decision was lawful and not tainted with bias because the rugby club had abandoned its interest in the land owned by the chairman before the decision was taken and the links which other members had with the rugby club were too insignificant. In reaching this decision Sedley J, applied the 'real danger of bias' test laid down in *R* v *Gough*, above, which he said applied not only to judicial and quasi-judicial bodies but also to administrative bodies.

Comment: The application of the 'real danger of bias' test is a departure from those authorities, such as *Steeples* v *Derbyshire County Council*, above, which had applied the test of unlawful fettering of discretion rather than bias in the case of planning decisions. Sedley J, was persuaded of the need for the additional test of bias by the fact that, increasingly, administrative decisions could radically affect the interests of individual citizens just as much as those that might be classified as judicial or quasi-judicial:

'That is why modern public law, since the landmark decision in *Ridge* v *Baldwin* [1964] AC 40, has set its face against the partitioning of proceedings into judicial, administrative and something in between. The distinctions are not only increasingly hard to make in the variety of adjudicative processes in the modern state; they were historically mistaken.' (at p324e).

While the test for bias therefore becomes constant for All kinds of decision-making, the question of whether or not apparent bias has been established will depend on the significance of the interest and its degree of proximity to the issue being decided: per Sedley J, at p325h.

Effect of breach of natural justice: void or voidable?

Percy v *Hall* [1996] 4 All ER 523 (CA) – for facts and decision see chapter 2, section 2.3. In the context of invalidity of bye-laws Schiemann LJ, observed (at p545d–e):

'The policy questions which the law must address in this type of case are whether any and if so what remedy should be given to whom against whom in cases where persons have acted in reliance on what appears to be valid legislation. To approach these questions by rigidly applying to All circumstances a doctrine that the enactment which has been declared invalid was "incapable of ever having had any legal effect upon the rights and duties to the parties" seems to me, with All respect to the strong stream of authority in our law to that effect, needlessly to restrict the possible answers which policy might require. For instance, in the context of the present case had we held the byelaws to be invalid, as it seems to me a sensible answer might be that no remedy should be given against the policeman who acted in good faith but that a remedy should be given against a Secretary of State who put into circulation invalid byelaws with the perfectly foreseeable consequence that policemen would act on the assumption that they were valid. We are not required in the present case to decide whether that is the answer given by our law as it stands. I merely give it as a possibility.'

Brown, 'Trial, Bias and Whether a Defendant has Received a Fair Trial: *R* v *Gough*' (1995) 29 L Teach 237

Craig, 'Substantive and Legitimate Expectations in Domestic and Community Law' [1996] CLJ 289

Gordon and Ward, 'The Billowing Fog: Legitimate Expectations' [1996] PL 46

Himsworth, 'Legitimately Expecting Proportionality: *ex parte Hamble*' [1996] PL 46

10.4 Analysis of questions

First year constitutional law students should see chapter 15 for advice on this area. For the administrative law student procedural impropriety as a category of ultra vires throws up many interesting issues for analysis and is therefore regularly examined, either in problem-type questions or essay-type questions. Indeed, it is reasonable to anticipate more than one question being set on procedural impropriety in a typical examination paper. Some of the issues have distinct lines of authority and a detailed knowledge of the relevant case law will be required. There has been much recent interest in two specific issues: whether the doctrine of legitimate expectation has developed a substantive character and whether common law is in the process of developing a general duty on administrators to give reasons for decisions. These issues have been examined in several recent judgments and articles, which provide stimulating conceptual analysis. Solid research into these issues will pay dividends in terms of good grades for the ambitious student. The distinction between void and voidable has also been the subject of examination questions, though the effects of ultra vires are not confined to the category of procedural impropriety.

10.5 Questions

QUESTION ONE

Following a riot, a number of inmates at East Midland jail were subjected to a variety of sanctions as a punishment for their involvement.

Cecil P, Barry X, and Eamon Y appeared before the Board of Visitors accused of having assaulted a guard. Barry X was permitted to cross-examine prison guards concerning his role in the riot. However the Board did not allow him to call inmates to testify in his defence on the grounds that their testimony could not possibly be reliable. Eamon Y was not permitted to cross-examine the guards or call witnesses as the Board had seen TV film showing him punching a guard and felt there was nothing to be said in his defence. Neither prisoner was permitted legal representation during the hearing. Both prisoners suffered the loss of one year's remission.

Cecil P was a lawyer convicted of insider dealing. He was not permitted to speak in his own defence, on the grounds that his skills as an advocate would give him an unfair advantage over his peers. He was also punished with three months' loss of remission.

In respect of all three prisoners the Board gave as its reason for its decisions the fact that 'we have been presented with incontrovertible evidence that the men concerned have committed the offences of which they are accused'.

Two days after the hearing the Home Office published a circular recommending that all Board hearings allow prisoners to be legally represented if the Board intended to impose a punishment in excess of loss of six months' remission. The circular gave formal approval to a policy that had been running on an informal basis in many prisons, including East Midland, for some months.

The prison governor additionally determined to withdraw 30 days remission from John B and Sid A for failing to assist prison officers to restore order during the riot. Both prisoners were permitted to speak for one minute in mitigation of their punishment, but not to challenge the assumption that they were guilty.

Advise the prisoners if they might successfully challenge these various decisions through judicial review.

University of London LLB Examination
(for External Students) Administrative Law June 1994 Q8

General Comment

This problem requires consideration of the rules of natural justice as they apply to disciplinary hearings. The problem is directed principally at what constitutes a fair hearing, although the rule against bias does feature, as do legitimate expectations. Much of the discussion in this problem is common to each of the individual prisoners, so that it is possible to set out the law in a general discussion and then apply it to each of the individuals concerned, rather than dealing with each individual in turn.

Skeleton Solution

- Do the rules of natural justice apply?
- Requirements of natural justice – a fair hearing.

- Content of a fair hearing.
- Infringement of the right to a fair hearing.
- The rule against bias.
- Legal representation – legitimate expectation.

Suggested Solution

Judicial review will lie against boards of visitors and against prison governors if, in the exercise of their disciplinary powers, they fail to apply the rules of natural justice (*R* v *Hull Prison Board of Visitors, ex parte St Germain (No 2)* (1979); *R* v *Deputy Governor of Parkhurst Prison, ex parte Leech* (1988)). Thus a challenge is available to each prisoner provided he has suitable grounds for making it.

The fundamental principle of natural justice applicable to all of these decisions is the right to a fair hearing, which is a rule of 'universal application' in the case of decisions affecting rights (*Ridge* v *Baldwin* (1964)). This means that each prisoner should have been told of the case against him and should have been given a proper opportunity to rebut that case (*Chief Constable of the North Wales Police* v *Evans* (1982)). This requirement includes a duty to disclose the charge or case against each prisoner to him in reasonable time to allow him to prepare his defence (*R* v *Thames Magistrates' Court, ex parte Polemis* (1974)). It is not clear that this has been done in respect of any of these prisoners.

Each of these hearings appears to have been oral. In oral hearings, there are a number of procedural requirements which must be observed if the requirements of natural justice are to be complied with. The board of visitors and the prison governor should thus have considered all the relevant evidence any of these prisoners wished to submit; should have informed each prisoner of all the evidence to be taken into account; should have allowed each prisoner to question the witnesses; and should have allowed each prisoner to comment on the evidence and present argument on the whole case (*R* v *Deputy Industrial Injuries Commissioner, ex parte Moore* (1965)). In authorities involving prisoners it has been held that prisoners should be allowed to call witnesses and they should be allowed to question their own witnesses and comment on the evidence (*ex parte St Germain (No 2)*). It is likely that these procedural requirements also include a right to cross-examine unfavourable witnesses, given the fact that the prisoners' rights are at stake.

In each of these cases, one or more of these requirements has been infringed. Thus Cecil P has clearly been denied a fair hearing by not being permitted to speak in his defence, although we do not know whether he was permitted to call evidence or cross-examine the witnesses against him. The fact that his advocacy skills may have given him an advantage may strengthen the case for allowing the other prisoners legal representation, but it was a fundamental breach of natural justice to deny Cecil P the opportunity to present his case. Barry X may challenge the decision against him on the basis that he was not permitted to call witnesses in his favour. We do not know whether he was allowed to comment generally on the evidence or speak in his defence, but if he was not permitted to do so, he will have further grounds of challenge. Eamon Y was not permitted to defend himself at all, and we do not know whether the TV film was shown to him. John B and Sid A were denied any possibility of defending themselves from the charges against them. An opportunity to speak for one minute in mitigation of their punishment probably would not satisfy the requirements of a fair hearing, even assuming that their guilt had been properly established.

Further, there seems to have been an element of bias in the findings of the board and the approach of the governor. For instance the board held that the evidence of inmates 'could not possibly be reliable' and that the evidence of the prisoners' guilt was 'incontrovertible'. It appears that the board of visitors had made up its mind in advance of the hearing. The governor had clearly made up his mind in advance, and thus was not prepared to consider the possibility of Sid A's and John B's innocence. This apparent bias, by predetermination, provides a further ground of challenge to each prisoner (*R* v *Kent Police Authority, ex parte Godden* (1971)), provided the court is satisfied that this amounts to a 'real danger' of bias: *R* v *Gough* (1993).

Natural justice does not generally require that legal representation be permitted, but it has been held that if serious allegations are made and a prisoner is unlikely to be able to present his own case, then consideration should be given to whether the interests of fairness require such representation (*R* v *Secretary of State for the Home Department, ex parte Tarrant* (1985)). Such consideration may not have been necessary in the case of Cecil P, but the other prisoners may be able to argue that they were prejudiced by the lack of representation. Furthermore, a legitimate expectation may arise out of settled policy (*Attorney-General of Hong Kong* v *Ng Yuen Shiu* (1983)) so that where there is an established policy of permitting legal representation in certain cases, that policy may give rise to a legitimate expectation that such representation will continue to be permitted. Such a policy existed in East Midland jail in respect of the punishments imposed upon both Barry X and Eamon Y, so that they may be able to claim the benefit of such a legitimate expectation. The Home Office circular does not strengthen their claim per se, having been published after the event, but it does approve the policy and thus may be of evidential assistance to Barry X and Eamon Y.

On the basis of the above authorities it is clear, therefore, that each of these prisoners does have substantial grounds for seeking to challenge the decision against him on the basis of breach of natural justice.

QUESTION TWO

The (fictitious) Administrative Law (Fair Licensing) Act 1993 requires designated bodies to ensure that their decision-making processes 'accord with the requirements of natural justice'.

You are approached by several designated bodies to assist them in ensuring that their administrative behaviour meets legislative requirements.

The Gaming Board (GB) seeks advice concerning the licensing of casino operators. The (newly established) National Parole Board (NPB) requests assistance in respect of its power to release long-term prisoners on parole. The British Airports Authority (BAA) wishes to devise new procedures for licensing taxi-drivers to collect passengers from airports.

All three clients ask for general advice, but request you to pay particular attention to applicants' access to the information on which decisions are based, the necessity of an oral hearing, the availability of legal representation at such hearings, and the revocation or non-renewal of licences.

Advise GB, NPB and BAA.

University of London LLB Examination
(for External Students) Administrative Law June 1993 Q7

General Comment

This problem requires consideration of the content of natural justice. Many of the cases in this area deal with the question of *whether* the rules of natural justice apply. Avoid dealing with these, since the question states that they *do* apply. What are the requirements of natural justice? Do they differ from case to case? What are the minimum requirements that will exist in every case? Deal with each of the four specific points raised.

Skeleton Solution

- The requirements of natural justice.
- The right to a hearing.
- Disclosure of information.
- Does a hearing have to be oral:
  - GB and BAA;
  - NPB.
- Requirements where hearing is oral.
- Legal representation.
- Revocation of licences.
- Taxi-drivers' legitimate expectation.

Suggested Solution

It is assumed that the (hypothetical) Administrative Law (Fair Licensing) Act 1993 does not contain any definition of natural justice or any specific procedural requirements that the designated bodies must observe. If there are such statutory procedures then following them will usually suffice in meeting the criteria of natural justice. In the absence of such procedures, the common law rules must be applied.

GB, NPB and BAA should be aware that the common law requirements of natural justice at their simplest impose a duty to act with procedural fairness. The requirements of natural justice will vary from case to case, depending upon the subject-matter involved (see Lord Denning MR in *R* v *Gaming Board for Great Britain, ex parte Benaim and Khaida* (1970)). There are certain requirements that will exist in nearly every instance of decision-making, and will apply to all three of the bodies seeking advice, but these requirements will themselves be more or less stringent depending upon the case.

It has been held that the right to a hearing is 'of universal application' in cases involving the rights of individuals (*Ridge* v *Baldwin* (1964)). This has been extended to include licensing cases, so GB, NPB and BAA must each give a hearing to applicants. The necessity to give a fair hearing will also require that information on which the authorities' decisions are to be based should be disclosed to the applicant in question. This requirement will apply both when an application is made for the first time and when an application to renew a licence is made, and in particular objections to the grant of a licence must be disclosed to the applicant (*R* v *Secretary of State for the Home Department, ex parte Fayed* (1997)). There is no obligation to disclose confidential sources of objections, if there are good reasons in the public interest for not doing so, but the applicant must be told of the substance of objections raised against him (*R* v *Gaming Board for Great Britain, ex parte Benaim and Khaida*). Disclosure of information must occur in such a way as to give the applicant sufficient time to consider the objections and to prepare answers to them (*R* v *Thames Magistrates' Court, ex parte Polemis* (1974)).

Although there is a general obligation on GB, NPB and BAA to give a hearing when considering applications for licences, such a hearing does not necessarily have to be oral (*Lloyd* v *McMahon* (1987)). The requirement for a hearing means that each applicant must have a fair opportunity to present his application and to meet objections to it. This can quite properly be done in writing, even where the objections might involve allegations of a serious nature. If an oral hearing is given then it must be conducted with procedural fairness; the applicant must have an opportunity to consider all the evidence, to call relevant witnesses and to question witnesses called by his opponents, and to comment and present argument on the case (*R* v *Deputy Industrial Injuries Commissioner, ex parte Moore* (1965)). In view of these requirements, it will probably be more appropriate for GB and BAA to adopt a written procedure than an oral one; but NPB may consider that, in view of the fact that its decisions will have an effect on the liberty of subjects, it is appropriate to give an oral hearing, although it is not necessary to do so. It has been held that a potential parolee only has a legitimate expectation that his case will be considered individually in the light of prevailing policy (*Findlay* v *Secretary of State for the Home Department* (1984) and *R* v *Secretary of State for the Home Department, ex parte Hargreaves* (1977)), and this implies that the prisoner's rights are quite weak, so it is a matter of discretion whether NPB does grant oral hearings or not. If an oral procedure is adopted it is not a general requirement of natural justice that legal representation be permitted. However, if objections are serious, or serious allegations are made about a prisoner's character or conduct, and if that prisoner is unlikely to be able to present his own case, then the NPB should consider whether it is in the interests of fairness to permit legal representation (cf *R* v *Secretary of State for the Home Department, ex parte Tarrant* (1984) and *R* v *Secretary of State for the Home Department, ex parte Hargreaves* (1997)).

The above requirements of natural justice are of general application to each of GB, NPB and BAA, and apply where applications are made for the first time. The requirements will apply more stringently where it is sought to revoke or not to renew a licence, as an existing licence holder may have a legitimate expectation that his licence will not be revoked or that it will be renewed (*McInnes* v *Onslow-Fane* (1978)).

Finally, it is noted that BAA wishes to change its licensing procedures; before it does so, it should consult existing licence holders whose interests may be prejudiced by such a change, as they have a legitimate expectation that existing policy will continue (*R* v *Liverpool Corporation, ex parte Liverpool Taxi Fleet Operators' Association* (1972)). This legitimate expectation gives rise to the requirements of natural justice.

QUESTION THREE

'The rules of natural justice require only that a decision be fair in all the circumstances.' Discuss and illustrate.

University of London LLB Examination
(for External Students) Administrative Law June 1991 Q3

General Comment

A difficult question in that it gives the candidate very little to go on. The principal issue to highlight is that the rules of natural justice are strictly speaking concerned with procedure, whilst the fairness or otherwise of a decision is an aspect of its merits, and thus outside the scope of judicial control. The candidate must demonstrate the link between unfair procedures and unfair decisions.

Skeleton Solution

- Nature of the ultra vires doctrine.
- No review of merits.
- Extent to which circumstances alter requirements of fairness.
- *Ridge* v *Baldwin*, *McInnes* v *Onslow-Fane*.
- Link between fairness and reasonableness.

Suggested Solution

It is traditional to view the two 'rules' of natural justice as being the 'right to be heard' and 'the rule against bias'. This distinction is inevitably somewhat artificial in that the 'right to be heard' must encompass the right to be heard by an unbiased tribunal in any event.

The statement under discussion has to be questioned since it suggests that judicial review on the ground that there has been a breach of the rules of natural justice is in some way concerned with the merits of the decision in question. In theory, of course, the rules of natural justice are concerned with the procedure leading up to a decision, and provided that procedure is not defective, the decision itself should not be impugned. The traditional view of judicial review is that it is there to deal with illegality, not to provided a 'better' or 'fairer' decision than the original decision-maker.

An initial problem is that the statement assumes the existence of 'rules' of natural justice. This is suggestive of a rigidity in approach and application which one is unlikely to find mirrored in the decided cases. It is not a 'rule' that one always has the right to a hearing before a decision affecting one's interests is taken, in the same sense that it is a 'rule' that motorists stop at red traffic lights. Similarly there is no 'rule' that one has the right to have decisions taken by an unbiased tribunal.

If one attempts to identify what natural justice requires, perhaps three elements emerge as being of most significance: that one should be allowed a hearing; that a decision should be free from bias; and that decision makers should act fairly. It is the latter element that creates uncertainty. Is the 'duty to act fairly' a quick way of summarising the content of the first two elements, or is it actually something different? Is it a duty that has to be observed in those situations where the traditional 'rules' of natural justice are deemed not to apply? A tribunal can certainly provide a fair hearing without an individual being given the opportunity of putting his case orally. But can the duty to act fairly be satisfied where a tribunal is biased?

It is submitted that the key to the problem posed in the question is provided by linking the procedure leading up to a decision with the decision itself. If a decision is seen to be unfair, the person challenging it will do so by alleging that this has resulted from the decision maker making some error, such as failing to hear evidence, or not allowing cross-examination, or not allowing legal representation. The suggestion is that without these procedural problems, a 'better' decision would have been arrived at.

If one accepts this link between the fairness of a decision and the procedure adopted, it becomes important to consider what procedural safeguards the courts require administrators to observe.

In *Ridge* v *Baldwin* (1964), Lord Reid suggested that the application of natural justice should be determined not by the source of the power under examination, but by reference to what was at stake for the complainant. One had to look at the right or interest affected. This somewhat restricted approach was developed by Megarry VC in *McInnes* v *Onslow-Fane* (1978) wherein he suggested that three categories could be identified (in relation to decisions of a licensing body). Where the circumstances were that the decision maker was faced with a 'mere applicant', assuming that the refusal of an application did not amount to a slur on his character, he merely had the right to a decision taken without bias or caprice. Natural justice did not require a hearing in support of the application. Secondly, there were what his Lordship described as the 'expectation' cases, where an individual had some legitimate ground for believing, either that he would be allowed a hearing, or possibly an expectation that a decision might be taken in his favour. Thirdly, there were the 'forfeiture' cases, such as where a licence was revoked. Here it was felt that natural justice would normally require a hearing, especially if the decision affected an individual's opportunity to pursue his livelihood, and was taken by a body having monopoly control over a particular trade or profession.

It is submitted that this approach bears out the contention in the question that circumstance is important. Megarry VC recognises as much himself where he states:

'I do not think that much help is to be obtained from discussing whether "natural justice" or "fairness" is the more appropriate term. If one accepts that "natural justice" is a flexible term which imposes different requirements in different cases, it is capable of applying appropriately to the whole range of situations indicated by terms such as "judicial", "quasi-judicial" and "administrative".'

It is clear, therefore that a decision can be 'fair' without, for example, an oral hearing being granted: see *Central Council for Education and Training in Social Work* v *Edwards* (1978), where it was held that an individual applying for a place on a college course did not have a right to be heard. If, however, a hearing, in the form of an interview, is granted, then it must be conducted fairly. Hence as the circumstances change so do the requirements of a fair decision. It appears that even a bare applicant has the right to be told of information unfavourable to his case: *R* v *Gaming Board for Great Britain, ex parte Benaim and Khaida* (1970) and *R* v *Secretary of State for the Home Department, ex parte Fayed* (1997).

A denial of cross-examination may not be unfair where it would not have served any useful purpose: see *Bushell* v *Secretary of State for the Environment* (1981).

In conclusion it is submitted that the issue of fairness may not relate solely to issues of natural justice. A decision may be unfair because it is irrational or unreasonable. This relates to more general issues concerning the abuse of power. The denial of legal representation may lead to an unfair process and a flawed decision, but the actual decision to deny representation can be attacked on the ground that it was unreasonable given the gravity of the case: *R* v *Secretary of State for the Home Department, ex parte Tarrant* (1984).

QUESTION FOUR

Assess the arguments for and against judicial recognition of a common law requirement that government bodies offer reasons for their decisions.

University of London LLB Examination
(for External Students) Administrative Law June 1995 Q3

General Comment

There are many different arguments for and against a general common law duty to give reasons. Most of the arguments are in favour, but that does not mean the arguments against are without validity. Consider the practical effects of such a duty if it were applied to every kind of administrative action. Where is such a duty most needed?

Skeleton Solution

- Contrast between statutory duty for tribunals and absence of general common law duty.
- JUSTICE-All Souls' recommendations.
- Effect on administrators; increased bureaucracy.
- Cases where rights are involved and natural justice applies.
- Reasons given before the decision is made.
- Reasons given once the decision is made.
- Contrast between rights cases and routine administration.

Suggested Solution

Whilst most tribunals and inquiries are subject to statutory duties to give reasons for their decisions (see, for instance, the Tribunals and Inquiries Act 1992), it is clear that there is no common law requirement that government bodies in general should give reasons for their decisions: *R* v *Higher Education Funding Council, ex parte Institute of Dental Surgery* (1994). While few people could quarrel with the counsel of perfection that all decision-makers should be prepared to give reasons for their decisions, this counsel of perfection has to be tempered with the ideal that administrators should perform their tasks efficiently and expeditiously. At the heart of the debate on whether there should be a general duty to give reasons lies a tension between these two ideals. As with many things in administrative law, the answer ultimately has to be something of a compromise. There are cases in which the arguments for giving reasons are compelling, but others in which the benefit of giving reasons may be outweighed by the adverse effects upon the operation of administrative powers.

The JUSTICE-All Souls report (1988) argues strongly for the incorporation of a general duty to give reasons into English administrative law, and proposes that this be done by legislation. The main arguments relied upon by the report are that reasons would improve the quality of decision-making, would satisfy the citizen's desire for just and fair treatment, and would enable the citizen to decide whether the decision may be challenged in the courts. These themes have been picked up by the courts in various cases, but the report also argues that government should be open and that citizens should have a right to be kept fully informed about the actions of administrative bodies. As a matter of principle, this is a powerful argument. Much day-to-day administration is carried out by civil servants or local government employees. These administrators are not elected but yet they exercise sweeping powers. It is an important part of the democratic ideal that they should be accountable for their exercise of those powers. Civil servants' accountability to Parliament through the doctrine of ministerial responsibility, and the accountability of local government employees to the elected councillors, are not enough, in practical terms, to guarantee that administrative powers are exercised properly on a day-to-day level. If administrators were subject to a duty to give reasons, they would have to justify their decisions and this would undoubtedly increase their accountability to those affected.

Despite this ideal, however, it is equally true that if administrators were subject to a duty to justify every decision they made, then the administrative process would inevitably be slowed down and bureaucracy would increase. The danger is that, motivated by the possibility of legal challenge, administrators would spend more time justifying their decisions than actually making them. If this became widespread, then the day-to-day administration of government might ultimately grind to a halt. There is certainly something to be said for the need for administrators to be able to make their decisions quickly and efficiently: that is, after all, what they are employed and expected to do. Furthermore, countless administrative decisions are made every day, some of which have very little impact on individual citizens and their rights. It would be very inefficient to require reasons to be given for every one of these decisions. While the reason-giving exercise might improve the quality of each individual decision, it would damage the quality of the overall administration.

While this argument may be made with some force in the context of low-level purely administrative decision making, government bodies do also have powers that interfere with the rights and interests of individual citizens. In the context of these kinds of decisions, the giving of reasons will be much more important, and a number of arguments may be made in support of a common law duty to give reasons in such cases. It should be borne in mind that reasons may be necessary at two stages in the process. The first of these is before the decision is finalised. In this situation, the giving of reasons may be a vital function of natural justice. It is a principle of natural justice that a person whose rights are to be adversely affected by a decision should have a right to a hearing on the matter. Reasons will clearly be a necessary adjunct to this right. Unless reasons for the decision are given at this stage, the affected citizen will not know what case is being made against him and therefore what objections he has to meet. A duty to give reasons in such cases is plainly necessary if the right to a hearing is not to be pointless: *Malloch* v *Aberdeen Corporation* (1971).

The giving of reasons may also be desirable once the decision has been finalised. The courts have been less enthusiastic about imposing a general common law duty to give reasons at this stage of the process, but strong arguments may be made for doing so. Some of these relate to the ability to subject decisions to the scrutiny of the court. A duty to give reasons may be justified on the basis that the giving of reasons enables those affected by a decision to ascertain whether there are any grounds for challenge. For this reason, in *Save Britain's Heritage* v *Number 1 Poultry Ltd* (1991) it was stated that the duty to give reasons is the counterpart in natural justice of the common law rule that justice must not only be done, it must be seen to be done. Similarly, decision-makers have a duty to act reasonably, and the court may not be able to tell whether they have done so or not in the absence of any reasons for a decision. To give reasons in these circumstances is to recognise that judicial review is a legitimate means for the individual citizen to challenge governmental decisions. On the other hand, if government bodies are unwilling to give reasons, that may suggest that they are being evasive and are unwilling to allow their actions to be scrutinised by the courts. Reasons are an effective way of bringing government actions and decisions out into the light of day. It should also be remembered that an applicant for judicial review bears the burden of proof: he has to prove that the decision is unlawful. This may be impossible to do if reasons are not provided for decisions.

In cases where individual rights and interests are affected to a great extent, it is submitted that the above arguments for a duty to give reasons are compelling. It may be inconvenient to administrators to give reasons, but that cannot outweigh the requirements of natural justice. The courts are willing to impose such a duty in cases where rights are affected, particularly where the decision under attack affects 'strong' rights (such as the right to liberty), or is in the nature of a judicial decision (eg *R* v *Civil Service Appeal Board, ex parte Cunningham* (1991); *R* v *Secretary of State for the Home Department, ex parte Doody* (1993)). In purely administrative cases, there is less demand for a general duty to give reasons, although this may be desirable in the interests of fair and open government.

Ultimately it must be recognised that government bodies exercise decision-making powers on a scale that ranges from strong interference with individual rights at one end of the scale to purely routine administrative tasks at the other. A general duty to give reasons will not necessarily be desirable at both ends of the scale. Had Parliament wanted there to be such a general duty in relation to purely administrative duties, it could have enacted such a duty. On the other hand, it is clear that such a duty will be highly desirable where individual rights are being interfered with. Rather than creating a general common law duty, the courts have done well to recognise the compromises inherent in administrative law and to concentrate their powers of intervention, through natural justice, in the areas where they are most needed.

QUESTION FIVE

In what ways, and for what reasons, does administrative law ensure that government decision-makers are not motivated by 'bias'?

University of London LLB Examination
(for External Students) Administrative Law June 1995 Q1

General Comment

Before answering this question, it is necessary to define 'bias'. If this word is given its ordinary meaning, it is clear that some forms of bias will inevitably exist in administrative decision-making. Administrative law gives 'bias' a narrower meaning, that nobody should be a judge in his own cause. When will that form of bias lead to the quashing of a decision? Why do the courts allow some forms of bias to escape their intervention, and yet intervene in other cases? What test have the courts adopted to determine 'how much' bias must exist before they will intervene?

Skeleton Solution

- Bias inevitable.
- Bias by formation of policy.
- Bias by pre-determination.
- Nobody a judge in own cause.
- Administrative cases involving judicial considerations.
- Reasonable suspicion of bias, administrative cases.

Suggested Solution

The judicial regulation of bias in the context of administrative law is a function of natural justice. When judges apply the rules of natural justice they are concerned to avoid unfairness in the decision-making process. In its ordinary sense, the term 'bias' means a predisposition towards a particular point of view. This may describe a variety of different situations and some bias, in the broadest sense, will inevitably feature in modern governmental decision-making. Not all forms of bias will be objectionable, and the courts do not regulate all forms of bias with the same vigour; their principal concern is with those forms of bias which do unfairly affect the outcome of the decision-making process.

An example of bias inevitable in modern government is the formation of policy. Administrative bodies will often formulate policies which to a large extent predetermine the outcome of applications made to them. Thus, a government body with the power to make grants may set criteria for the allocation of those grants. The criteria adopted will exclude certain applicants, and in the broadest sense will bias the decision-maker against those applicants. When faced with situations like these the courts have to weigh up the apparent injustice to the individual applicant against the efficient administration of the grants that such policies allow. The courts recognise that such policies are a necessary and indeed an inevitable feature of the complex bureaucratic state. They also recognise that such forms of bias are hardly objectionable, and subject them to the relatively weak requirement that the decision-maker should give the applicant an opportunity to show any special features in his application that might justify a departure from the policy: see for instance *British Oxygen Co Ltd* v *Minister of Technology* (1971). The benefits to be gained from the formation of such policies greatly outweigh the disadvantage to any applicant who may not fulfil the criteria. Indeed, far from producing widespread unfairness, adoption of such policies will usually produce fairness of a different kind, since it may give applicants advance knowledge of the criteria to be satisfied and lead to greater consistency of approach between different applicants.

While the reference to a predetermined policy by a decision-maker exercising discretionary powers is a relatively innocuous form of bias, other forms of preconception may be more objectionable. This will be most clearly so where judicial power is being exercised. If a decision-maker acting in such a capacity has predetermined a case without reference to its merits, then the decision will be set aside for bias. Thus, where a magistrate refused to grant a licence, because he belonged to a strict temperance sect and felt that to grant the licence would be treachery to his strict views, the refusal was set aside because he had clearly been biased from the outset: *R* v *Halifax Justices, ex parte Robinson* (1912). Not all preconceptions will invalidate a decision, however. They will only do so where they lead to a predetermined result that disregards the evidence. The expression of preconceived opinions by the judge or decision-maker does not by itself constitute bias, for it does not follow from such opinions that the evidence will be disregarded. To some extent, all judges and decision-makers are bound to have some preconceived opinions from time to time. The real question is whether they lead to an unfair result, which disregards the evidence.

It is clear, then, that bias may be more or less objectionable depending upon the circumstances of the case. At this point it becomes necessary to distinguish between the broad meaning of bias, and a narrower meaning used in administrative law. The narrower sense of bias states that no person may be a judge in his own cause, and administrative law tends to include all objectionable forms of bias within this narrow definition. This limb of natural justice has a long history and originates in appeals from judicial decisions. It is clearly objectionable that any judge should literally have a personal interest in the outcome of the case, and where this is so his judgment will be invalid whether or not he has actually allowed that interest to affect his decision. The appearance of bias will be enough to invalidate the judicial process. This will be so whether the interest is pecuniary, as in *Dimes* v *Grand Junction Canal Proprietors Ltd* (1852), or whether the interest is non-pecuniary as in *R* v *Sussex Justices, ex parte McCarthy* (1924). In such judicial cases it is important that justice is not only done, but is seen to be done. In such circumstances it is clearly improper that the judge's decision should be, or appear to be, influenced by any personal interest in the matter. This principle will clearly extend beyond the courtroom to administrative decisions of a judicial nature, and will apply not only where the judge has a personal interest in the matter, but where the judge is advised or influenced by some person with an interest in the matter. Thus in *R* v *Barnsley Metropolitan Borough Council, ex parte Hook* (1976), where a market trader's licence was revoked for misconduct, the decision of the appeal committee which heard his appeal was quashed because the prosecuting officer sat with the appeal committee while they made their decision.

While this narrow interpretation of bias is revealed most clearly in cases of a judicial nature, it also applies to administrative decisions that have a judicial character. Thus a fair rent set by a rent assessment committee in respect of one tenant's flat was quashed because the chairman's father was also a tenant of an associated landlord, albeit in a different block of flats, and the chairman had previously advised his father and other tenants in fair rent proceedings issued by the landlord. It was thought that the chairman's involvement in proceedings involving the associated landlord might have prejudiced the determination of the fair rent: *Metropolitan Properties Co (FGC)* v *Lannon* (1968). Even though it was not alleged that there was any actual bias, the question was whether bias might reasonably have been suspected.

Metropolitan Properties is an important case, not only in illustrating the application of the rule against bias in the administrative, as opposed to judicial, context but also in clarifying the extent to which appearances are important. Although justice must be seen to be done, it is important to define the point at which the appearance of bias will nullify a decision. A balance must be found whereby justice will be seen to be done, on one hand, but decisions are not attacked merely because of a far-fetched suspicion of bias on the other. The courts have wavered between two tests, 'real likelihood' of bias, and 'reasonable suspicion' of bias. Recently the House of Lords came down in favour of a 'real likelihood' of bias test, although the Law Lords preferred to re-label it as the 'real danger of bias' test to emphasise the need to show a real possibility, rather than a probability of bias. The test was held to apply to all judicial and quasi-judicial decision-making: *R* v *Gough* (1993). In administrative decision-making a different approach may be necessary. In *R* v *Amber Valley District Council, ex parte Jackson* (1984) suggests that the two possible tests are the same, but distinguishes between policy-based decisions, such as those made by planning authorities, and decisions of a more judicial character such as those made by rent tribunals. In that case, an authority had made contracts with developers for the exploitation of land which the authority owned. Part of the bargain was that the authority would do its best to procure planning permission, to be granted by itself. Although there was no suggestion of actual bias in the grant of planning permission, there was clearly a reasonable likelihood or suspicion of bias. The court held that to be irrelevant in this 'administrative' case: the justification for this approach is that to subject such policy-driven aspects of administration to the stringent test for bias would effectively shackle the exercise of administrative power and prevent decisions from being made in such cases.

However, this authority was not followed by Sedley J, in the recent case of *R* v *Secretary of State for the Environment, ex parte Kirkstall Valley Campaign Ltd* (1996), involving a planning decision. Sedley J, applied the 'real danger of bias' test of *R* v *Gough*, above, which he said applied to administrative decision-making as well as to judicial decisions. In Sedley J's view administration ought to be subject not only to the principle that their discretion must not be fettered (an aspect of illegality or *Wednesbury* unreasonableness) but also to the test for bias because administrative decisions could radically affect the interests of individual citizens just as much as those that might be classified as judicial or quasi-judicial. There is thus a conflict of authority as to whether administrative authorities are subject to a bias test, and it will require the decision of a higher court to resolve it.

QUESTION SIX

On what basis does administrative law distinguish between 'void' and 'voidable' decisions? What purposes does this distinction serve, and is the law on this question in need of reform?

University of London LLB Examination
(for External Students) Administrative Law June 1994 Q6

General Comment

This is quite a difficult question in conceptual terms. It highlights the underlying paradox of administrative law, that certain decisions may be ultra vires, and thus without legal validity but they will remain effective unless and until set aside by the court. The terms 'void' and 'voidable' appear in the law of contract, so use your knowledge of them in that context to supply a legal definition which can be used to test their application in administrative law. Distinguish between the legal and the practical effects of the ultra vires doctrine, and examine the discretionary element of judicial review.

Skeleton Solution

- 'Void' and 'voidable' defined.
- Ultra vires means 'void'.
- Error on the face of the record – does it still exist?
- The practical aspect of judicial review:
  – time limits;
  – discretionary relief.
- Resolving the paradox – legal and practical effects distinguished.

Suggested Solution

The terms 'void' and 'voidable' have been imported into administrative law from the law of contract. They distinguish between those acts which have no legal validity or effect ab initio, and those which have legal validity or effect ab initio but which are liable to be set aside by a court of competent jurisdiction at the instance of a party to an action. Because of the peculiarities of administrative law, these concepts do not translate well into the administrative law context. While at one time the distinction between void and voidable may have had some value, it will be argued that it is of little relevance to the modern framework of administrative law.

Judicial intervention in administrative decisions or actions is based upon ultra vires. If an authority has made a decision outside of its jurisdiction or powers, then that decision will be quashed as being ultra vires. Logically, that decision can only be considered to be 'void'. Once it is quashed, it is shown to have had no legal validity or effect ab initio. For this reason it has been held by the House of Lords that where administrative action is ultra vires 'there are no degrees of nullity'. If the decision is ultra vires, then it is void; it cannot be anything else (*Anisminic Ltd* v *Foreign Compensation Commission* (1969)).

Historically it was possible to distinguish between decisions which were quashed as ultra vires, and decisions which were intra vires but nonetheless liable to be quashed. This latter category of decisions only arose in the context of error on the face of the record. Where a public body or, particularly, a tribunal made an error of law which was within its jurisdiction, the court would quash its decision if that error appeared on the face of the record. Technically, such decisions were intra vires and therefore could properly be described as 'voidable'; the decision had legal validity ab initio but was liable to be quashed when the record was produced to the court. Since all errors of law have been held to be jurisdictional as a result of *Anisminic* and the subsequent reasoning of the House of Lords, culminating in *O'Reilly* v *Mackman* (1983), it follows that there is no longer any need for a distinct jurisdiction to quash for error on the face of the record. This has been confirmed in the case *R* v *Greater Manchester Coroner, ex parte Tal* (1984). For this reason there is equally no reason to distinguish between the 'void' and 'voidable' decisions of a public body; there is no longer any such thing as a voidable decision.

There are two sources of confusion which have disturbed the logic of this conclusion. The first, and now less serious, was a current of judicial support for the notion that even ultra vires decisions might be 'voidable' rather than 'void'. This approach was favoured by Lord Denning MR in particular. Thus in *R* v *Secretary of State for the Environment, ex parte Ostler* (1977) he stated that bad faith or a breach of natural justice would only make an order voidable, and not void. Yet the court could only quash the order on the grounds of ultra vires, so this reasoning is not coherent.

The second, more serious source of confusion in using the terms 'void' and 'voidable', is the constitutional nature of judicial review. Although a decision may be ultra vires, it will only be quashed at the direction of the court. Before it is quashed, it must be presumed to be valid and therefore must be acted upon. Whether a particular decision is ever quashed may depend upon a number of purely practical factors. An example of this is a case where there is a statutory time limit after which a decision may not be challenged (as in *ex parte Ostler*); if the decision is not challenged within that time limit then the court will not be able to set it aside later, even if it is ultra vires. In the meantime, the decision enjoys a presumption of validity, but is liable to be set aside if a challenge is brought within the statutory time limit. It may be thought then that such decisions are merely 'voidable' and not 'void'.

Similar considerations arise because of the discretionary nature of judicial review remedies. Thus even where a decision is brought before the court and the court decides that it is ultra vires, it may nonetheless decline to quash the decision. In *Percy* v *Hall* (1996) Schiemann J, commenting on the invalidity of bye-laws, said that the effects of invalidity raised policy questions as to 'whether any and if so what remedy should be given to whom against whom in cases where persons have acted in reliance on what appears to be valid legislation'. He deprecated a rigid doctrine of absolute nullity, despite the strong stream of authority to that effect.

This apparent paradox is more illusory than real. To describe ultra vires decisions as 'voidable' is a misuse of legal jargon. It is true that all decisions appear to be only liable to be set aside but, as a matter of law, such decisions are not valid ab initio, they are merely presumed to be valid. They do not acquire validity in law by the operation of time limits or the discretion of the court. Time limits and the court's discretion merely remove such invalid decisions from the bounds of challenge. In effect, they set practical considerations above the purely legal effects of ultra vires decision-making. The paradox of 'void' decisions being in fact 'voidable' can thus be resolved if the legal effects of the ultra vires doctrine are separated from the practical reality of the administrative state, which requires that there be a degree of certainty in the decision-making process. Administrative decision-making would become wholly unworkable if public bodies had to await the possibility of a successful challenge each time they made a decision. Thus there is a need for a presumption of validity; there is a need for statutory time limits in certain important areas, such as where large and expensive public projects are undertaken; and there is a need for judicial review to be exercised in a discrete manner.

It is clear from the above discussion, however, that the terms 'void' and 'voidable' do not fit happily into the context of administrative law. Indeed, any distinction between the two appears to be redundant, and to serve no practical purpose. In view of this, the only reform that may be necessary is to abandon the use of these terms, and to refer only to ultra vires decisions which are presumed to be valid unless and until they are set aside by the court in the exercise of its discretion, a statement which appears to reflect accurately the realities of administrative law.

11 Irrationality (Total Unreasonableness) and Proportionality

11.1 Introduction

a) *Total unreasonableness or irrationality*

In *Associated Provincial Picture Houses Ltd* v *Wednesbury Corporation* [1948] 1 KB 223 Lord Greene MR, said at p228: 'if a decision on a competent matter is so unreasonable that no reasonable authority could ever come to it, then the courts can interfere'. He went on to say, at p229, that an unreasonable decision is one which is 'so absurd that no sensible person could ever dream that it lay within the powers of the authority'. It is not for the judge to set aside a decision merely because he believes that it goes further than is prudent or necessary or convenient because it is not accompanied by some qualification or exception which he thinks ought to be there; the supervisory jurisdiction of the High Court is one of review, not appeal. This approach had been established in regard to the review of bye-laws: see *Kruse* v *Johnson* [1898] 2 QB 91 per Lord Russell. The approach sets the applicant for review a very high threshold and provides the judge with a low intensity of review in order to preserve the constitutional separation of law from politics: see per Lord Lowry in *R* v *Secretary of State for the Home Department, ex parte Brind* [1991] 1 All ER 720 (HL) at pp737–738 especially.

In *Council of Civil Service Unions* v *Minister for the Civil Service* [1985] AC 374 at p410 Lord Diplock agreed with the *Wednesbury* test of total unreasonableness but preferred to use the word 'irrationality' instead of 'unreasonableness' to describe this category of review. He thought it better conveyed the sense of absurdity that needs to exist about the decision in order for the reviewing court to set it aside. Lord Diplock described as irrational 'a decision so outrageous in its defiance of logic or of accepted moral standards that no sensible person who had applied his mind to the question to be decided could have arrived at it'. However, this makes it very difficult for the applicant to prove an abuse of power under this category of review, and some judges have expressed concern that setting such a high threshold may inhibit the ability of the courts to protect fundamental rights from misuse of executive power. Hence, some judges have suggested a lowering of the threshold and a higher intensity of review (a 'hard look' approach) where fundamental rights, such as the right to life, are at stake. For example, Lord Bridge has spoken of the need to give decisions affecting the right to life 'the most anxious scrutiny': *Bugdaycay* v *Secretary of State for the Home Department* [1987] 1 All ER 940 at 952. Laws J, adapted this approach to the issue of medical treatment for terminally ill patients, though he was reversed on appeal: *R* v *Cambridge DHA, ex parte B* [1995] 2 All ER 129: see chapter 1, section 1.3.

At the other extreme, some judges have suggested a raising of the threshold and an even lower intensity of review where high-level government policy decisions of a sensitive nature are being challenged. This approach has been described as the 'super-*Wednesbury*' test. For example, Lord Scarman in *Nottinghamshire County Council* v *Secretary of State for the Environment* [1986] AC 240 at p247 suggested that an examination by the court of ministerial regulations laid before Parliament and affirmatively approved 'would be justified only if a prima facie case were to be shown for holding that the Secretary of State had acted in bad faith, or for an improper motive, or that the consequences of his guidance were so absurd that he must have taken leave of his senses'.

However, these views as to the variable character of the test of unreasonableness or irrationality have not always been followed and, indeed, doubt has been cast on them in some of the cases that are examined later in this chapter: see 11.3 below.

b) *Proportionality*

In *Council of Civil Service Unions* v *Minister for the Civil Service*, above (the GCHQ case), Lord Diplock suggested that proportionality might one day become a ground for review. To some extent the concept is already part of the *Wednesbury* test because a disproportionate penalty may be set aside as being *Wednesbury* unreasonable: *R* v *Barnsley Metropolitan Borough Council, ex parte Hook* [1976] 3 All ER 452 (CA). However, Lord Diplock probably had in mind the European concept of proportionality, which has been part of public law on the continent for many years. Under it, a judge is able to set standards against which to measure administrative action in order to decide whether a decision is manifestly wrong or out of proportion to that required. The test requires a reasonable proportion between the administrative objective and the means used to achieve it, with a requirement that the measures taken by the administration should be the least restrictive of individual human rights compatible with the objective being pursued. Under this approach the primary judgment, subject only to a limited 'margin of appreciation' for the decision-maker, is for the court rather than the executive, ie the constitutional balance shifts by allowing the judges to evaluate the merits. Traditionally in English law judges exercise only a secondary judgment to review the legality of administrative action. For this reason Lord Diplock's suggestion has been received with great caution and some hostility, with some judges suggesting that proportionality cannot become a separate ground for review unless Parliament gives the judges clear authority for using it, eg by incorporating the European Convention on Human Rights into English law: see per Lords Ackner and Lowry in *R* v *Secretary of State for the Home Department, ex parte Brind* [1991] 1 All ER 720, at pp735 and 737–739 respectively. However, in the same case the other Law Lords (Lords Bridge, Roskill and Templeman) gave the concept of proportionality a more sympathetic treatment, leaving open the possibility that common law might develop it as a separate ground for review, particularly as the influence of membership of the European Union continues to affect aspects of English law; the principle is part of the jurisprudence of the European Court of Justice and has already infiltrated English law in cases involving direct application of European laws. Even where no direct application of European law is involved it can be argued that, as part of the process of harmonisation, all Member States of the European Union should apply common judicial standards in the area of public law.

11.2 Key points

a) The concept of *Wednesbury* total unreasonableness or irrationality sets a high threshold of review, with the result that cases which have successfully established this ground are rare.

However, the concept is sufficiently flexible to take account of changes in attitude and moral standards. In the *Wednesbury* case itself, the decision of a local authority to impose a licensing condition which required local cinemas to exclude children under 15 on Sundays was held lawful in the prevailing moral climate of 1948, but it is likely that changes in attitudes since 1948 could lead to a different result on the same facts if repeated in the 1990s.

b) It is arguable that the test of *Wednesbury* unreasonableness or irrationality changes character at two extremes: where fundamental human rights are at stake the judges might be prepared to adopt a higher intensity of review, but where high-level government policy of a politically sensitive nature is being challenged the judicial capacity for review becomes extremely limited and almost impossible to establish without proof of bad faith or insanity on the part of the relevant government minister!

c) The *Wednesbury* principles (which are considered further in chapter 12) apply to most forms of delegated discretionary power, even those conferred in wide subjectively-phrased language such as 'if the minister is satisfied that ...'. Such a phrase is interpreted to mean 'if the minister is [reasonably] satisfied that ...': *Secretary of State for Education and Science* v *Tameside Metropolitan Borough Council* [1977] AC 1014.

d) The concept of proportionality is not yet a separate ground of review, although disproportionate penalties may be set aside as *Wednesbury* unreasonable or irrational. Constitutional objections based on the distinctions between review and appeal, legality and merits, and law and politics stand in the way of common law development of such a concept. The Law Lords in *R* v *Secretary of State for the Home Department, ex parte Brind* [1991] 1 All ER 720 were divided on the weight of such objections.

In *NALGO* v *Secretary of State for the Environment* (1992) The Times 2 December Neill LJ extracted the following principles from the *Brind* judgments:

i) the European Convention on Human Rights is not part of English law and a court when reviewing the exercise of executive discretion could not interfere with such exercise on the ground that it had not been exercised consistently with the Convention;

ii) nevertheless, where fundamental human rights, such as freedom of expression, were being restricted by the exercise of executive discretion, the executive would need to show an important competing public interest which was sufficient to justify the restriction;

iii) the primary judgment on that question was for the executive, and the court was only entitled to exercise a secondary judgment by asking whether a reasonable authority, on the material before it, could reasonably make that primary judgment; and

iv) the court was not entitled to lower the threshold of unreasonableness merely on the ground that the particular case concerned an important human rights' dimension. (This is difficult to reconcile with Lord Bridge's dictum in *Bugdaycay* v *Secretary of State for the Home Department* [1987] AC 514.)

Neill LJ went on to observe that he saw great difficulty in applying the principle of proportionality to the decisions of government ministers because of the delicate constitutional balance between the courts and the central executive. Further, he said, apart from cases involving disproportionate penalties, it was unclear how far a court would be able to apply the principle of proportionality to the exercise of administrative judgment because, whilst the principle allowed the decision-maker a margin of appreciation, it did not cover so many degrees of latitude as that afforded by the traditional *Wednesbury* doctrine.

However, other judges have been less hostile to the importation of proportionality from European public law systems: see per Sedley J in *R* v *Secretary of State for the Home Department, ex parte McQuillan* [1995] 4 All ER 400 at pp422e–423a (below).

11.3 Recent cases and articles

R v *Ministry of Defence, ex parte Smith and Others* [1996] 1 All ER 257 (CA); [1995] 4 All ER 427 (QBD) – held (CA upholding QBD) that the prerogative policy of dismissing persons of homosexual orientation from the armed forces was justiciable but not reviewable on ground of *Wednesbury* unreasonableness or irrationality. In the Court of Appeal Sir Thomas Bingham MR (as he then was) said that the policy had been supported by both Houses of Parliament and by professional advisers in the military and that, at the time when the particular dismissals occurred (1994), the policy was not incompatible with prevailing moral standards. Major policy changes should be the product of mature reflection not instant reaction. In the Queen's Bench Division Simon Brown LJ, having held that the dismissals were not irrational because there was still room for two views on the issue, went on to observe that in view of changing attitudes towards homosexuality the tide of history was against the Ministry and that it was probable that the policy would die an early death. In both the Queen's Bench Division and the Court of Appeal, the ordinary test of *Wednesbury* unreasonableness or irrationality was applied: the threshold was not lowered because of the human rights' dimension, but it was also not raised to the 'super-*Wednesbury*' level because of the sensitivity of the prerogative policy. In the Court of Appeal Sir Thomas Bingham MR opined (at All ER pp263–264) that the *Wednesbury* test is sufficiently flexible to cover all situations: in judging whether a decision-maker has acted unreasonably in the *Wednesbury* sense the human rights context is important: the more substantial the interference with human rights, the more the court will require by way of justification before it is satisfied that the decision is reasonable in the *Wednesbury* sense. At the other extreme, the greater the policy content of a decision, and the more remote the subject-matter of a decision from ordinary judicial experience, the more hesitant the court must necessarily be in holding a decision to be irrational; further, where decisions of a policy-laden, esoteric or security-based nature are in issue, even greater caution than normal must be shown in applying the test.

R v *Secretary of State for the Home Department, ex parte McQuillan* [1995] 4 All ER 400 (QBD) – held statutory exclusion orders made against the applicant on grounds of national security were not ultra vires on the ground of *Wednesbury* unreasonableness or irrationality. However, the proceedings would be stayed to await the outcome of references to the Court of Justice of the European Union to decide whether such exclusion orders were compatible with EU Directives on freedom of movement. In the course of his judgment Sedley J observed that, if it had not been for the issue of national security (which prevented the court from knowing the Minister's reasons for making the orders), he would have been prepared to follow the dictum of Lord Bridge in *Bugdaycay* v *Secretary of State for the Home Department* [1987] AC 514, and give the most anxious scrutiny to the evidence to decide whether the orders lay within the band of rational decisions. The right to life, to freedom of movement and the right not to be subjected to inhuman treatment by executive action were fundamental values of the common law, and it was the duty of the court to scrutinise administrative decision-making which infringed such rights to ensure that all relevant considerations had been taken into account. Sedley J also commented on the growing influence of the European Convention on

Human Rights, the principles of which now inform the law of the European Union. Accordingly, where it falls to a United Kingdom court to apply principles of European law, the principles and standards set out in the European Convention can be said to be a matter of which English law now takes notice in setting its own standards. Whilst this approach falls well short of incorporation of the Convention (and thus does not undermine the ratio of *Brind*) it does enable the text of the Convention to be used as a reference point in the practical development of public law. Accordingly, the legal standards by which the decisions of public bodies are supervised can and should differentiate between those rights which are recognised as fundamental and those which, though known to the law, do not enjoy such a pre-eminent status ... the standard of justification of infringement of rights and freedoms by executive decision must vary in proportion to the significance of the right which is at issue. Such an approach is indeed already enjoined by *Bugdaycay* in relation to a predominant value of the common law – the right to life – which, as it happens, the Convention reflects. Whether this in itself is a doctrine of proportionality I do not now pause to ask; if it is, the House of Lords has long since contemplated its arrival with equanimity' (at pp422j–423a).

R v *Secretary of State for the Home Department, ex parte Pierson* [1996] 1 All ER 837 (CA) – the applicant was a convicted murderer. The trial judge and Lord Chief Justice had recommended that he should serve a minimum of 15 years before he could be considered for release on licence from his mandatory life sentence. This recommendation was not accepted by the Home Secretary in 1988 who fixed the penal term at 20 years because of 'aggravating features' in the case. In 1994 a different Home Secretary reconsidered the matter and concluded that there were no aggravating features. Nevertheless, he took the view that 20 years was still appropriate. The applicant sought judicial review, contending, inter alia, that this decision was irrational. It was *held* that, given the wide statutory discretion conferred on the Home Secretary, his decision could not be stigmatised as irrational. The Home Secretary's function in this context was not an orthodox sentencing function. He was not bound by the recommendations of the relevant judges and was entitled to reach the view that 20 years was an appropriate period even without the aggravating features which had persuaded his predecessor to fix such a period: per Sir Thomas Bingham MR, (as he then was) at p849e–f. (The decision is subject to appeal to the House of Lords.)

R v *Cambridge District Health Authority, ex parte B* [1995] 2 All ER 129 (CA) – see chapter 1, section 1.3.

Beyleveld, 'The Concept of a Human Right and Incorporation of the European Convention on Human Rights' [1995] PL 577

Foster, *'ex parte Smith'* (1996) 30 L Teach 224

Hare, 'Military Bases and Military Biases: *ex parte Smith'* [1996] CLJ 179

Himsworth, 'Legitimately Expecting Proportionality?' [1996] PL 46 (at pp 74–75 especially)

Irvine, Lord, 'Judges and Decision-makers: The Theory and Practice of *Wednesbury* Review' [1996] PL 59 (at pp 60–67 especially)

Norris, '*ex parte Smith*: Irrationality and Human Rights' [1996] PL 590

Walker, 'What's Wrong with Irrationality?' [1995] PL 556

Wintemute, Sexual Orientation and Military Employment: *ex parte Smith'* [1995] NLJ 1477

11.4 Analysis of questions

First year constitutional law students should see chapter 15 for advice on this area. For administrative law students it can be said that usually *Wednesbury* unreasonableness or irrationality is examined along with other grounds of review as part of a lengthy problem-type question (see examples in chapter 16). However, sometimes it is examined as an essay-type question, usually with the objective of bringing out discussion of the constitutional sensitivities surrounding its own definition, scope and use. The same comments apply to the developing doctrine of proportionality, where interest is being continually provoked by judicial observations of the kind made by Sedley J in *R* v *Secretary of State for the Home Department, ex parte McQuillan*, above. Consequently, careful analysis of recent judgments, and acquaintance with some of the leading academic articles on these topics, are important in tackling such questions.

11.5 Questions

QUESTION ONE

Suppose that the facts of the 1948 *Wednesbury* case were repeated today. Advise the cinema owners as to whether an argument based on proportionality would enable them to succeed in an application for judicial review of a ban on under 15 year-olds entering cinemas on Sundays.

University of London LLB Examination
(for External Students) Administrative Law June 1989 Q9

General Comment

This is a difficult question which requires a discussion of the concept of proportionality including the extent to which it constitutes a ground for judicial review and its possible application to a modern version of the facts which were considered in the Wednesbury case.

Skeleton Solution

- Outline of *Wednesbury* decision.
- Reformulation in GCHQ case.
- Outline of concept of proportionality.
- Examples of cases involving absence of proportionality.
- Possible rationale for exclusion of under 15s on Sundays.
- Lack of proportion to hardship imposed.
- Conclusion.

Suggested Solution

The decision in *Associated Provincial Picture Houses Ltd* v *Wednesbury Corporation* (1948) concerned the exercise by a local authority of a power to grant permission for the opening of local cinemas subject to such conditions as it saw fit to impose. The plaintiff cinema operators sought a declaration that a condition imposed on the grant of permission for them to open one of their cinemas, namely that no child under 15 years was to be allowed to attend without adult accompaniment on Sundays, was ultra vires because it was unreasonable. The court, however, in rejecting this argument, was influenced by the fact that the authority had been entrusted with the discretion to impose conditions on the grants of licences because it could be expected to be aware of and understand the needs and the views of the local inhabitants. The court therefore concluded that it should be slow to quash any such condition unless it was so unreasonable that no reasonable authority would have imposed it.

The test of unreasonableness enunciated in the *Wednesbury* case has since been reformulated in terms of irrationality by Lord Diplock in *Council of Civil Service Unions* v *Minister for the Civil Service* (the GCHQ case) (1984). In his view a decision would be invalid on the ground of irrationality if it was so outrageous in its defiance of logic and of accepted moral standards that no sensible person who had applied his mind to the question could have arrived at it. Once again this is a very stringent test.

An alternative ground for invalidating administrative decisions, which is similar to unreasonableness in the sense of examining the quality or content of the decision but which is less stringent in its operation, is proportionality. This concept, although well established in Europe, first received explicit judicial recognition in the GCHQ case where Lord Diplock cited it as a possible future head of judicial review. It basically requires that the effect of any order must be in proportion to the end which it is designed to achieve.

Prior to the GCHQ case there were a number of decisions where the UK courts appear to have been influenced by considerations of proportionality (see, for example, *R* v *Barnsley Metropolitan Borough Council, ex parte Hook* (1976)). In *Bromley London Borough Council* v *Greater London Council* (1983), the House of Lords appears to have been influenced by considerations of lack of proportionality in holding a decision to be invalid although the concept of proportionality was not specifically invoked. The decision which was considered in that case involved an arbitrary reduction in transport fares without due regard to ordinary business principles. The court held that the burden which was placed on ratepayers was excessive and that insufficient regard had been paid to their interests; in other words, that the burden imposed on ratepayers was out of proportion to that which could reasonably be expected to result from the implementation of an electoral promise. The decision was, however, invalidated on the basis that there had been a failure to take into account a relevant consideration, namely that the council owed a fiduciary duty to ratepayers.

The possibility of an application for judicial review based on an allegation of lack of proportionality was considered by the House of Lords in *R* v *Secretary of State for the Home Department, ex parte Brind* (1991). Two Law Lords (Lords Ackner and Lowry) ruled out a proportionality test as undermining the process of review and substituting a process of appeal on the merits. But the majority (Lords Bridge, Roskill and Templeman) did not rule it out.

In the case of the fact situation which is required to be considered, it is arguable that the restriction imposed by the council was out of all proportion to any objective which was intended. It is in fact difficult to see what a council might be seeking to achieve in banning children under 15 from entering cinemas on Sundays. For example, if it is intended to ensure that children attend church then it is difficult to see why it is not confined to Sunday mornings or why the age limit of 15 years has been selected. Alternatively, if it is intended to ensure that Sunday is treated as a family day it is difficult to see why it is confined to a specific age group. Another possibility is that it is intended to promote the interests of adults in ensuring that they do not have to compete with children for seats, are not interrupted by their presence and are provided with adult-orientated films. In any of these cases the end which the condition sets out to achieve is out of all proportion to the hardship imposed on children, who are banned from participating in a legitimate and popular leisure activity on one of the two days of the week when they are most free to do so.

In view of this the cinema owners should be advised that there are good grounds for arguing that the condition imposed by the council is lacking in proportionality. Dicta of Sedley J in *R* v *Secretary of State for the Home Department, ex parte McQuillan* (1995) were sympathetic to the use of a proportionality test, but as there has not as yet been any decision where the courts have been prepared to apply a test of proportionality as a separate ground for review, it would be wise to raise other alternative grounds for invalidity. For example, the lack of proportionality may arguably support a finding of unreasonableness since the condition here would appear to be irrational and unreasonable in the social and moral conditions of today which are in stark contrast to those which prevailed in 1948 and in the context of which the *Wednesbury* case was decided.

QUESTION TWO

Would the introduction of 'proportionality' as a ground of review in administrative law necessarily embroil the judiciary too closely in an examination of the 'correctness' rather than simply the 'legality' of government decisions?

University of London LLB Examination
(for External Students) Administrative Law June 1995 Q4

General Comment

This is quite a difficult question because it involves consideration of a principle that is basically foreign to English law, and there is very little case law on the matter. It is important to be very clear on what is meant by 'proportionality'. In what sense would it involve consideration of the merits of a decision? If it would do so, would that be a bad thing? How would such consideration compare with the other grounds of intervention that exist in the English concept of judicial review?

Skeleton Solution

- Opening argument.
- Proportionality defined.
- Why the courts may not consider the merits of a decision.
- Proportionality compared with unreasonableness and breach of natural justice.
- No necessary consideration of merits except in a presently occurring inoffensive manner.

Suggested Solution

In his leading analysis of the principles of judicial review in *Council of Civil Service Unions* v *Minister for the Civil Service* (1985) Lord Diplock attempted to open the way for the introduction of the European doctrine of proportionality into English administrative law. Despite a certain amount of academic support for the doctrine, a subsequent leading case effectively shut the door on proportionality. In *R* v *Secretary of State for the Home Department, ex parte Brind* (1991) the House of Lords did not favour the adoption of a separate principle of proportionality into English administrative law. The main justifications for this point of view were that the doctrine of reasonableness was sufficiently flexible to deal with situations where proportionality was in issue, and that if proportionality was to be given a life separate from unreasonableness 'an inquiry into and a decision upon the merits cannot be avoided' (per Lord Ackner). If that were to happen, judicial review would become an appeal instead of a review, and so trespass into forbidden territory (per Lord Lowry). This point of view was unnecessarily cautious, however, and there are two arguments which may be made against it. First, there are principles inherent in judicial review which come close to a consideration of the merits, but the courts have been able to define those in legalistic terms so as to avoid any genuine consideration of the merits. Secondly, even if proportionality would inevitably entail some consideration of the merits, this would not necessarily be objectionable.

The doctrine of proportionality is one which exists in European systems of public law. It means that an appropriate balance must be maintained between the adverse effects which an administrative authority's decision may have on the rights, liberties or interests of the person concerned, and the purpose which the authority is seeking to pursue. The principle of proportionality is part of the formal system of checks and balances which exists in continental constitutional law. It recognises that there is room for officials to abuse their powers by making otherwise lawful decisions which interfere disproportionately with the rights of individual citizens. Proportionality thus seeks to draw an appropriate balance between the competing demands of the administration and the individual citizen. Where the impact on an individual is disproportionate to the objective sought to be achieved, the decision will not be permitted to take effect.

One of the main difficulties the courts have in deciding whether proportionality should be introduced into English law is that there is no formal system of checks and balances in the English constitution. The courts therefore have no tradition of intervening on the basis that the balance between the executive and the individual has not been struck correctly. Within English administrative law the ultra vires doctrine reigns supreme, and is the foundation of judicial intervention into administrative activities. This concentration of the grounds for judicial review upon the doctrine of ultra vires is one reason why the courts are scrupulous to avoid any suggestion that they are examining the merits of a decision, and their insistence upon classifying even irrationality and procedural impropriety as species of ultra vires.

This practice is unhelpful because it disguises the fact that unreasonableness and natural justice are concepts that come close to an examination of the merits of decisions. Yet the courts have skilfully defined these questions so as to avoid any suspicion that they are indeed examining the merits. Reasonableness is notoriously difficult to define in common law, and inevitably is a question of fact involving thorough consideration of the merits of any particular course of action. In the context of judicial review the courts have been able to define this concept with reasonable certainty and in a more or less legalistic fashion on the basis of the principles forged in *Associated Provincial Picture Houses* v *Wednesbury Corporation* (1948). Despite the closeness of reasonableness to an investigation of the merits, the courts have thus been able to redefine it in a way which is not objectionable. There is no real reason to suppose that the courts would not be able to do this for proportionality. There is also no reason why proportionality should necessarily involve untoward consideration of the merits. The courts should be able to define it in legal terms as a balancing exercise that will lead to a finding of ultra vires in an appropriate case. The court is not required to investigate the merits of a particular decision, merely to ask whether the adverse effects of a decision are proportionate to the ends it is desired to achieve. Such a balancing exercise recognises that in a democratic society administrative bodies should be accountable and should be made to account for their actions where they have strong adverse effects on individual rights and liberties.

It is nonetheless true that the above balancing exercise must come near to an investigation of the merits of a decision. Even where it does so, this will not always be objectionable. It is necessary to distinguish two different ways in which the court may be said to be considering the merits of a decision. The first way is something that occurs often enough on the basis of the second limb of *Wednesbury* unreasonableness and on the basis of natural justice. If the court concludes, for instance, that a decision is void because no reasonable decision-maker could have made it, or because it is motivated by bias, then the court is in reality making a judgment about the merits of that decision. Even though the court will classify its judgment in terms of ultra vires, the fact remains that it is stating that the decision is 'wrong', that it is without merit. While the court will then leave it to the decision-maker to reconsider its decision, curing any irregularity that the court identified, the decision-maker will clearly not be able to arrive at the same decision where that is a decision that no reasonable decision-maker could have made. Where a consideration of the merits of a decision occurs in this sense, it is not objectionable: the court is not substituting its own view about what the 'right' decision should be for that of the decision-maker, it is merely stating that the decision under attack is 'wrong' and that the decision-maker must reconsider its position.

The second sense in which the court may be said to be considering the merits of a decision is in acting in an appellate role by substituting its own decision for that of the decision-maker. For the court to do this on an application for judicial review would genuinely be objectionable, for it would contravene the sacred principle that judicial review is not an appeal. There is no need for the doctrine of proportionality to involve this kind of consideration of the merits of a case. Where the court considered that proportionality had been infringed, it would remit the decision to the decision-maker for reconsideration; it would not substitute its own view of what the decision ought to be. This is what occurs time after time without objection in the context of unreasonable-ness and natural justice. There is no reason why it should not occur in the context of proportionality. Furthermore, it is clear that some sort of concept of proportionality does exist and does operate in this way, even if it is not formally recognised as a distinct principle. Thus the House of Lords in *ex parte Brind* held that proportionality did exist within the concept of reasonableness. In another case it has been held that the court has always had power to quash an excessive (disproportionate) punishment: *R* v *Barnsley Metropolitan Borough Council, ex parte Hook* (1976). The courts would be better to recognise this principle overtly than to resort to other grounds of review which disguise its importance.

There is no reason, then, why the principle of proportionality should be offensive to the sacred rules of judicial review any more than the principles of reasonableness and natural justice are. Of course, it is evident that there will be a sense in which proportionality involves consideration of the merits of a decision, but this is in the relatively weak and unobjectionable sense of saying that a decision is 'wrong' because of the lack of proportionality. The courts are well equipped to develop the principle, if adopted, in a way that satisfies the need to avoid any suspicion of an appellate role. The adoption of the principle of proportionality would add an important weapon to the courts' arsenal and enable them to ensure that power is not used in such a way that, although lawful, it grossly infringes individual rights and interests. The important democratic principle of protecting minority rights from unnecessary interference by the majority amply justifies the introduction of proportionality into English law.

12 Illegality and Unreasonableness

12.1 Introduction

An unlawful or unreasonable exercise of power may occur in a number of ways. Common law has developed certain classifications of excess or abuse of power, but they are not clear cut and often overlap with each other. Judges have rarely attempted to list them in any logical way, though lists are given in the judgments of Lord Greene MR in *Associated Provincial Picture Houses Ltd* v *Wednesbury Corporation* [1948] 1 KB 223 and by Lord Reid in *Anisminic Ltd* v *Foreign Compensation Commission* [1969] 2 AC 147 (HL). Lord Greene said that proof of any of the heads of ultra vires would render a decision unreasonable and a nullity, though total unreasonableness itself is also a separate basis for review (see chapter 11). Lord Reid said that proof of any of the heads of ultra vires, including total unreasonableness, would render a decision void on the basis of jurisdictional error (see chapter 9). Sometimes a distinction is drawn between procedural ultra vires and substantive ultra vires (covering irrationality and illegality), but such distinctions are for purposes of classification only, since the effect of any type of ultra vires decision is to render it subject to judicial review. For purposes of convenient classification irrationality (or total unreasonableness) has been discussed in chapter 11 and the remaining heads of illegality (or aspects of *Wednesbury* unreasonableness) are discussed in this chapter.

12.2 Key points

a) *Relevant considerations (an aspect of* Wednesbury *unreasonableness)*

A decision may be set aside if it was taken on the basis of irrelevant considerations, or as a result of failure to take account of relevant ones. The definition of what is relevant in a particular context will depend on the statute conferring the discretionary power being exercised, since the statute will set out the aims and objects of the power and the circumstances in which it may be exercised. If the decision-maker is motivated by an improper purpose or ulterior motive, this will also be treated as an irrelevant consideration: *Congreve* v *Home Office* [1976] QB 629.

Under many statutes the discretion conferred is extensive and the courts will not restrict it artificially by limiting the considerations that are relevant. This explains why, in some areas, the discretion will usually be unreviewable under this category of illegality, eg traditionally, the area of police operational discretion: *R* v *Metropolitan Police Commissioner, ex parte Blackburn* [1968] 2 QB 118.

The problem of reviewing decisions on the test of relevant considerations becomes very sensitive where the decision has been taken by an elected and representative body. The courts will leave a 'margin of appreciation' to the decision-making body in order to allow that body sufficient discretion to decide how much weight to give to a particular relevant factor when assessing all the factors and striking a balance. It is only when the balancing exercise has been carried out unreasonably in the *Wednesbury* sense that judicial review will be granted.

The margin of appreciation approach means that a decision will not be illegal even though some irrelevant factors were taken into account, provided that the dominant considerations which decided the issue were relevant ones: this is known as the 'dominant purpose rule': *Westminster Corporation* v *London and North Western Railway Co* [1905] AC 426 (HL) and *R* v *Secretary of State for Social Services, ex parte Wellcome Foundation* [1987] 2 All ER 1025. The fiduciary duty which local authorities owe to council tax payers is a dominant factor to consider when carrying out political commitments: *Bromley London Borough Council* v *Greater London Council* [1982] 1 All ER 129 (HL). Political pressure from the local community is a relevant factor in the exercise of local authority discretionary powers but cannot be relied on to justify interference with the lawful conduct of a person or group to which sections of the local community have voiced objections: *Wheeler* v *Leicester City Council* [1985] 2 All ER 1106 (HL). See also *R* v *Coventry City Council, ex parte Phoenix Aviation* [1995] 3 All ER 37 in 12.3 below.

Moral, ethical and humanitarian considerations may be relevant and carry weight depending on the context. For example, a power to make a bye-law for the preservation of public decency would permit local councillors to take account of the moral offence caused by some kinds of public behaviour, because the moral aspect is inherent in the very purpose for which the power is granted. By contrast, in other contexts, the statute conferring the power may define the purpose narrowly so as to exclude moral and ethical considerations, eg the imposition of planning conditions for land development must be on the basis that the stipulated conditions fairly and reasonably relate to the development being permitted: see *R* v *Hillingdon London Borough Council, ex parte Royco Homes Ltd* [1974] 2 All ER 643. For a recent analysis of the relevance of moral considerations in a non-planning context see *R* v *Somerset County Council, ex parte Fewings* [1995] 3 All ER 20 in 12.3 below.

b) *The sufficient evidence rule (an aspect of* Wednesbury *unreasonableness)*

This head of illegality (sometimes called the no evidence rule) requires that the discretionary power must be exercised on at least a minimum core of objective fact, supported by sufficient, relevant, probative evidence. In the absence of such a basis of fact and in the absence of any reasons for the decision, the court will treat the decision as unlawful: *Padfield* v *Minister of Agriculture* [1968] AC 997 and *Coleen Properties* v *MHLG* [1971] 1 WLR 433. A finding of fact for which there is no sufficient evidential basis is treated as a jurisdictional error: see chapter 9.

c) *Bad faith (mala fides) (an aspect of* Wednesbury *unreasonableness)*

Deliberate misuse of power for reasons of bribery, corruption or personal prejudice or spite will be unreasonable and illegal and, apart from being subject to judicial review, may give rise to civil proceedings for the tort of misfeasance in a public office: *Dunlop* v *Woollahra Municipal Council* [1982] AC 158; see also *Three Rivers District Council* v *Bank of England (No 3)* [1996] 3 All ER 558 in chapter 7, section 7.3. Cases of bad faith are rare, partly because of a rebuttable presumption that ministers of the Crown act in good faith at all times. A rare example in the context of local government is *R* v *Ealing London Borough Council, ex parte Times Newspapers Ltd* (1986) 85 LGR 316, where a library ban on *The Times* newspaper in support of a printers' dispute with the proprietors of that newspaper was described as an example of 'bad faith and vindictiveness'. However, this was not the sole head of ultra vires found in that case and usually the courts are content to review the decision under a different head rather than cast doubt on the good faith of public decision-making.

d) *The rule against delegation ('delegatus non potest delegare': a delegate may not delegate his decision-making powers) (an aspect of illegality)*

Where unlawful delegation occurs it cannot be validated by a later ratification of the decision by the responsible authority: *Barnard* v *National Dock Labour Board* [1953] 2 QB 18. A delegation of administrative work will be lawful if the decision on which it is based is taken after a proper exercise of discretion by the responsible body: *Selvarajan* v *Race Relations Board* [1975] 1 WLR 1686.

Lawful delegation may occur under statute, eg local authorities are permitted to delegate many kinds of executive power to appropriate council officials under local government legislation: Local Government Act 1972, s101. Common law also recognises the legality of a delegation of power by a minister to an appropriate civil servant even though there may be no statutory authority for it, since the convention of individual ministerial responsibility to Parliament provides the constitutional safeguard of accountability for the action of the civil servant; indeed, in strict theory no 'delegation' has occurred since the Minister and the civil servant are treated in law as one entity: *Carltona* v *Commissioners of Works* [1943] 2 All ER 560 and *R* v *Secretary of State for the Home Department, ex parte Oladehinde* [1990] 3 All ER 393 (HL).

e) *The rule against fettering of discretion (an aspect of illegality)*

Unlawful fettering may occur in a number of ways: by policy; by contract; by making a representation or otherwise. The crucial test in each case is whether the discretion survives the adoption of the policy or the making of the contract or representation. The judges will leave a 'margin of appreciation' to public bodies so that they may adopt policies in order to structure their discretionary decision-making and so that they may make contracts or representations in order to obtain commercial services or other benefits. No unlawful fettering occurs if the body in question has retained an open mind and is willing to make exceptions to its adopted policy, or even to change that policy: *British Oxygen Co Ltd* v *Minister of Technology* [1971] AC 610 (HL). Similarly the making of ordinary commercial contracts will not amount to unlawful fettering of discretion provided that there is no restriction on the ability of the public body to take future action which may be required for the public good: *Ayr Harbour Trustees* v *Oswald* (1883) 8 App Cas 623, *Rederiaktiebolaget Amphitrite* v *R* [1921] 3 KB 500 and *Birkdale District Electricity Supply Co Ltd* v *Southport Corporation* [1926] AC 355 (HL). The rule against fettering discretion explains why it has proven difficult to plead a substantive legitimate expectation resulting from a representation made by a public body: see chapter 10. The same difficulty has stood in the way of pleading promissory estoppel against a public body which has made a representation: see (f) below.

Finally, fettering may occur in a manner hitherto unprecedented, eg the recent case where the Home Secretary tried to use the royal prerogative to legislate contrary to existing legislative discretion: *R* v *Secretary of State for the Home Department, ex parte Fire Brigades Union* [1995] 2 All ER 244 (HL): see chapter 3.3.

f) *Estoppel in public law (an aspect of illegality)*

There are three types of estoppel which may be relevant in public law:

i) Issue estoppel – this is based on the principle of res judicata: the courts will permit a fettering of discretion if an administrator has exercised a power to make a determination in order to resolve a dispute between two or more parties. The parties to that dispute will in general be unable to seek a fresh determination later once all appeals have been exhausted: *Thrasyvoulou* v *Secretary of State for Environment* [1990] 1 All ER 65 (HL).

ii) Primary estoppel – this occurs where a public body has exercised a power to decide a matter of fact affecting a person's rights and that person has relied on that determination. The decision cannot be revoked without that person's consent and so a lawful fettering of discretion will occur once the power has been exercised: *Robertson* v *Minister of Pensions* [1949] 1 KB 227.

iii) Promissory estoppel – sometimes it has been suggested that a public body may commit an abuse of power if it tries to revoke a decision which confers a discretionary benefit on a citizen in circumstances where that citizen has relied on the exercise of the power, and where revocation of the decision will cause him loss or inconvenience. However, this conflicts with well-established principles to the effect that estoppel cannot prevent a public body from performing its public duties or exercising its discretionary powers for the public good: see especially per Lawton LJ in *Laker Airways Ltd* v *Department of Trade* [1977] QB 643 at p707. It is certainly well established that the doctrine of estoppel cannot be used to 'clothe' a public body with powers it does not legally possess. Consequently, the preferred approach is that where a breach of representation has given rise to a substantive legitimate expectation that the decision will not be changed, then, provided that the representation is intra vires the authority making it, the authority may be prevented from revoking it, not because of an estoppel but because it would be unfair and procedurally ultra vires to permit such revocation: see chapter 10.

Finally, attempts by Lord Denning to import promissory estoppel into public law under the general doctrine of ostensible authority appear to have failed because of the difficulty of reconciling the doctrine (borrowed from private law) with the rule that statutory powers cannot be extended by an estoppel. An attempt by Lord Denning to apply the doctrine in the field of planning law (*Lever Finance Ltd* v *Westminster (City) London Borough Council* [1971] 1 QB 222) has been drastically modified so as to apply only to the rare case of clear evidence of a formal delegation of authority from the local planning authority to its planning officials: *Western Fish Products Ltd* v *Penwith District Council* [1981] 2 All ER 204.

12.3 Recent cases and articles

R v *Somerset County Council, ex parte Fewings* [1995] 3 All ER 20 (CA) – held (Simon Brown LJ dissenting) that a local authority ban on deer hunting on land over which it had statutory powers of management was illegal because (per Sir Thomas Bingham MR and Swinton Thomas LJ) the local authority had failed to take into account the main relevant consideration under the statute in question (namely, whether this use of the land was for its benefit, improvement or development) and because (per Swinton Thomas LJ) the authority had taken into account an irrelevant consideration, namely moral and ethical objections to the sport of deer hunting. Swinton Thomas LJ (at pp35h–36e) opined that the issue of blood sports was a sensitive national issue best left to parliamentary regulation. Whilst the local authority could ban deer hunting to protect rare flora or an endangered species on the land in question they could not ban deer hunting purely on humanitarian grounds. Sir Thomas Bingham MR agreed that the ban was unlawful but opined (at p28a–b) that the statutory language was sufficiently broad so that, if the authority had considered what was for 'the benefit of their area', moral considerations would not have been necessarily irrelevant. Simon Brown LJ, in his dissenting judgment (at p31c–j) thought that the cruelty to animals argument was a relevant consideration in deciding what was for the benefit of the area, and that since the councillors were elected by, and representative of, the local community they were entitled to regard the cruelty argument as decisive: see further Lindsay [1995] NLJ 412.

R v *Coventry City Council, ex parte Phoenix Aviation* [1995] 3 All ER 37 (QBD) – held illegal for public authorities operating air and sea ports to ban flights or shipments of livestock by animal exporters in order to avoid the disruptive consequences of unlawful protests by animal rights demonstrators. The export of live animals was lawful and the exporters should not be penalised as a result of the authorities wishing to surrender to political pressure. Whilst short-term security measures were lawful, long-term bans of the kind imposed in this case were not lawful, for otherwise it would be the end of the rule of law.

Cragg and Low-Beer, 'Moral Considerations' [1995] NLJ 1342

Freedland, 'The Rule Against Delegation and the *Carltona* Doctrine in an Agency Context' [1996] PL 19

Lindsay, 'Blood Sports and Public Law' [1995] NLJ 412

12.4 Analysis of questions

First year constitutional law students should see chapter 15 for advice on this area. For administrative law students it can be said that aspects of *Wednesbury* unreasonableness and of illegality are usually examined as part of lengthy, problem-type questions, which also usually involve other categories of ultra vires such as procedural impropriety and irrationality (total unreasonableness). Knowledge of the procedural rules under RSC O.53 and of the law on remedies may also be part of such questions. Examples are found in chapter 16. Occasionally specialised aspects of illegality may be examined in either problem-type or essay-type questions, notably on the rules about fettering discretion and their relationship to the doctrine of estoppel in public law. Examples are set out in section 12.5 below. Cases involving illegality or *Wednesbury* unreasonableness are reported on a regular basis so it is important to keep up to date with new decisions which might re-awaken interest in a particular area of illegality, or which may stimulate fresh academic debate, eg recent case law on whether humanitarian considerations are relevant to the exercise of public powers: *ex parte Fewings* in section 12.3 above.

12.5 Questions

QUESTION ONE

The Secretary of State at the Department of Trade and Industry (DTI) is given statutory power to make substantial grants to firms in designated 'special zones', a substantial part of whose business has been in defence or defence-related industries. The purpose of the grants is to enable the firms to modify their machinery and retrain their staff for other kinds of production. Because a very large number of applications is expected, the senior official at the DTI in charge of the programme decides that priority should be given to firms which have previously supported a scheme run by another government department, the Department of Education and Science (DES), which encouraged firms to give time to allow their staff to attend training and further education courses. The clerk at the DTI who processes applications is instructed that, unless there are exceptional features, grants should be awarded only to firms which are certified by the DES as having a good record under the previous scheme.

Advise Thor Industries plc, whose application for a grant is turned down. It is agreed that Thor Industries are located in a special zone and that a substantial part of their business has been in defence-related production, but they have not been certified by the DES.

University of London LLB Examination
(for External Students) Administrative Law June 1992 Q7

General Comment

This problem focuses on the exercise of ministerial discretion. To what extent may the Minister develop a policy? To what extent may his power be subdelegated? What considerations may or must he take into account? The principle of law developed in the cases must be set against the practical background of this problem.

Skeleton Solution

- Formulation of policy.
- Delegation of decision-making power.
- Discretion must be exercised.
- Purpose of power.
- *Wednesbury* unreasonableness.

Suggested Solution

Thor may be able to bring judicial review proceedings against the Secretary of State. Its first point of challenge will be that the Secretary of State has fettered his discretion. The Secretary is entitled to have a policy governing the allocation of grants to industries, but he must keep an open mind, and he must be prepared to listen to applicants with something new to say in the matter: *British Oxygen Co Ltd* v *Minister of Technology* (1971). There are two difficulties in the way of this case. First, the Minister has not altogether fettered his discretion, he has left open the possibility of 'exceptional circumstances'. Secondly, it is not clear how far Thor can claim to fall into the category of something new to say.

Another challenge to this decision lies in the nature of delegated authority. The statutory power is conferred upon the Minister. But the Minister has apparently exercised no discretion in the matter, since the policy in question has been formulated by a senior official at the DTI, whilst the ultimate decision has been taken by a clerk. This complaint will be difficult to sustain with reference to the senior official since a Minister is entitled to act by an official in his department (*Carltona Ltd* v *Commissioners of Works* (1943), but the fact that the final decision was taken by the clerk in circumstances where the clerk was following rigid instructions may add weight to the inference that there was no genuine consideration of Thor's case. As far as the clerk is concerned, it may be possible to challenge his action on the principle delegatus non potest delegare. Whilst it is permissible for the Minister to act *through* his official, it is not permissible for that official to delegate his authority to the clerk. The real test here will be whether the decision has ultimately been made by the person to whom Parliament conferred the power to make it. In this case at first glance it would seem not. A good deal of weight is added to this proposition when it is considered that the Minister has effectively bound himself to follow the advice of the DES save in exceptional circumstances, and that therefore there has been no genuine exercise of his discretion. This is similar to the situation in *Lavender & Sons Ltd* v *MHLG* (1970), where the Minister of Housing was held to be not entitled to bind himself to follow recommendations of another minister.

The Minister's power will be construed in the light of the statute conferring it. Thus Thor may be able to say that the policy adopted by the Minister is not in accordance with the purpose of the statutory power. It is clear that the purpose of the grants is to fund retraining, broadly speaking it is thus educational. It is not clear that giving preferential treatment to those who have supported the previous scheme is in accordance with this purpose. Furthermore, the support given by these firms in the past would appear to be an irrelevant consideration and the department's policy may thus be challenged on *Wednesbury* (1948) grounds.

My advice to Thor is thus that there is a reasonable prospect of being able to challenge this decision in judicial review proceedings. There are a number of grounds that may be raised, but principally the Minister has failed to exercise his discretion, and has formulated a policy based on irrelevant and improper considerations. It should be remembered, as always, that the court cannot compel the Minister to make a grant to Thor, merely to review his decision.

QUESTION TWO

Does the current law on the question of applying the doctrine of estoppel to public bodies place too much importance on 'doing justice in the individual case' and too little importance on maintaining the integrity of the ultra vires doctrine?

University of London LLB Examination
(for External Students) Administrative Law June 1994 Q4

General Comment

This question is unusual in that it suggests the exact opposite of the law as it presently stands. At present, instances where estoppel binds public bodies are the exception rather than the rule, and the court is more concerned to uphold the ultra vires doctrine than to allow questions of justice to the individual case to dominate. Explain why estoppel is incompatible with the ultra vires doctrine. Is this incompatibility as strong as it is perceived to be? Should estoppel be permitted to operate nonetheless?

Skeleton Solution

- The general rule – estoppel will not operate.
- Theoretical incompatibility of ultra vires and estoppel.
- Fettering discretion.
- Exceptions to the general rule.
- Should estoppel be permitted? What does justice require?

Suggested Solution

As the law stands at present, the general rule is that estoppel will not operate so as to bind public bodies in the exercise of their public duties. There are few exceptions to this general rule. It will be argued that the courts have allowed theoretical considerations to obscure the practical injustice that arises when public bodies seek to retract representations or to break promises that have been relied upon, and that there is a need for reform in this area of the law.

The doctrine of ultra vires is the foundation stone for the general rule described above. Estoppel cannot operate either so as to give authorities powers that they do not possess in law or so as to prevent them from carrying out their statutory duties. Thus in a case where a planning officer represented that a plaintiff was permitted to use land for certain purposes, the planning authority was not estopped from later taking enforcement action to prevent that land use, even though the plaintiff had incurred expenditure in reliance upon the representations made (*Western Fish Products Ltd* v *Penwith District Council* (1981)). The planning officer's representations were ultra vires, since only the authority itself had power to make decisions on planning matters. If estoppel were permitted to operate in these circumstances, the effect would be to give such officers powers they do not possess in law.

It is this fear that public bodies, and particularly their officers, might acquire powers not conferred upon them by Parliament that has prevented the development of estoppel in administrative law. The threat of this occurring has on occasions been stated in very exaggerated terms. Thus, in an unreported case Lord Greene MR claimed that to permit estoppel to operate in administrative law would lead to the collapse of the ultra vires doctrine and would enable public officers to extend their powers at will (*Minister of Agriculture and Fisheries* v *Hulkin* (referred to in *Minister of Agriculture and Fisheries* v *Matthews* (1950)). Such is the force of this reasoning that the ultra vires doctrine has even prevented estoppel from binding a public authority acting in a private capacity, where it has acted ultra vires. The supremacy of the ultra vires doctrine in this respect has been extended beyond representations or promises which a body does not have jurisdiction to make to decisions which it makes in the exercise of its discretion. In this context, estoppel will not operate because the public body must not be permitted to fetter its discretion. Thus if an authority makes a discretionary grant on the basis of incorrect information, it cannot be estopped from later revoking that grant once the true state of affairs is discovered, however much hardship the later revocation causes.

There are limited exceptions to the general rule which prevents estoppel from binding public bodies. One of these is where a representation is made by an officer of the public body who has ostensible authority to make it. In *Lever Finance Limited* v *Westminster (City) London Borough Council* (1971), a planning authority was held to be bound by a mis-statement on the part of one of its officers. In this case, the authority had a practice of allowing its officers to make certain kinds of decision. The officer was therefore held to have ostensible authority and his decision was deemed to be intra vires, even though delegation of the authority's powers to him had not, as such, lawfully occurred. This case suggests that estoppel will operate where there is some special circumstance to justify the assumption that the officer has the power to bind the public body concerned, and consequent reliance upon that officer's representations; but it is not clear why in this case the mis-statement of the officer should be permitted to bind the authority on the basis of ostensible authority, whereas in the *Western Fish* case the officer was not held to have such ostensible authority. The contrast between these two cases highlights a fundamental difficulty with the concept of ostensible authority. Officers of public bodies will nearly always appear to have authority to make binding representations. An individual who relies upon the representations made cannot really be expected to look beyond this appearance to see whether such authority is indeed 'ostensible' or not, on the basis of the practice of the public body concerned.

A second exception to the usual rule operates where a public body has waived some procedural requirement: it will then be estopped from seeking to rely upon that lack of formality in deciding against an applicant. In this case there is no conflict with the ultra vires doctrine, provided that the public body has the power to make the decision in question.

It is doubtful whether public bodies need such strong general protection from the operation of estoppel. In the case of ultra vires decisions, there is a clear objection of principle to allowing estoppel to operate for it is true that authorities should not be allowed to exceed their powers. This objection of principle does not really apply to the exercise of discretion. In this latter case it is hard to see that any serious damage can be done by permitting estoppel to operate. To do so would not lead to any serious fettering of discretion in relation to future decisions of the public body concerned.

Even the more principled objection based on the concept of ultra vires can be overcome to a great extent when it is considered that judicial review remedies are discretionary in nature and, in different contexts, the court has declined to quash ultra vires decisions where the practical consequences made it undesirable to do so. When this is borne in mind, it becomes apparent that the ultra vires objection is not as fundamental as it has been presented to be. Just as the court has discretion to quash a decision or not, it should also have the discretion to declare that a representation was ultra vires, but should not be retracted in relation to a particular individual. It is submitted that the claim that this will enable officers of public bodies to extend their powers at will is simply far-fetched. Estoppel operates ex post facto, after scrutiny by the court, and this would make it extremely difficult for officers to extend their powers at will, even if they wished to do so. Like everybody, officers of public bodies do from time to time make mistakes. Individuals who rely upon their representations should not be forced to bear the burden of those mistakes. It is time for the judiciary to take a fresh look at the doctrine of estoppel, and to realise that, whatever the theoretical niceties of ultra vires, practical reality demands that justice should be done in individual cases. From that perspective the failure to develop the doctrine of estoppel in administrative law is a serious deficiency.

QUESTION THREE

Under what circumstances may a public body be estopped from altering an ultra vires decision? Do you consider this area of the law to be in need of reform?

University of London LLB Examination
(for External Students) Administrative Law June 1993 Q4

General Comment

This question requires a consideration of the nature of administrative decision-making. Is estoppel generally permitted (regardless of the vires of the decision in question)? What are the justifications for not allowing estoppel in cases where the decision is ultra vires? How should the balance be struck between individual hardship and the need for an authority to do its duties? What alternatives are there to estoppel, and are they effective? What reforms are needed?

Skeleton Solution

- Estoppel in administrative law.
- The ultra vires doctrine.

- Alternatives to estoppel:
  - – legitimate expectations;
  - – abuse of power;
- Reform:
  - – proportionality;
  - – allowing estoppel to operate.

Suggested Solution

As a matter of general principle, public authorities cannot be estopped from performing their public duties, or from exercising the powers conferred upon them. This principle will apply a fortiori where an individual seeks to found estoppel upon an ultra vires decision. This is an area in need of reform, however, since it is clear that in a number of cases individuals may suffer significant detriments as a result of reliance upon decisions made by public authorities.

Estoppel is thought to threaten the whole doctrine of ultra vires by purporting to give authorities, or their officers, powers which they do not possess. In *Minister of Agriculture and Fisheries* v *Hulkin* (cited in *Minister of Agriculture and Fisheries* v *Matthews* (1950)) Lord Greene MR stated that if estoppel were permitted in administrative law then the ultra vires doctrine would collapse and public officers would be enabled to extend their powers at will.

Thus in *Western Fish Products Ltd* v *Penwith District Council* (1981) an officer of a planning authority made representations about the legality of certain land uses on the plaintiff's land. It was held that the planning authority could not be estopped from issuing enforcement notices and stop notices to curtail that use even though the plaintiff had relied on the representations by carrying out works on the land. The rationale for this decision was that the officer was not authorised to make the representations as the planning authority alone could make decisions on planning matters. The officer's representations were therefore ultra vires. Had the authority delegated the power to make representations and decisions to the officer, then it might have been bound by those representations.

Justification for the decision in *Western Fish* may be derived from a consideration of the nature of the planning authority's duties. If estoppel were to operate in such a case, then individuals might effectively be able to develop land without planning permission in defiance of the public consultation process required by the planning legislation. Thus it is the public interest that is being protected through the ultra vires doctrine. Two objections may be put to this point of view. The first is that it is questionable whether an individual should bear the financial burden of reliance upon the representations of an official with apparent though not actual authority. In theory the public will suffer some intangible harm if the ultra vires doctrine is not strictly enforced, but in the majority of cases the impact of a decision will be lessened if borne by the entire community. Secondly, estoppel as traditionally formulated is not a sword but a shield. Thus, for example, estoppel should not allow members of the public to acquire planning permission, but simply to defend themselves against enforcement action in circumstances where the requirements for estoppel are met.

The unwillingness of the courts to acknowledge that estoppel can operate to prevent an authority from altering an ultra vires decision means that on occasions they have indulged in judicial sleight of hand. In *Lever Finance Ltd* v *Westminster (City) London Borough Council* (1971), which is similar to the *Western Fish* case, the planning authority was held bound by wrong statements made by its officers. Here the officer in question was held to have ostensible authority because of the authority's practice of allowing its officers to make certain kinds of decision. In effect, therefore, the statement was held to be intra vires. However, delegation had not occurred in accordance with the relevant statutory provisions so it is extremely doubtful that the statements were in fact intra vires. It is difficult to see how the officer in the *Western Fish* case had any less apparent authority than the officer in *Lever Finance*.

Although estoppel will not operate to prevent an authority from altering a decision made ultra vires, there are various devices by which the courts may exercise a limited control over their power to do so. Public authorities have a duty to act fairly and consistently. In some circumstances the authority's representations may give rise to legitimate expectations (see *Attorney-General of Hong Kong* v *Ng Yuen Shiu* (1983)). Legitimate expectations are sometimes thought of as a kind of estoppel, although usually legitimate expectations do not usually prevent an authority from altering its decisions; they give rise to certain requirements of natural justice, in particular that the individual concerned should have an opportunity to make representations if the decision is altered.

However sometimes an authority's failure to act fairly and consistently may be an abuse of power. The altering of the decision may in certain circumstances be itself in the nature of ultra vires action. In *Laker Airways Ltd* v *Department of Trade* (1977) Lord Denning MR stated that an authority would be misusing its powers if it exercised them in circumstances which worked injustice to an individual without any countervailing benefit to the public. In such a case the authority could be estopped. Here the court might be faced with the difficulty of weighing two opposite ultra vires actions to decide which should prevail. It is submitted that the courts should act to protect the individuals who may suffer detriment as a result of the revocation of decisions that have provided the foundation for investment.

Legitimate expectations and the doctrine of abuse of power supply only limited powers of control to the courts, and neither meets the problem head on. The difficulty is that, as has been noted, the courts have tended to lean towards protecting an anonymous public from the effects of ultra vires decisions rather than developing remedies to assist the individuals who are likely to suffer as a result of an authority resiling from those decisions. One avenue through which reform might take place is indicated by the *Laker Airways* decision cited above, and by general considerations of who should bear the burden of ultra vires decisions in particular cases. The development of the continental doctrine of proportionality referred to by Lord Diplock in *Council of Civil Service Unions* v *Minister for the Civil Service* (1985) would provide the courts with an effective means of balancing the public interest, which they seek to protect through the ultra vires doctrine, and the private interest of a particular individual. Where the detriment to the individual would be substantial, and the benefit to the public small, the authority would be prevented from resiling from its decision. However, the decision in *R* v *Secretary of State for the Home Department, ex parte Brind* (1991) means that proportionality is unlikely to find its way into English law as a distinct doctrine for a long time, if at all.

It may be that the simplest method of reform would simply be to lift the taboo that administrative law observes with respect to estoppel. Three justifications have been noted for not extending the doctrine of estoppel to cover ultra vires decisions. First, to do so would permit officers to extend their powers at will; second, authorities should not be prevented from exercising their powers; third, the public interest should be protected. It is submitted that the first of these justifications is simply far-fetched: it is unlikely that officers would be seeking to extend their powers through estoppel, and estoppel would not permit them to do so; it would simply provide a just solution to prevent hardship in an individual case. Similarly, estoppel in an individual case will require fairness in the exercise of powers; it will not prevent the future exercise of those powers other than in the area which the estoppel covers. As for the third justification, as has been suggested, where there is a pecuniary detriment the burden should be spread throughout the community as opposed to resting upon one individual. This might not prove satisfactory in every case, and it is submitted that from the point of view of public interest the doctrine of proportionality would provide a better solution. However, the concept of estoppel could possibly be expanded in administrative law to include notions of public interest. As has been indicated, some reform is necessary to prevent the hardship that can clearly occur when individuals rely upon the decisions of those who apparently have authority. Ultimately, it should be for the authority to exercise its powers properly in the first instance, and not for the individual to repair the damage later.

13 Remedies

13.1 Introduction

RSC O.53 permits the following remedies to be obtained in an application for judicial review. Each remedy has its own special rules and limitations resulting from its source and historical development:

a) the prerogative order of certiorari;

b) the prerogative order of prohibition;

c) the prerogative order of mandamus;

d) the common law remedy of damages;

e) the equitable remedy of injunction;

f) the equitable remedy of declaration.

The prerogative orders were always available in public law and, indeed, can only be obtained in a public law case (the prerogative writ of habeas corpus is available under O.54: see further Wade and Forsyth, *Administrative Law* (7th edn) at pp615–623). The common law and equitable remedies were not available in public law cases prior to the introduction of the reformed O.53 on 1 January 1978 but have a long history in private law. It does not follow that the same rules will apply to obtaining these remedies where they are sought under O.53. For example, in private law cases damages can be obtained as a free-standing remedy, but under O.53 it is available only as ancillary relief in support of another remedy.

Apart from damages, each remedy may be obtained singly. A combination of remedies may be granted at the court's discretion. The applicant need not specify the particular remedy he is seeking but instead simply ask for judicial review; the court will decide which remedy is appropriate to the particular case.

13.2 Key points

a) *Certiorari*

Certiorari is granted to quash an ultra vires decision. Normally this will be sufficient to ensure that the decision-maker will take a fresh decision in the light of the court's ruling on the law in question.

For a more detailed account of the history and scope of this remedy, see Wade and Forsyth, *Administrative Law* (7th edn) at pp623–643.

b) *Prohibition*

Prohibition is granted to prevent an ultra vires decision from being taken. Again, this will normally be sufficient to ensure that the decision-making process is re-started in the light of the court's ruling on the law in question. For a more detailed account of the history and scope of this remedy see Wade and Forsyth, *Administrative Law* (7th edn) at pp625–643.

c) *Mandamus*

Mandamus is granted to compel the performance of a public duty, including a duty to exercise a discretion according to law. For a more detailed account of the history and scope of this remedy see Wade and Forsyth, *Administrative Law* (7th edn) at pp643–659.

d) *Availability of prerogative orders against the Crown*

The prerogative orders of certiorari, prohibition and mandamus are not available against the Crown, but are available against ministers of the Crown in their official capacities: *Padfield* v *Minister of Agriculture* [1968] AC 997 (HL). However, it will usually be unnecessary (as well as discourteous) to grant a prerogative order against the central government which invariably respects non-coercive declarations made by the court: dicta in *R* v *Secretary of State for Employment, ex parte Equal Opportunities Commission* [1994] 1 All ER 910 (HL).

e) *User-friendly terminology*

The Law Commission in its 1994 Report (No 226) has recommended that the Latin names of the prerogative orders should be changed to make them more 'user-friendly': certiorari would become a 'quashing order'; prohibition would become a 'prohibiting order'; and mandamus would become a 'mandatory order'. The Commission recommends that each order should be available in interim as well as final form.

f) *Damages in public law*

The main problem is that this remedy can be granted only if damages would have been available in a private law action if such an action had been brought successfully in respect of the matter in question, ie the public law decision being challenged must have involved the commission of a private wrong (a tort) in order to give rise to the award of damages. (Breaches of contract are dealt with in private law but, exceptionally, unfair dismissal of a public office holder may be dealt with under O.53 and compensation for the breach may therefore be awarded if the dismissal was ultra vires.)

Ordinary torts will be dealt with in private law so that, for example, where a person has been unlawfully detained as a result of an ultra vires decision the appropriate remedy is the issue of a private law writ for damages for the tort of false imprisonment (release from ultra vires detention is secured by habeas corpus under O.54). It appears that there are only three torts which may be directly involved in ultra vires decision-making and which may be relevant under an O.53 review, namely, negligence, breach of statutory duty and the tort of misfeasance in a public office: see chapter 7, section 7.2 above.

g) *Injunctions in public law*

Here the main problem has been whether injunctions can be granted against ministers of the Crown. Under s21 Crown Proceedings Act 1947 compulsory orders in the form of injunctions and other coercive relief are declared unavailable against the Crown, and this ban applies in all private law proceedings against the Crown: see chapter 4. At one time the ban was also held to apply to public law proceedings brought against ministers of the Crown, but it is now established that such rulings were based on failure to take account of the relationship of s21 Crown Proceedings Act 1947, with the subsequent enactment of the judicial review process under s31 Supreme Court Act 1981. This means that, at least in principle, injunctions and other coercive relief (eg a committal for contempt of court) may be granted against ministers of the Crown in either their personal or official capacities: *M* v *Home Office* [1993] 3 All ER 537 (HL) especially per Lord Woolf. This decision is a landmark, not only for upholding the rule of law but also for ensuring a mechanism for the granting of interim relief in a judicial review application, since the injunction is the only remedy that may be granted in interim as well as final form. The need for interim relief is particularly important because of the general unavailability of damages under O.53 reviews. As an alternative to an interim injunction the court has discretion to order a stay of proceedings: *R* v *Secretary of State for Education and Science, ex parte Avon County Council* [1991] 1 All ER 282 (CA). However, a stay is more appropriate to a judicial decision, rather than an administrative one, and could work injustice by having the same effect as an interim injunction on a third party who was not before the review court. Accordingly, the Law Commission in its 1994 Report (No 226) has recommended that stays should only be available for the proceedings of courts and tribunals.

h) *Declarations in public law*

A declaration is a formal statement by a court pronouncing upon the existence or non-existence of a legal state of affairs. It is a non-coercive remedy. The declaration cannot be granted in interim form and this has been described as a 'serious procedural defect in the English system of administrative law': per Lord Diplock in *IRC* v *Rossminster Ltd* [1980] AC 952 at p1014. The Law Commission in its 1994 Report (No 226) recommends that interim declarations should be made available under O.53 reviews.

Declarations will not be granted on purely academic or hypothetical issues, but may be granted in advisory form to settle issues of important public policy or ones affecting future specific rights or duties. At one time the declaration could be granted only in lieu of one of the prerogative orders, but the recent growth in the practice of awarding advisory declarations has led to the development of the declaration as a free-standing remedy in public law, with a flexible and liberal test of locus standi. This development has been welcomed by academics and judges as an exciting one because the advisory declaration is regarded as a flexible and beneficial remedy: see, eg, *Royal College of Nursing of the United Kingdom* v *Department of Health and Social Security* [1981] AC 800; *Gillick* v *West Norfolk and Wisbech Area Health Authority* [1986] AC 112. An advisory declaration was also granted to contradict a minister's view that English law was compatible with European Union law on the matter of employment rights of part-time workers. Since his view had been contained in a letter to the Equal Opportunities Commission, rather than in a formal decision of any kind, a prerogative order would have been unavailable. Yet the advisory declaration, as a free-standing remedy, was granted because the matter was not purely academic or hypothetical: *R* v *Secretary of State for Employment, ex parte Equal Opportunities Commission* [1994] 1 All ER 910, discussed by Villiers and White (1995) 58 MLR 560 at pp566–568 especially. For a general account of the effect of advisory declarations see Laws (1994) 57 MLR 213 at pp213–219 especially. The Law Commission in its 1994 Report (No 226) has welcomed the emergence of the advisory declaration for cases of general public importance in O.53 reviews.

For remedies available in respect of partial invalidity see 2.2(g) above. The remedies are available in respect of judicial and administrative actions, as well as delegated legislation.

13.3 Recent case and articles

R v *Secretary of State for the Environment, ex parte Royal Society for the Protection of Birds* (1995) The Times 10 February (HL). In this case Lord Jauncey made some discouraging observations about the granting of declarations in interim form:

a) it could leave the executive facing administrative chaos by being unable to take a decision until the court finally declared the proper basis upon which it could be taken;

b) it would frustrate implementation of executive policy without the court being able to compel a cross-undertaking in damages from the party seeking the declaration (a cross-undertaking is available for other remedies); and

c) the interim declaration could not declare anything in terms of rights and obligations but would be designed as a way of neutralising the executive, ie it had the real purpose of serving as an interim injunction without having the safeguards for the defendant from abuse of such a serious compulsory order.

Algazy, 'Interim Relief Against the Crown' [1996] NLJ 591

Bamforth, 'Reform of Public Law: Pragmatism or Principle?' (1995) 58 MLR 722

Hare, 'The Law Commission and Judicial Review: Principle Versus Pragmatism' [1995] CLJ 268

13.4 Analysis of questions

First year constitutional law students should see chapter 15 for advice. For the administrative law student it can be said that usually the availability of particular remedies is required for discussion as part of a general piece of advice to a client in a problem-type question. Indeed, nearly every piece of advice will require specification of the likely remedy to be granted by the court. Traditionally the London LLB (External) examinations have treated the subject of remedies in that way. However, recent developments in the fields of injunctions and declarations, and the continuing controversy over the general unavailability of damages under O.53 reviews, may lead to questions being set in essay form, requiring a critical analysis of the scope and potential of individual remedies, and other syllabuses, eg Wolverhampton LLB, have begun to include such questions in their examination papers.

13.5 Questions

Students are referred to discussions of availability of particular remedies in questions covered in chapters 8 to 12 inclusive, and in chapters 15, 16 and 17.

14 The Parliamentary Commissioner for Administration

14.1 Introduction

The concept of an 'ombudsman' originated in Sweden. It is a Scandinavian word for officer or commissioner. The concept has been adapted by other countries, including the United Kingdom, as a further method of control over the exercise of administrative powers. In the United Kingdom the traditional methods of control through Parliament and the courts proved to have serious limitations in uncovering abuses of power. The Crichel Down Scandal (1953) Cm 9176, discussed by Griffith (1955) 18 MLR 557, was probably the starting point of the serious campaign for the introduction of an ombudsman into the British parliamentary system. Members of Parliament were generally unenthusiastic about such reform since it appeared to undermine their rôles as redresssers of constituents' grievances and eventually a compromise reform was adopted in 1967.

The Parliamentary Commissioner Act 1967 created the office of Parliamentary Commissioner for Administration (PCA). The office is conceptually different from that of the Swedish ombudsman, who may be contacted directly by Swedish citizens and who can investigate all manner of administrative errors which cause injustice, with power to order remedies to enforce his findings. The United Kingdom concept is designed to fit within the peculiar constitutional doctrines of parliamentary sovereignty and ministerial responsibility to Parliament. The PCA was designed to become a powerful weapon 'with a sharp cutting edge' at the disposal of MPs to investigate administrative errors. A select committee of MPs was established to help and advise the PCA.

The PCA has proven to be a valuable adjunct to administrative law because he involves no cost to applicants and is more informal than the courts, with facilities for investigation and access to evidence not available to litigants. He supplements the work of the Council on Tribunals (of which he is an ex officio member), and is more powerful and influential than that body. Further, the PCA strengthens rather than undermines the role of MPs by acting as their servant in uncovering administrative errors. A former holder of the office, Sir Cecil Clothier, thought that the device had transplanted well into the United Kingdom's constitutional arrangements: [1986] PL 204 at p209. Other ombudsmen have been created in other fields as the popularity of the device became evident, eg for local government (under the Local Government Act 1974) and for the National Health Service (currently the PCA also holds the office of Health Service Commissioner: Health Service Commissioners Acts 1993 and 1996). Even private institutions have voluntarily established ombudsmen, eg insurance and banking. A Legal Services Ombudsman (to deal with complaints about solicitors and barristers) was created by the Courts and Legal Services Act 1990. There are also compulsory ombudsmen schemes for building societies, conveyancing practitioners and the pensions industry. An Ombudsman for prisoners has also been appointed.

14.2 Key points

a) *Jurisdiction of PCA*

Section 5(1) Parliamentary Commissioner Act 1967 provides that in order to be eligible for investigation by the PCA complaints must be directed against actions taken 'in the exercise of administrative functions'. Complaints about the making of primary or delegated legislation are therefore outside his jurisdiction, though the PCA is prepared to look at the *effects* in terms of administering statutory instruments and other statutory orders.

Schedule 2 to the 1967 Act (as amended) sets out the list of government departments and other public bodies which fall within his jurisdiction. The original list has been extended by the Parliamentary and Health Service Commissioners Act 1987 to cover about 50 non-departmental public bodies ('quangos'), such as the Welsh Development Agency, the British Library, the Equal Opportunities Commission, the Commission for Racial Equality and Industrial Training Boards. All executive agencies set up by the government under the 'Next Step' programme of civil service reform since 1988 are also brought within the PCA's jurisdiction. The Parliamentary Commissioner Act 1994 expanded his jurisdiction to cover, inter alia, the work of administrative staff at tribunals, as well as the general work of social security, disability and medical tribunals and the controversial Child Support Agency Appeal Tribunal. Jurisdiction was also extended to cover the new regulatory offices for water and the National Lottery. The PCA has also become the arbiter of government refusals to divulge information to the public under the government code on the the release of official papers. The present holder of the office of PCA, Mr William Kennedy-Reid, has criticised the need for primary legislation to extend his jurisdiction each time a new regulatory body appears: [1993] PL 221.

Schedule 3 to the 1967 Act declares various activities of government to be outside the PCA's jurisdiction: foreign affairs, extradition, crime, passports, the prerogative of mercy, the granting of honours, legal proceedings generally, and any matter on which the citizen has a remedy in the courts which it is reasonable to take. Two controversial areas of exclusion under Schedule 3 are in paragraphs 9 and 10, namely, the contractual and commercial undertakings of the Crown generally (para 9), and personnel matters arising within the civil service, armed forces or for other Crown appointments (para 10).

The other main limitation on the jurisdiction of the PCA is set by s12(3) of the 1967 Act, which provides that 'nothing in this Act authorises or requires the Commissioner to question the merits of a decision taken without maladministration by a government department ... in the exercise of a discretion vested in that department'. The effect is to confine the investigations of the PCA to cases of 'maladministration', which, though not specifically defined by the Act, is a concept based on the manner in which a decision was taken rather than on the policy behind the decision. Note the 'Crossman Catalogue' of examples of maladministration made by Richard Crossman in the House of Commons during the second reading of the Bill which passed into the 1967 Act: 'bias, neglect, inattention, delay, incompetence, ineptitude, perversity, turpitude, arbitrariness, and so on'. However, in 1968 the PCA was encouraged by the Commons Select Committee to treat a 'thoroughly bad decision' as the product of maladministration by inferring from the quality of the decision that there must have been an element of maladministration in the taking of it: 'the doctrine of constructive maladministration'. Also, again in 1968, the PCA agreed with the Select Committee to comment adversely on a 'bad rule' which was causing injustice without maladministration. He would then inquire as to whether the relevant Department had taken any action to review the rule and, if not, he would again comment adversely, but leaving it to the Department whether to maintain such a rule. Such approaches helped to overcome the jurisdictional barrier set up by s12(3), though too much adventurism on the part of the PCA has occasionally met with defeat, eg the Court Line Affair (1975) when Mr Tony Benn, Secretary of State for Trade, robustly rejected findings of maladministration by criticising the PCA for infringing s12(3). Mr Benn argued strongly that the merits of decisions were for Parliament, not the PCA. He subsequently won a vote of confidence on his handling of the Court Line Affair.

b) *Access to the PCA: the filter system*

A citizen is required to complain via an MP to the PCA. This MP filter is designed firstly to retain the role of the MP as the redresser of grievances, and secondly to ensure that the PCA is not flooded with trivial or vexatious complaints, or ones that fall outside his jurisdiction. However, it has been argued that the filter system deters complainants and inhibits the investigation of public grievances. Successive holders of the office of PCA have urged Parliament to give them the power to initiate their own investigations and to receive complaints direct from members of the public.

c) *Powers of the PCA*

Following receipt of a complaint it is for the discretion of the PCA alone whether to begin an investigation, to continue or discontinue it: *Re Fletcher's Application* [1970] 2 All ER 527. During an investigation he has a right of access to government departmental files and the records of other public bodies within his jurisdiction. He may examine civil servants and ministers (in private). A refusal to give evidence to the PCA may be referred by the PCA to the High Court where it can be punished as a contempt. If the PCA finds evidence of maladministration he must make a report to that effect, sending a copy to the Select Committee and a copy to the MP who referred the complaint to him. The Select Committee may refer the report to the whole House if it thinks fit. The PCA has no power to enforce his findings, though it is rare for a central government department to reject his recommendations totally. Sometimes the minister has publicly disagreed with the findings of maladministration but nevertheless accepted the report and paid compensation, eg in the Sachsenhausen Affair (1969) and in the Barlow-Clowes Affair (1989). Unless an ex gratia payment is made the citizen will be without remedy because no damages are payable for maladministration in the courts of England and Wales: *R* v *Knowsley Metropolitan Borough Council, ex parte Maguire* (1992) The Times 26 June (QBD). In Northern Ireland a person may use a report by the Northern Ireland Local Commissioner as a basis for a civil action if the local authority fails to comply with the Commissioner's recommendations. It has been argued that this right should be extended to England and Wales, or that enforcement powers should be given to the PCA. One former holder of the office of PCA, Sir Cecil Clothier, disagrees: 'The threat of a report to both Houses of Parliament in a case of unremedied injustice is as good an enforcing power as any reasonable Ombudsman could wish for': [1986] PL at 210.

d) *Controls over the PCA*

The PCA, like any other public institution, is subject to judicial review if he exceeds his jurisdiction: *R* v *Parliamentary Commissioner for Administration, ex parte Dyer* [1994] 1 All ER 375 (QBD). He is also subject to the political control of Parliament, though his relationship with the Commons Select Committee is one of partnership rather than master and servant. By s1 of the 1967 Act he is appointed by the Queen on the advice of the Prime Minister and holds office until the age of 65. His salary is charged on the Consolidated Fund and he may be removed from office only on an Address from both Houses of Parliament.

14.3 Recent articles

Bradley, 'The Parliamentary Ombudsman Again: a Positive Report' [1995] PL 345

Clothier, 'Fact Finding in Inquiries: the Commissioner's Perspective' [1996] PL 384

Woolf, Lord, 'Civil Justice is Important as Well' [1996] NLJ 1701 at 1702 (on the Ombudsman's relationship with the Courts)

14.4 Analysis of questions

For first year constitutional law students the topic of the parliamentary ombudsman would be relevant to general essay-type questions on calling government to account. For administrative law students it can be stated that the PCA is not directly examined by the Wolverhampton LLB syllabus, but is frequently examined by the London LLB (External) and other syllabuses. The emphasis is usually on an essay-type question requiring critical analysis of the effectiveness of the PCA in terms of jurisdiction, accessibility and powers. A useful research article is by Drewry and Harlow (1990) 53 MLR 745, examining the issue of whether the PCA as a powerful weapon with a sharp cutting edge was merely empty rhetoric. The PCA may be examined together with other ombudsmen under a general umbrella question, or with other remedies, such as tribunals.

14.5 Questions

QUESTION ONE

How important a role is played by ombudsmen in promoting good government? How might their role be reformed?

University of London LLB Examination
(for External Students) Administrative Law June 1993 Q5

General Comment

An answer to this question should be based on a thorough knowledge and understanding of the modern function of the ombudsmen. How does their role promote good government, as opposed to simply providing a grievance mechanism? Are the Ombudsmen effective in promoting good government? How could their role be made more effective in doing so?

Skeleton Solution

- History of the ombudsmen.
- Maladministration defined.
- Comparison with judicial alternatives.
- The Ombudsmen's methods.
- Suggested reforms.

Suggested Solution

Although the ombudsmen are often thought of as having a mainly remedial role, their role in promoting good government is one that should not be underestimated. They provide a vital intermediary between members of the public and administrative organisations in cases where redress through the courts is not appropriate. The ombudsmen's role is so defined as to give them broad powers of penetration into the workings of central and local government, and although there may be a need for some reform, their functions are peculiarly well suited to resolving the types of complaint that they deal with.

The history of the ombudsmen itself shows the importance with which their role is viewed. The first ombudsman to be established in England and Wales was the Parliamentary Commissioner for Administration, created by the Parliamentary Commissioner Act 1967, with jurisdiction to investigate complaints of maladministration in central government. It was realised very early on that the ombudsman was having a beneficial effect, as is shown by the creation within seven years of two further offices – the Health Service Commissioner, established by the National Health Service Reorganisation Act 1973, and the Local Commissioner for Administration, created by the Local Government Act 1974. Two decades on, these three Commissioners provide a well-established means of scrutiny into a broad range of governmental decision-making.

It has been mentioned that the role of each ombudsman is to investigate and report on complaints of *maladministration* within his particular jurisdiction. This term was originally conceived as including 'bias, neglect, inattention, delay, incompetence ... arbitrariness, and so on' (the Crossman Catalogue). In fact, 'maladministration' is a necessarily vague term which quite literally means 'bad government', so that it is clear from the very definition of the ombudsmen's role that it is linked to the promotion of good government. To some extent each ombudsman will himself be responsible for determining what 'bad government' means in any particular set of circumstances, so he has the broadest possible powers of penetration.

The task of investigating maladministration is particularly important when considered alongside the judicial alternatives. Maladministration provides a very broad avenue of complaint, as has been noted. The public law remedies by way of judicial review are comparatively narrowly defined and depend upon proof of some specific act of illegality, irrationality or procedural impropriety (cf *Council of Civil Service Unions* v *Minister for the Civil Service* (1985)). Similarly, the private law remedies that are available against public law bodies will typically depend upon specific breaches of more or less narrowly defined tortious or contractual duties. Pursuit of these remedies is time-consuming and costly. There is a definite need for a means of complaint and redress that covers those situations where the governmental organisation concerned has behaved badly but not unlawfully. Each ombudsman is in fact constrained by statute from investigating complaints where there is a remedy before a court or tribunal, but provides an important means of dealing with cases where such remedies do not exist, or where in all the circumstances it is unreasonable to expect the complainant to pursue them. Through his investigation of these types of complaint the ombudsman discourages bad or unfair behaviour on the part of the authorities concerned.

The ombudsmen's offices are well suited to the investigation of complaints of the type under consideration. They are able to probe to the heart of the inner workings of the administrative body complained against – something that is exceptionally difficult for the complainant to do even in cases before the courts where discovery of documents can be obtained. Each ombudsman carries out his investigation at no cost to the complainant, thus encouraging members of the public to report their complaints of maladministration, a factor which underlies the promotion of good government – this being in the interest of the entire community, not just of the individual. Furthermore, the ombudsmen are able to recommend the payment of compensation, and to make reports which are submitted to a Member of Parliament, or to a member of the local authority, as the case may be. In the case of the Parliamentary Commissioner, his authority is backed by his power to report to the Select Committee of the House of Commons, so that the parliamentary authority complained against simply cannot afford to ignore his recommendations. This increases the accountability of public authorities, an important aspect of the rule of law, and, in terms of promoting good government, as opposed to simply redressing individual complaints, the ombudsmen's mere presence is important, since the existence of a watchdog almost certainly encourages authorities to take greater care in their decision-making.

However, despite the importance and success of the ombudsmen in promoting good government, there are reforms which could be made to their role. Although it has been noted that the ombudsmen can recommend that compensation be paid in particular cases, they are unable to quash a decision or to compel the administration to perform its duties. Although it is true that these particular powers lie with the courts, and are the result of legal process, the ombudsmen's powers should perhaps include at least being able to compel an authority to reconsider its decision in cases where its maladministration has caused hardship of a kind that cannot be compensated for financially. Similarly, the ombudsmen have no powers of enforcement. In the case of the Parliamentary Commissioner this is perhaps less important since, as has been noted, he is backed by the Select Committee of the House of Commons. But in the case of the Local Commissioner it is specifically recommended by the JUSTICE – All Souls report 1988 ('Administrative Justice – Some Necessary Reforms' at p84) that his recommendations be enforceable through the courts, as is true of the Commissioner for Complaints in Northern Ireland. This recommendation is based on research that shows that in a number of cases the Local Commissioner's recommendations are simply ignored, or there is delay in responding to them. Clearly, such powers of enforcement would substantially increase the Local Commissioner's efficacy.

The Parliamentary Commissioner's jurisdiction is still subject to the rule that all complaints must be routed through a Member of Parliament; the Commissioner may not entertain complaints received directly. In practice this rule is circumvented because where the Commissioner does receive a complaint directly, he refers it to the Member of Parliament concerned, who then refers it back to the Commissioner. This is simply wasteful, and the rule should be abolished, as it no longer serves any useful function.

Subject to these suggested reforms, it can be seen that the Ombudsmen have a very important role to play in promoting good government. Indeed their jurisdiction is defined in the broadest way to enable them to tackle all aspects of governmental behaviour and thus to nurture administrative fairness.

QUESTION TWO

'The ombudsman system should not be seen as a cheap substitute for courts. Its role should be quite different.'

Discuss.

University of London LLB Examination
(for External Students) Administrative Law June 1992 Q4

General Comment

To answer this question requires a sound knowledge of the origins, development and modern status of the ombudsman within the English administration. It is important to compare and contrast the different roles and procedures of the ombudsman and the courts in the context of administrative law. How does the ombudsman's role compare with that of the courts? What are the differences? Are there similarities or areas of overlap? Why should the ombudsman not be a cheap substitute for the courts? How does the ombudsman function? What powers of redress does he have? Is the ombudsman a success?

Skeleton Solution

- Origins.
- Constraints.
- Manner of dealing with grievances.
- Type of complaints dealt with.
- Redress.
- Success.

Suggested Solution

The role of the ombudsman is to investigate and report on the complaints that members of the public have against the administration. There is some overlap in his function with that of the courts as both provide a mechanism for resolving disputes and grievances that arise out the dealings of the civil service and other public bodies. The reality is that, in many cases, the ombudsman is an effective and cheap alternative to litigation. But an alternative is not the same thing as a substitute; whilst the functions of the courts and the ombudsman may overlap, they are nonetheless distinct and there are clearly cases where one procedure should be used rather than the other.

The first ombudsman to be established in England and Wales was the Parliamentary Commissioner for Administration, created by the Parliamentary Commissioner Act 1967. His jurisdiction is confined to the investigation of complaints of maladministration in central government. A Local Commissioner for Administration was established by the Local Government Act 1974, to provide similar control over local authorities. Mention should also be made of the Health Service Commissioner, established by the National Health Service Reorganisation Act 1973. It may perhaps be observed that the creation of two further commissioners in the mid 1970s is a sign of the early success of the ombudsman and of confidence in his role.

That the ombudsman is not to be regarded as a mere cheap substitute for the courts is demonstrated by the provision that the ombudsman may not investigate complaints where there is a remedy before a court or tribunal. This constraint is contained within the statutory powers of all three commissioners although it is subject to the proviso that the commissioner may nonetheless investigate the complaint if he is satisfied that in the circumstances of a particular case it is not reasonable to expect the complainant to pursue such remedies. The existence of this escape clause means that the distinction in function between the ombudsman and the courts is blurred at the edges although reaffirmed by the main provision set out above.

There are important reasons why the ombudsman should be distinct from the courts. The first of these is a result of the manner in which the ombudsman functions. His success depends upon the informality of his investigative powers. When a court sits it must hear the evidence of both parties and the submissions of lawyers before it can make a determination based on rules of law applied to the facts. Where the administration is challenged the difficulty is often that all the evidence lies in the hands of the public authority. The ombudsman's role, on the other hand, is investigative. He is able to look at the whole matter in the round before reaching his own conclusion as to the merits of the complaint.

This blends into the second reason for the utility of a grievance mechanism that is distinct from the courts. There are many instances where a complaint or grievance about the behaviour of the administration is quite justified, but does not give rise to a remedy at law. It may be said that judicial review is only really effective in the clearest cases of unlawfulness, unreasonableness, and so on. The ombudsman is able to provide assistance in the cases where the administration has behaved badly, but not unlawfully. Thus the ombudsman's powers are defined under the various statutes as being the investigation of maladministration and not unlawful behaviour. Maladministration is a word covering a multitude of sins. It quite literally means bad administration and it was initially conceived as including 'bias, neglect, inattention, delay, incompetence … arbitrariness and so on' (the Crossman Catalogue). The truth is that it is a deliberately vague term, maximising the ombudsman's powers of penetration.

It can be seen then that the ombudsman does not act as a judge, and nor does he deal with law. But that does not make him a paper tiger. He is a skilled mediator between the administration and the citizen. Where maladministration is found to exist, he is able to recommend that compensation be paid, although he has no power to reverse a decision made by a public authority. Further, he is able to make reports which are submitted to a Member of Parliament or to a member of the local authority as the case might be. In the case of the Health Service Commissioner the reports are sent to the Secretary of State for Health. This in itself provides a means of increasing accountability for the actions of the administration. But the inability to quash a decision or compel the administration to perform their duties is an important distinction in his role compared with that of the court. Where the administration have made a decision unlawfully, it is important that such a decision is challenged in a forum where it may be set aside. A similar line of reasoning applies where an allegation is made that there has been some breach of statutory duty or even negligence giving rise to damages. In such cases there will be disputes of fact and law which only a court is qualified to decide; it would be contrary to principle to allow the ombudsman to be the determiner of disputes involving legal claims as opposed to administrative ones.

There is only one rule which might be thought to hinder the functions of the ombudsman, and that is the rule that now only exists in relation to the Parliamentary Commissioner; he may not accept a complaint sent to him directly by a citizen, all complaints must be routed through a Member of Parliament. This rule was clearly designed to act as a filter to dispose of inappropriate cases at an early stage. In reality this rule has no significant effect. Where complaints are submitted directly to the Parliamentary Commissioner, the rule is circumvented by the Commissioner bringing the complaint to the attention of the appropriate member, who then refers it back.

The ombudsman is an effective form of control over the activities of the administration. But this form of control is not in any sense judicial; it is a role involving mediation and negotiation. The ombudsman has a great deal of room for manouevre and is able to produce satisfactory compromise and balance between the conflicting requirements of bureaucracy and accountability to the public. Above all, whereas the courts are principally concerned with legality, the ombudsman's role nurtures administrative fairness. Thus the ombudsman is not a cheap substitute for the courts, but nor is he a poor relation; his role is a vital one within the provision of a high quality administration.

QUESTION THREE

Critically assess the system of ombudsmen in the United Kingdom. Illustrate your answer by reference to specific investigations.

University of London LLB Examination
(for External Students) Administrative Law June 1990 Q1

General Comment

A question calling for a discursive general overview of the operation of the various ombudsmen. Some background is required, but not a complete run through of the legislation. The matters emphasised are largely a matter of taste. The author here has chosen to relate most of the shortcomings of the systems to the enabling Acts. It is suggested that the lion's share of the answer be devoted to the Parliamentary Commissioner.

Skeleton Solution

- Brief background to Parliamentary Commissioner.
- Development of maladministration.
- Growth in jurisdiction.
- Examples of successes.
- Note existing problems.
- Brief notes on other ombudsmen, highlighting shortcomings.

Suggested Solution

The origins of the Parliamentary Commissioner for Administration ('the ombudsman') and his cousins, the Health Service Commissioner, the Local Commissioners, and the Northern Ireland Complaints Commissioner, can be traced back to the scandal surrounding the 'Crichel Down affair' in the 1950s and the Justice Report of 1961, calling upon the government to emulate the Scandinavian system of ombudsmen.

The Labour government of the 1960s responded by enacting the Parliamentary Commissioner Act 1967, under which the newly constituted ombudsman was empowered to investigate complaints against the administration. The other ombudsmen were created by legislation passed in the following seven years, to deal with complaints concerning local government and the provision of state health care. It is thus 30 years since the system was introduced, and it is now possible to look at the operation and achievements of the various ombudsmen to assess whether the institution has been a success.

The Parliamentary Commissioner

It is generally agreed that since 1967 that the Parliamentary Commissioner has established himself as a useful and respected watchdog over central government. It is submitted that this is in some respects in spite of, rather than because of, the enabling legislation passed by Parliament. The Parliamentary Commissioner Act 1967 ('the 1967 Act'), refers, in s5(1)(a), to the ombudsman having the power to investigate:

'... action taken by ... a government department ... in the exercise of administrative functions ..., in any case where ... a member of the public ... claims to have sustained injustice in consequence of maladministration in connection with the action so taken.'

What the 1967 Act does not go on to do is to provide a definition of what is meant by maladministration. This omission may have been a deliberate one on the part of Parliament, in that if a definition had been provided, the concept of maladministration might have become more limited. During the second reading, in the House of Commons, of the Bill which came to be passed as the 1967 Act, Richard Crossman suggested that the term maladministration might be taken to cover such matters as: 'bias, neglect, inattention, delay, incompetence, ineptitude, perversity, turpitude, arbitrariness, and so on ...'

This has become known as the 'Crossman Catalogue' and is now generally regarded as the authoritative definition of maladministration, at least to the extent that it is possible to arrive at such a thing. The ombudsman is further hampered by s12(3) of the 1967 Act which provides that:

'... nothing in this Act authorises ... the Commissioner to question the merits of a decision taken without maladministration ...'

The House of Commons Select Committee which shadows the work of the ombudsman was quick to correct the first incumbent, Sir Edmund Compton, who had expressed his view that the effect of the subsection was that it prevented him from investigating unfair decisions where the procedure leading up to the decision had been unimpeachable. It is to their credit that subsequent holders of the office appear to have adopted a much more robust view as to the concept of maladministration.

There is no doubt that the ombudsman has carried out a number of successful investigations which have attracted considerable publicity. The value of these investigations in keeping government departments 'on their toes' is probably considerable.

Notable achievements include the investigation of the Department of Trade and Industry's licensing of the failed financial group Barlow Clowes. Sir Cecil Clothier investigated the delay on the part of the Home Office in reviewing the safety of convictions of prisoners that had been obtained on the basis of forensic evidence supplied by the subsequently discredited Home Office scientist Dr Alan Clift, an investigation which led to over 1,500 convictions being re-examined, and compensation being paid to those wrongly convicted. There have been many other investigations into more mundane matters which have nevertheless been significant for the individual citizens involved, and may also have led to a general improvement in administrative practices. For example, investigations into the giving of incorrect advice on tax liability by the Customs and Excise, errors by the Passport Office which enabled a complainant's divorced wife to take their child out of the country, and the incorrect classification of prisoners of war which led to their being denied war pensions.

The strength of the ombudsman's role has been evidenced by the decision to extend his jurisdiction. In 1987, by the Parliamentary and Health Service Commissioners Act 1987, he became empowered to investigate complaints concerning 'quangos'. Criticisms can still be made of the ombudsman's role, however. He cannot investigate matters on his own initiative. He is prohibited from investigating the actions of certain bodies, such as those under the control of the Charity Commissioners, the nationalised industries, and professional bodies. Bodies such as the Criminal Injuries Compensation Board and the Civil Aviation Authority are excluded from his jurisdiction on the basis that they are, in reality, tribunals. Similarly, the Boundary Commission and the Monopolies and Mergers Commission are excluded on the basis that they perform purely advisory roles.

It has to be concluded, however, that in respect of those areas of government falling within his jurisdiction the ombudsman can provide a far quicker and more cost effective way of extracting compensation, albeit on an ex gratia basis, from a government department than can ever be achieved by the courts.

The Health Service Commissioners

The health service ombudsman can investigate complaints concerning the failure by a health authority to provide services. Any criticisms of his functions would have to be directed at the authors of the enabling legislation, rather than the individuals who have occupied the post.

He cannot, for example, investigate complaints concerning individual general practitioners. The Annual Reports of the Health Service Commissioner reveal some of his achievements. He has dealt with allegations of maladministration arising from the closure of surgeries, the inadequate provision of pharmaceutical services, wrong information being given to the families of patients resulting in their suffering unnecessary distress, and improper disclosure of medical records.

The House of Commons Select Committee has also helped support the health service ombudsman by requiring the attendance before it of practitioners who have not cooperated with his investigations.

The Local Commissioners, and the Northern Ireland Complaints Commissioners

The greatest weakness of the system of Local Commissioners in England and Wales is that they have no means of enforcing their findings of maladministration. Reports indicate that there are some 10 per cent of cases where local authorities reject his findings and leave the complainant without any redress. This is to be compared with the Northern Ireland system where the courts can be called upon to give effect to the Local Commissioner's recommendations. Once again the criticisms levelled at the Local Commissioners concerning their ineffectiveness would be better directed to those responsible for the enabling legislation which left them without the power to intervene in certain aspects of local government.

15 Advice for LLB Constitutional Law Students on Judicial Review of Administrative Action

15.1 Introduction

Judicial review of administrative action is a vast and complex topic that can only be dealt with superficially when studied as part of a typical first year constitutional and administrative law syllabus. Students will therefore only be expected to know the general principles of judicial review and one or two cases to cite as illustrations of these principles. Students must know the procedure for seeking judicial review – the public law/ private law divide, the exclusion of judicial review and the grounds upon which administrative action may be challenged – the doctrine of ultra vires and the requirements of natural justice.

15.2 Key points

The most likely examination question is a problem-solving exercise in which students are asked to advise three or four separate applicants as to whether he/she can complain by way of judicial review about a particular administrative action. Such a question should be approached by asking and answering the following four questions for each individual applicant:

a) *Is the decision being complained about a public law matter, ie is it susceptible to complaint by way of judicial review as opposed to the ordinary appeal procedure?*

You must understand and be able to apply what has become known as the public/private law divide: *O'Reilly* v *Mackman* [1983] AC 237.

The test for deciding whether it is a public law matter is not exclusively from where does the source of power derive but predominantly whether the decision affects sufficient members of the public generally so as to be properly described as being a 'public law' matter: *R* v *Panel on Take-overs and Mergers, ex parte Datafin* [1987] 1 All ER 564.

Look, in particular, for the following situations:

i) A body exercising statutory authority which only affects private rights (eg a prison hospital giving negligent treatment to an inmate) – this affects no-one else other than the individual inmate and therefore would not be a public law matter.

ii) A body exercising non-statutory authority which affects the public generally (as in the *Datafin* case) – this would be a public law matter. Note however that the courts have rejected any attempts to use *Datafin* as the basis for allowing domestic bodies such as sporting clubs to be challenged by way of judicial review.

b) *Assuming it is a public law matter, is the applicant barred from bringing judicial review proceedings because:*

i) He lacks 'sufficient interest': *IRC* v *National Federation of Self-Employed and Small Businesses* [1982] AC 617.

Note here that as regards complaints of breach of natural justice at least 'legitimate expectation' will be sufficient to allow a person to bring judicial review proceedings: *R* v *Deputy Governor of Parkhurst Prison, ex parte Leech* [1988] AC 533.

or

ii) He has delayed: note here the three month rule in O.53.

or

iii) The error is not a jurisdictional error: *Anisminic Ltd* v *Foreign Compensation Commission* [1969] 2 AC 147; *Re Racal Communications Ltd* [1980] 2 All ER 634.

For example in:

Pearlman v *Keepers and Governors of Harrow School* [1979] QB 56

Was the installation of central heating a 'structural alteration' so as to entitle a reduction in rates? The judge decided (wrongly on the facts) that it was not a structural alteration. But that was a mistake that he was given power to make – it was not a mistake that was outside his powers so as to be deemed an ultra vires decision which was subject to judicial review as opposed to the ordinary appeal procedure.

or

iv) There is an ouster clause.

Note distinction between:

- a complete ouster – the decision shall not be called into question at all

  'A decision which is a nullity is not a decision at all': *Anisminic Ltd* v *Foreign Compensation Commission* [1969] 2 AC 147.

and

- a time limit clause

  'After six weeks the decision shall be final': *R* v *Secretary of State for Environment, ex parte Ostler* [1977] QB 122.

c) *Assuming it is a public law matter and the applicant is not barred, what are the grounds of complaint?*

You must know the three grounds of attack laid down by Lord Diplock in the GCHQ case (*Council for Civil Service Unions* v *Minister for the Civil Service* [1984] 3 All ER 935) and what type of wrong comes within each ground. These give an excellent structure for examining what complaint or complaints each individual may make. Lord Diplock's three grounds of attack were:

i) Illegality

ii) Irrationality

iii) Procedural impropriety

i) Illegality: examples include:

- No reasons: *Padfield* v *Minister of Agriculture* [1968] AC 997.
- No evidence: *Coleen Properties* v *MHLG* [1971] 1 All ER 1049.
- Irrelevant considerations: *Roberts* v *Hopwood* [1925] AC 578.
- Ulterior or wrong purpose: *Congreve* v *Home Office* [1976] QB 629.
- Fixed policy: *British Oxygen Co Ltd* v *Minister of Technology* [1971] AC 610.

ii) Irrationality

You must understand what is meant by '*Wednesbury* unreasonableness', in particular how the courts will apply the concept of reasonableness to the following administrative actions:

- Formulation of test: *R* v *Ministry of Defence, ex parte Smith* [1996] 1 All ER 257 (CA).
- Bye-laws: *Kruse* v *Johnson* [1898] 2 QB 91.
- The exercise of power given by statute/regulation: *Associated Provincial Picture Houses Ltd* v *Wednesbury Corporation* [1948] 1 KB 223.
- The power (ie regulation) itself: *R* v *Secretary of State for the Environment, ex parte Nottinghamshire County Council* [1986] AC 240.

iii) Procedural impropriety

- Failing to comply with procedural requirements

  Note practical distinction between mandatory and directory requirements.

  Look for consultation, notice, advertising requirements in the statute/regulation.

- Breach of the rules of natural justice (or fairness)

  Note the two limbs of natural justice ie:

  1) A fair hearing

     The extent of the hearing depends upon what is at stake, ie if the decision means loss of livelihood then something near a full court hearing with the right to a personal hearing and to cross-examine witnessess would be required. On the other hand, if all that is being sought is a privilege then the duty may be only to allow written representations to be made: *Ridge* v *Baldwin* [1964] AC 40. Note the development of the doctrine of legitimate expectation on this point: *R* v *Devon County Council, ex parte Baker* [1995] 1 All ER 73.

  2) By an unbiased tribunal

     The test is whether there is a real danger of bias: *R* v *Gough* [1993] AC 646 (HL). The test applies to judicial *and* administrative decisons: *R* v *Secretary of State for the Environment, ex parte Kirkstall Valley Campaign Ltd* [1996] 3 All ER 304.

     Note that the principle has widened out to be one of a duty to act fairly – the arrival at a decision may be unfair because reasons are not given or legal representation has been refused. Note also the effect of a failure to give reasons for decisions in particular contexts: *R* v *Secretary of State for the Home Department, ex parte Doody* [1993] 2 All ER 92.

d) *Assuming one or more of the grounds of complaint are satisfied what are the possible remedies?*

You should know the basic procedure for obtaining remedies as laid down in RSC O.53.

You must, for each person you are advising in a problem question, state what remedy or remedies he/she might be entitled to.

i) Note discretionary nature of remedies.

ii) Public law remedies

- certiorari
- prohibition
- mandamus

iii) Private law remedies

- damages
- injunction
- declaration

15.3 Analysis of questions

It is most likely that the examination question on this area will be a problem-solving exercise requiring the candidate to show an understanding of the basic grounds upon which an administrative act may be attacked by judicial review. Accordingly the key points section (15.2) deals with the important principles and cases within a problem solving structure. Occasionally, an essay-type question is set; this usually requires the candidate to show an understanding of the role of the High Court when exercising its judicial review jurisdiction, ie to check not the quality of the decision but merely the quality of the decision making process. Examples of both types of possible examination questions are in section 15.4.

15.4 Questions

QUESTION ONE

The (fictitious) University Complaints Commission was set up under the Education Act 1994 to receive and investigate complaints from students on 'academic matters'. In May 1994, Jane, a final-year student reading History at the New World University, was accused of removing legal articles from the library, contrary to university regulations. Following internal disciplinary proceedings, at which Jane was not represented, Jane was expelled from the University.

Jane complained to the UCC requesting an investigation. The Commission wrote to Jane stating that it did not have jurisdiction to investigate her complaint, as her expulsion from the University related to a disciplinary rather than academic matter.

Jane wishes to apply for judicial review of the decision of the University to expel her and the decision of the University Complaints Commission.

Advise her.

University of London LLB Examination
(for External Students) Constitutional Law June 1994 Q6

General Comment

A reasonably straightforward problem question on judicial review. Such difficulty as there is lies in separating Jane's two possible challenges although there is a considerable overlap between the two. As ever, it is important in the answer to make it clear that Jane is actually being advised; do not, therefore, treat the question as a general essay. Structurally, the approach taken here is, it is submitted, appropriate for most problem questions on judicial review.

Skeleton Solution

- Public law or private law?
- Procedural matters: leave, delay and sufficient interest.
- Grounds for challenge: GCHQ (illegality, irrationality and procedural impropriety).
- Remedies.
- Relevant case law: *ex parte Aga Khan; ex parte Datafin; R* v *Lord President of the Privy Council, ex parte Page; ex parte Brind.*

Suggested Solution

Jane has a number of hurdles to cross before she can apply for judicial review of the decisions of the New World University (NWU) and the University Complaints Commission (UCC). In the first place, she will need to establish that, in respect of both, her claim lies in public, rather than private, law. Second, assuming this requirement is satisfied, she will need to ensure that she satisfies the various procedural requirements. She will then have to establish the grounds on which she may challenge the decisions; and, finally, she will need to consider what remedies she seeks. It is proposed to examine each of these in their turn.

With respect, first, to the NWU, it might seem that Jane's relationship to the University is primarily contractual. Jane would have to consider whether the NWU is established by Royal Charter, rather than statute, in which case her claim would normally arise in private law under contract. If the charter provided for the resolution of disputes by a Visitor, these would probably fall within the Visitor's exclusive jurisdiction. There is insufficient information given in the problem to be certain, but on the assumption that the NWU and its disciplinary powers find their source in statute then, as a public body discharging public functions, this could be enough to establish that Jane's claim arose in public law. With respect to the UCC, established under statute, it seems clear that, whether one adopts a 'source of power' (see, eg, *R* v *Disciplinary Committee of the Jockey Club, ex parte Aga Khan* (1993)) or functional test (see, eg, *R* v *Panel on Take-overs and Mergers, ex parte Datafin plc* (1987)), decisions of the UCC may be said to impact on the realm of public law. It would seem, therefore, that she may apply to challenge both decisions.

Jane must be advised of the importance of compliance with procedural requirements. Thus, Jane must act without delay, since a court can refuse to grant leave to apply for judicial review, or any relief sought, if there has been undue delay in making the application; the period is three months (Supreme Court Act 1981 s31(6); RSC O.53, r3(4)). There is no indication from the facts given that Jane falls outwith this period but, obviously, she must ensure she does not. Second, Jane must establish that she has locus standi to challenge either or both decisions since a 'court shall not grant leave to make ... an application [for judicial review] unless it considers that the applicant has a sufficient interest in the matter to which the application relates' (Supreme Court Act 1981 s31(3); RSC O.53, r3(7)).

Generally, whether the applicant does have sufficient interest is a matter of common sense – does the decision affect her? Some interests will be more sufficient than others – eg a financial interest in the decision taken, but no test is definitive, and it is always a matter of all the facts and circumstances. Here, it would seem that Jane clearly has the requisite sufficient interest. Finally, it is important to note that the court has a discretion whether to grant leave or not (Supreme Court Act 1981 s31(3); RSC O.53, r3(1)). Jane may yet fall foul of this requirement, though it would seem on the facts that her claim is not without merit.

The grounds on which a challenge to the decision of a public body may be made were conveniently laid down by Lord Diplock in the GCHQ case (*Council of Civil Service Unions* v *Minister for the Civil Service* (1985)): these are illegality, irrationality and procedural impropriety. It seems from the facts that Jane's grounds of challenge are different for the two bodies and it is thus necessary to consider them separately.

With respect to the decision of the NWU, there is a suggestion here of procedural impropriety, in the sense that Jane was not represented at the hearing of her case. Under the rules of natural justice, there is a right to a fair hearing (audi alteram partem). There is a variety of matters of which courts take account in deciding whether a hearing is fair, including adequate notice, oral hearings, a right to legal representation and the requirement of reasons. It always depends on all the facts and circumstances whether a hearing is fair. Given that we are told Jane was 'not represented' (which may mean either she was not actually present or, while present, she was denied legal representation), it would seem arguable that either constitutes a breach of the rules of natural justice. In *R* v *Lord President of the Privy Council, ex parte Page* (1993) the House of Lords held that, even in the case of a university established under charter, a Visitor's decisions could be challenged by way of judicial review for procedural impropriety.

It is also possible that a challenge might lie in the sense that the punishment imposed – expulsion – was disproportionate to the nature of the alleged offence. While it is unlikely following the decision of the House of Lords in *R* v *Secretary of State for the Home Department, ex parte Brind* (1991) that proportionality is a separate head of review, it is still arguable that the decision could be categorised as irrational in the sense of *Wednesbury* (*Associated Provincial Picture Houses Ltd* v *Wednesbury Corporation* (1948)) unreasonableness.

A challenge to the decision of the UCC refusing to investigate Jane's claim could lie on the grounds that in misinterpreting the phrase 'academic matters' in the Education Act 1994, the UCC has made an error of law in deciding that it does not have jurisdiction. In *Page*, the House of Lords explained that, where Parliament has conferred a decision-making function on a public body, this could only have been done 'on the basis that it was to be exercised on the correct legal basis: a misdirection in law in making the decision therefore rendered the decision ultra vires'. Whether or not Jane may succeed on this ground will depend on whether or not disciplinary matters fall within the meaning of 'academic matters' in the Act. It is impossible to say what a court might decide here, but Jane has at least an arguable case.

Finally, it remains to consider the remedies that might be available to Jane. The most appropriate remedies would be certiorari to quash the decision of the NWU expelling Jane. Certiorari would also seem to be the most appropriate remedy vis-à-vis the UCC, requiring it to reconsider Jane's complaint.

In conclusion, Jane may well be able to challenge the decisions of both the NWU and the UCC. Whether or not she will be successful in her challenge will depend on all the facts and circumstances of her case. We do not have sufficient information here to reach a definitive conclusion.

QUESTION TWO

'In making sense of the inconsistencies in the application of the rules of natural justice, it should never be forgotten that natural justice is not intended to be a precise and uniform code of procedure.' (de Smith).

Discuss.

University of London LLB Examination
(for External Students) Constitutional Law June 1992 Q9

General Comment

This question allows a review of natural justice authorities, with a fairly general discussion.

Skeleton Solution

- Definition.
- The development of natural justice.
- Duty to act fairly.
- Audi alteram partem.
- Nemo iudex in causa sua.
- Conclusion.

Suggested Solution

Natural justice is concerned with procedural impropriety. It is one of the principles of administrative law that certain powers must be exercised in accordance with natural justice. However, as with the curate's egg, it depends how you look at the problem with which you are dealing. There are too many variables to allow a precise and uniform code of procedure and this has led to inconsistencies in approach. Whether that is inevitable is another matter.

While natural justice has a long history, its modern development stems from the leading case of *Ridge* v *Baldwin* (1964) where the House of Lords applied the rules of natural justice to administrative functions, as well as judicial ones, the test being what was at stake for the individual whose rights were being affected by the decision. It is significant – in terms of this discussion – that Lord Reid made the point that the application of the rules varied, depending upon the nature of the dispute in question.

The emphasis upon an overriding principle of natural justice as opposed to a precise code is shown in the case of *Re HK (An Infant)* (1967). While the rules – discussed below – may be applied in certain situations, there is also a duty to act fairly. While this duty may be implied in subsequent judgments rather than expressed, it might explain inconsistent application of the rules.

The first of the rules is the right to a fair hearing: audi alteram partem. There are various aspects of this rule, so one might take two areas as examples. Firstly, a person has the right to notice of the case against them. For example, in *Glynn* v *Keele University* (1971), a student was fined for breaching university rules without being told why or being given a hearing. This was a breach of the rule, although for other reasons, no remedy was given – a reminder of the discretionary nature of remedies. Secondly, there is the right to make representations. This is a more difficult area, because the court may be dealing with a body that determines its own procedures or be in a situation where representations will be futile. For example, in *Cinnamond* v *British Airports Authority* (1980), car-hire drivers who had been flouting the law received little sympathy from the court. However, a reluctance to apply the rules of natural justice, rather than to apply them but find other reasons for denying a remedy – while it may amount to the same thing – weakens the principle.

The other rule of natural justice is that no man should be a judge in his own cause: nemo iudex in causa sua. The clearest statement of the dangers when someone sitting in judgment has an interest is in *Dimes* v *Grand Junction Canal Proprietors Ltd* (1852), where the Lord Chancellor's involvement as a shareholder and trustee in the canal company led to his decrees in the case being set aside. No allegation of partiality was made, but the existence of the interest was sufficient. This is a more straightforward breach for the courts to consider and allows the courts to be more consistent.

Another aspect of this rule – and a harder one for the courts – is the question of bias. In *R* v *Sussex Justices, ex parte McCarthy* (1924), Hewart LCJ said, 'Nothing is to be done which creates even a suspicion that there has been an improper interference with the course of justice'. The test has been seen in two ways: either that there is a reasonable suspicion of bias or that there is a real likelihood of bias. The reasonable suspicion test was easier to establish than the real likelihood test. The latter has now been preferred for all kinds of judicial decision-making and has been re-labelled 'the real danger of bias' test: *R* v *Gough* (1993). The test also extends to administrative decison-making: *R* v *Secretary of State for the Environment, ex parte Kirkstall Valley Campaign Ltd* (1996).

In conclusion, this brief survey of natural justice shows the difficulties that the courts face. The nature of the cases leads to an uneven application of the rules, but that is because concepts such as fairness and bias are harder to apply evenly. However, the principles are long-established and it is doubtful if they could ever be applied uniformly, given the diversity of the subject matter.

QUESTION THREE

The Highways and Byways Act 1990 (a fictitious Act) s12 provides that:

1) A local authority must protect and maintain existing public rights of way within its area.
2) Where the closure of a public right of way is necessary in the interests of promoting the efficiency of road traffic, a local authority may:
    a) close that right of way and redevelop the land as a road for motor traffic, provided that:
        i) public notice has been given in the local press for a period of not less than three months; and
        ii) all local residents have been informed by written notice, and have been given an opportunity to make representations.
3) The decision to close the right of way and redevelop the land must be made by the Planning Committee of the local authority.

In December 1990, the Kingshire County Council Planning Committee decided to exercise its power under the Act to provide routes for cyclists and motor-cyclists only. The Committee invited Mr Fitt, Secretary of the Blankshire Two Wheel Club, to attend the meeting and investigate and report on the matter. Mr Fitt recommended that the towpath alongside the

River Thames should be developed for this purpose, and further, that part of the adjacent recreation ground should be developed as a training and racing track for cyclists and motorcyclists.

In February Mr Fitt reported his findings to the Committee, but unfortunately, because of the bad weather conditions only the Chairman and Mr Fitt were present at the meeting. They agreed to the plan and the Chairman asked Mr Fitt to proceed.

Mr Fitt requested his secretary, Miss Able, to prepare the necessary notices for the press, and the mailing to local residents. Miss Able did this, but failed to write to several families who were living in the caravans at the side of the towpath. Mr and Mrs Jones, who live in a caravan, have heard of the plans and wish to challenge the legality of the Kingshire Council's action. Advise Mr and Mrs Jones.

University of London LLB Examination
(for External Students) Constitutional Law June 1991 Q6

General Comment

A detailed question requiring reference to several different grounds for review. It is suggested that the procedural matters be mentioned at the outset, and the possible grounds of review considered in turn. It is important to use case law to illustrate the points made.

Skeleton Solution

- Procedural matters.
- Abuse of power.
- Delegation.
- Bias.
- Failure to give press notice.
- Failure to notify residents.
- Inquorate meeting.
- Intermingling of functions.

Suggested Solution

Mr and Mrs Jones would be advised to seek judicial review of the local authority's decision to adopt the Fitt recommendations.

Under O.53 RSC they would be regarded as having sufficient interest in the matter to which the application relates, and thus should be regarded as having locus standi. They should ensure that they make their application without delay, and in any event within three months of the impugned decision. The following outlines the grounds upon which they could seek review of the decision, and request an order of certiorari which if granted would have the effect of quashing it.

a) The power under the Act is to close a right of way to develop the land for motor traffic. On this basis can the power be used to develop routes for two-wheeled traffic only? Even if it can, is it a reasonable decision to make? The discretion must be exercised with regard to the duty imposed upon the authority by s1 of the Act to protect and maintain existing rights of way. A general ground of challenge might be that the authority is failing to have regard to the aims and objects of the legislation under which it purports to act.

b) The planning committee delegated the function of investigating the feasibility of the cycle route scheme to Mr Fitt. Local authorities do have the power to delegate functions under s101 Local Government Act 1972, provided they reserve to themselves the right to exercise those functions if they so wish. The problem with appointing Mr Fitt to exercise this function is that he has a vested interest in the proposed routes being approved. It may be alleged that there is an appearance of bias. Given that the function in question is classified as administrative, the test to be applied, on the basis of *Steeples* v *Derbyshire County Council* (1985), would be to ask whether there the interest in the matter amounted to an unlawful fetter on the exercise of discretion by the local authority. If the answer were in the affirmative, the subsequent proceedings may have been vitiated. It had been thought that the additional test for bias was not appropriate for this kind of administrative decision-making but in *R* v *Secretary of State for the Environment, ex parte Kirkstall Valley Campaign Ltd* (1996) Sedley J, said that the unlawful fettering of discretion was a distinct and separate ground of review and should not be a substitute for a test of bias in this area. Accordingly he extended the 'real danger of bias' test laid down for judicial decisions (*R* v *Gough* (1993)) to administrative decisions. This would strengthen the challenge in the present case since Mr Fitt's involvement would appear to give rise to a real danger of bias.

c) The statute requires three months notice to be given in the local press. This seems not to have been complied with.

In *R* v *Swansea City Council, ex parte Quietlynn* (1983), the local authority was required to give notice in the local press of the introduction of a licensing scheme for sex shops. Notice had to be given at least 28 days before the scheme was to come into effect. Certiorari was granted to quash the scheme when the local authority conceded that the time limit had not been complied with. The time limits were regarded as mandatory, as they were designed to give users of premises the opportunity of avoiding the commission of a criminal offence by applying for a licence. Relief was granted even though no prejudice had been suffered by the applicants in that case.

It is submitted that the failure of Kingshire CC to comply with this requirement would of itself be sufficient to invalidate the whole process.

d) The statute requires local residents to be consulted. This requirement has not been fully complied with. A statutory requirement of consultation is normally regarded as mandatory. Failure to comply invalidates any subsequent decision making; see *Grunwick Processing Laboratories Ltd* v *ACAS* (1978). An exception will be made where the decision-making body has acted in good faith in trying to notify all those likely to be affected, and those not notified are unable to point to any prejudice suffered as a result of non-notification. In *Coney* v *Choyce* (1975), regulations required the posting of notices in the vicinity of schools which were to be re-organised under a policy of comprehensivisation. In the case of two schools, the requisite notices were not posted. It was held that the procedural requirement of giving notice had been substantially complied with, and there was no evidence of anyone suffering substantial prejudice as a result, hence the Secretary of State's action (in approving the scheme for reorganisation) was lawful.

The applicants in the present case have not been prejudiced by the failure to notify as they have heard of the decision anyway; thus normally the court might be minded to condone the authority's failure to comply with the requirement of notification. It should be remembered, however, that the authority has also failed to comply with the requirement of notice in the press, and in such circumstances the court may feel that there is not enough evidence that it was acting in good faith in trying to discharge its statutory duties.

e) The decision of the planning committee appears to have been taken by the chairman acting alone. There are a number of challenges that could be brought in respect of this procedure. First, it is likely to be a breach of the authority's standing orders to proceed without a quorum of members. The lowest figure for a quorum is normally three. Secondly, the facts state that the Chairman and Mr Fitt agreed to the plan. Mr Fitt is not, on the evidence given, a member of the committee, thus should not have taken any part in its processes. Thirdly, Mr Fitt's presence at the meeting may also give rise to an impression of bias. As the investigator and reporter he should not also be involved in the decision making process, notwithstanding that he may not even be a member of the committee; see *R* v *Barnsley Metropolitan Borough Council, ex parte Hook* (1976).

In conclusion it is submitted that there are several grounds upon which the applicants would succeed in persuading the court to quash the decision.

QUESTION FOUR

A University Law Faculty has 100 places for its LLB course but receives 2,000 applications. The Sub-Dean for Admissions asks her secretary to choose the 100 candidates with the best 'O' Level results. The secretary does this by looking at the application forms. The Sub-Dean then writes to the unsuccessful applicants saying that 'after the most careful consideration, we have reluctantly decided not to offer you a place. If you would like to discuss this with me, please arrange an appointment through my secretary.' All 1,900 disappointed applicants try to arrange appointments. The Sub-Dean writes again to withdraw her offer to meet applicants because of 'pressure of work'. She adds that 'applicants have no right to a hearing before or after a decision to refuse them admission.'

Have there been any breaches of the principles of administrative law?

University of London LLB Examination
(for External Students) Constitutional Law June 1988 Q7

General Comment

A question requiring consideration of four aspects of the ultra vires principle, the rule against delegation, irrational selection policy, estoppel, and natural justice. The rubric accompanying the question does not specifically invite discussion of whether the matters in question should be challenged by way of writ or an application for judicial review, so it is suggested that a discussion of the public/private dichotomy is not required here.

Skeleton Solution

- The rule against delegation.
- No abdication of power.
- Irrational basis for selection.
- Extent to which the University is bound by the unilateral undertaking.
- Whether any breaches of natural justice have occurred.

Suggested Solution

It is submitted that there are four grounds upon which the proceedings outlined in the above question might have involved a breach of the principles of English administrative law. Each will be considered in turn.

a) *The rule against delegation*

The rule against delegation, or the rule against sub-delegation as it should perhaps be described, operates to ensure that power is exercised by the body in whom it has been vested.

If, for example, a tribunal has been empowered under statute to determine claims for a benefit of some sort, and in the absence of any express power to do so it delegates this function to some other organisation, a violation of the ultra vires principle will occur, since a body which has not been properly empowered to act will in fact be taking the decisions. Prima facie the delegation of the task of selecting students, by the Sub-Dean for Admissions, to a secretary, would appear to be a violation of the rule against delegation, since it involves a sub-delegation of powers vested in the Sub-Dean by the University.

However, it could be contended that the facts under consideration do not involve delegation of a decision making function, but merely the use of an agent ie the secretary, by the Sub-Dean. Such an argument might meet with approval in the courts provided the ultimate decision making power still rests with the Sub-Dean, and also the responsibility for the decisions made; compare *Ellis* v *Dubowski* (1921) with *Mills* v *London County Council* (1925).

Generally, it is submitted that the key question is not whether the Sub-Dean can delegate tasks to her secretary, but whether this particular type of task can be delegated. The act of delegation itself might be more properly challenged on the ground of irrationality (considered below).

b) *Irrational basis of selection*

The decision of the Sub-Dean to select university entrants on the basis of their 'O' Level grades could be impugned upon the ground that it involves the over-rigid application of an irrational policy. Administrative agencies are permitted to exercise discretion according to policies, in order to achieve fairness and consistency, but this must not result in the exercise of discretion becoming 'straight-jacketed' by the policy, and the policy itself must be sound. The facts of the question suggest that the policy of referring to applicant's 'O' Level grades is being applied with considerable rigidity. This could be challenged on the basis that the university has 'shut its ears' to applicants who, despite poor 'O' Level grades, might have 'something new to say': *R* v *Port of London Authority, ex parte Kynoch Ltd* (1919). Against this, it has to be recognised that the Sub-Dean is dealing with a large number of applications, and in such circumstances the House of Lords has recognised that the adoption of a policy may be desirable, so that the administrative machinery can operate more efficiently: *British Oxygen Co Ltd* v *Minister of Technology* (1971). Perhaps a stronger ground of challenge is that the policy itself is unreasonable or irrational. A complainant would have to show that the basis of selection was one that no reasonable university admissions tutor would have adopted: *Associated Provincial Picture Houses Ltd* v *Wednesbury Corporation* (1948). Alternatively, the selection process could be described as 'irrational' in the sense outlined by Lord Diplock in *Council of Civil Service Unions* v *Minister for the Civil Service* (1985), wherein his Lordship spoke of a decision being challengeable because of its defiance of logic and moral standards, being one that no sensible person who had applied his mind to the matter in issue could have arrived at.

Given that most of those applying to university will not yet have their 'A' level grades, reference to 'O' level grades may be perfectly sensible, but it is perhaps irrational to ignore such matters as references from head teachers, and the work experience of mature applicants.

c) *Estoppel*

Can the Sub-Dean lawfully withdraw her offer to deal with enquiries from all the unsuccessful applicants? It might be contended that she is estopped from going back on her unilateral undertaking, see for example *Lever Finance Ltd* v *Westminster (City) London Borough Council* (1971). It should be borne in mind, however, that estoppel is 'a shield not a sword', and that any party wishing to raise the issue must show that they have acted in reliance upon the undertaking. It is submitted that a better approach would be to suggest that the undertaking of the Sub-Dean to deal with disappointed applicants gave rise to a legitimate expectation on their part that they would be given a hearing, and that the refusal of any such hearing amounts to a breach of natural justice: *Attorney-General of Hong Kong* v *Ng Yuen Shiu* (1983). In that decision the Privy Council held that where a public body makes a unilateral public statement as to the way in which it intends to act, those likely to be affected have a legitimate expectation that the undertaking will be observed, unless it would involve the public body in acting contrary to its public law powers and duties. In principle there is no reason why the sub-Dean should not be required to act according to her original undertaking, but it might be pointed out that a hearing would be unlikely to achieve any result for those applicants who have not been successful.

d) *Breach of natural justice*

Should all 2,000 applicants have been given a hearing? Natural justice does not require that an oral hearing should be given to every person whose interests are to be affected by a decision. Broad guidelines as to the treatment that should be given are provided by the decision in *McInnes* v *Onslow-Fane* (1978), wherein Megarry VC identified three types of case. First there is the 'forfeiture' case where the individual in respect of whom the decision is being made, stands to lose some existing right or privilege. Secondly, the 'legitimate expectation' case, where the individual expects to receive some benefit because of past conduct or treatment. Thirdly there are the cases concerning 'mere applicants' who, in the words of the Vice-Chancellor, do not have any right to heard as such, but who can expect their cases to be handled in good faith, without bias or caprice. It is submitted that the present question is concerned with this latter category. Applicants are entitled to be told of information unfavourable to their case: *R* v *Gaming Board for Great Britain, ex parte Benaim and Khaida* (1970).

The failure to interview all applicants does not, therefore, constitute a breach of natural justice, especially as the rejection of an application does not cast any particular slur on the reputation of the applicant, bearing in mind that there are other institutions of higher education to which the applicants can apply. This view is further supported by *Central Council for Education and Training in Social Work* v *Edwards* (1978), wherein it was held that an applicant for a place at a polytechnic does not have a right to an interview prior to any decision being made, but if an interview is granted it should be conducted in accordance with the rules of natural justice.

16 Advice for LLB Administrative Law Students on Judicial Review of Administrative Action

16.1 Introduction

This chapter contains a selection of problem-type questions raising points covered by chapters 8 to 13 inclusive.

16.2 Analysis of questions

These questions range over the whole field of judicial review of administrative action. They illustrate the need for students to be able to link the grounds for review to the procedures for obtaining review and the remedies which implement review. Administrative law should not be studied as if it were comprised of watertight compartments. The issues covered in chapters 8 to 13 inclusive may arise as aspects of a single problem, and it is important to be able to cope with them in giving a single piece of advice to the client in question. Some exam papers may make at least one such question compulsory,

16.3 Questions

QUESTION ONE

A market and funfair is held each month in Barchester. A limited number of licences is available for those who wish to set up stalls and sideshows. The licences are awarded by the Barchester District Council and each licence is valid for a year.

George applied for one of the licences. His application was photocopied and copies were distributed to the members of the licensing committee. By mistake the last few lines of one page of the application were cut off in the photocopying process and the members of the committee wrongly concluded that George did not have sufficient experience to meet the council's requirements. In any case the committee knew that George held many political views which were unpopular in Barchester. They therefore rejected his application.

Harold was awarded an annual licence in January. In April the council were informed that he was selling toys at his stall which did not meet approved safety standards and, without offering Harold an opportunity to explain, revoked his licence.

Advise George and Harold what remedies, if any, may be available and whether they would be entitled to compensation for any losses they have suffered.

University of London LLB Examination
(for External Students) Administrative Law June 1991 Q7

General Comment

Essentially a natural justice problem question, with additional elements relating to unreasonableness. Note that it is impossible to deal with the 'political views' point with any certainty since the examiner does not indicate the precise nature of the problem. As to remedies, it is worth pointing out that if the revocation of Harold's licence was ultra vires, he still has one, and can thus carry on trading.

Skeleton Solution

George

- *McInnes* v *Onslow-Fane* classification.
- Mere applicant.
- What is he entitled to?
- Livelihood case.
- Irrelevant considerations in referring to local politics.

Harold

- Clearly a forfeiture case.
- Whether a hearing required.
- Remedies by way of AJR.
- Harold could do nothing.
- Problem of damages.

Suggested Solution

George

George has been refused a licence. There would appear to be two errors in the procedure leading up to this decision. The committee did not have before it all the relevant evidence before arriving at its decision, and may have taken into account irrelevant factors in referring to his political views.

The local authority committee concerned is a public body exercising what are presumably statutory powers. In relation to the committee George may have few if any private law rights that could give rise to a private law cause of action, but he may have certain rights arising in public law. In short he will claim that the committee is at least under a duty to consider his application fairly, without abusing its powers. What is he entitled to expect in the way of natural justice? Some guidance may be provided by the judgment of Megarry VC in *McInnes* v *Onslow-Fane* (1978). In that case his Lordship identified a number of different situations, the application of natural justice varying according to the context. In particular he identified a class of litigant whom he referred to as the 'mere applicant'. This would be a case where the individual was seeking a right or privilege, not defending one. In such cases there was rarely any right to be heard, but only a right to an unbiased consideration of the application. The mere applicant may also have the right to be informed of matters unfavourable to his application: *R* v *Gaming Board for Great Britain, ex parte Benain and Khaida* (1970).

It is submitted that George would be regarded as coming within the 'mere applicant' category. As a result the licensing committee is under a duty to act fairly, but this does not mean that it should have granted him an oral hearing. Megarry VC suggests that in such cases the applicant can expect no more than that the body making the decision does so honestly, without bias and caprice. It should be noted that more may be required if the refusal of a licence could be interpreted as casting a slur on George's character, but that may not be the case here.

By not looking at all the evidence George can argue that the committee has not given a proper consideration to his case, this matter being of particular relevance given that his livelihood is at stake.

George should contend that by paying regard to his political views the council committee has taken into account an irrelevant consideration. George's political views are a 'pre-eminently extraneous consideration' (*R* v *Board of Education* (1910)). If the committee is attempting to show its support for or opposition to a particular view by way of its licensing decision then that would involve an abuse of power: *R* v *Ealing London Borough Council, ex parte Times Newspapers Ltd* (1986). Perhaps some thought needs to be given to the nature of George's political views and the nature of the people who live in Barchester. If, for example, George advocated extreme right wing policies in regard to race relations and immigration, and a large proportion of Barchester's inhabitants were of Asian or Afro-Caribbean extraction, the committee may feel that allowing him to operate a stall would be contrary to good race relations. The committee could then point to its statutory duty under s71 of the Race Relations Act 1976 to promote good race relations. In such circumstances its actions may not be unreasonable. On a more general level the committee may have acted reasonably in refusing a licence to George if it felt that to do so might result in public disorder.

Harold

Harold has been granted a licence which is then revoked without his being given any notice of the decision or any opportunity to make representation cases. Again, following the classification offered in *McInnes* (above), Harold's case could be regarded as falling within the 'forfeiture' category. In such cases Megarry VC thought that there was a right to an unbiased tribunal, notice of the charges, and the right to be heard. It should be noted again that the committee has monopoly control over an issue that relates to livelihood, thus emphasising the need for it to act fairly.

By not allowing him to answer the case against him, the committee has not adhered to what the common law would require in the way of a fair procedure. It is not being suggested that he should necessarily have been allowed to appear in person before the committee. In fact, an oral hearing is the exception, not the rule. In many cases an individual can put all necessary evidence before a decision making body in the form of written representations: see *Selvarajan* v *Race Relations Board* (1975).

A leading authority on this issue is the decision of the House of Lords in *Lloyd* v *McMahon* (1987). Lord Keith indicated that an oral hearing would clearly be essential in the interests of fairness where, for example, an informer wanted to place some personal knowledge of facts indicative of wilful misconduct on the part of another before a tribunal. Justice would demand that the accused be given an opportunity to depone to his own version of the facts. It is submitted that if there is likely to be a substantial dispute as to fact, thus necessitating cross-examination, it is better for the tribunal concerned to permit an oral hearing.

Even if an oral hearing is not granted, *R* v *Army Board of the Defence Council, ex parte Anderson* (1991), provides that the individual adversely affected by a decision should be given the opportunity to respond to a tribunal's finding of fact, when the proceedings could be classified as 'disciplinary'.

In short, it is submitted that the committee's failure to inform Harold of the 'case against him' could be fatal to the validity of its decision.

Remedies

In both cases the committee's decisions should be challenged by way of an application for judicial review. George could apply for an order of mandamus compelling the committee to exercise its discretion according to law. Note that it would still not have to decide in his favour. Harold has two options. The conventional advice would be to suggest he applies for an order of certiorari to quash the revocation of his licence, thus leaving him with the licence originally granted. Alternatively Harold could ignore the revocation, on the basis that it is clearly ultra vires, and carry on trading. In the event of his being prosecuted for unlicensed trading he could refer to the invalidity of the revocation by way of defence. It is submitted that to do so would not constitute an abuse of process: see *R* v *Oxford Crown Court, ex parte Smith* (1989).

As regards financial compensation, George and Harold would only be able to obtain damages by way of an application for judicial review, if they could show that damages could have been obtained by way of a private law action in respect of the same matter: see O.53, r7. Damages are not available simply because a public body has acted ultra vires: see *Dunlop* v *Woollahra Municipal Council* (1982). The only situations in which damages would be available, would be where George and Harold are able to point to a deliberate abuse of power on the part of the decision maker: *Three Rivers DC* v *Bank of England (No 3)* (1996), and, possibly, if the negligence was so extreme as to render the decision unreasonable in the *Wednesbury* sense see dicta of Lord Browne-Wilkinson in *X* v *Bedfordshire County Council* (1995).

QUESTION TWO

The (fictitious) Billet Act 1990 sets up regional Billet Boards with powers to require householders in certain circumstances to provide accommodation for members of the armed forces and emergency services. The Boards have power in respect of 'houses, flats and other premises appearing to the Board to be wholly or mainly used for domestic purposes'. The occupier may be required to accept persons housed by the Board 'if it appears to the Board that there is space which is not reasonably required for the accommodation of the occupier, his family or others residing permanently with him.' The Board may in exceptional circumstances grant an exemption and there is a right of appeal against a refusal of exemption; notice of this right must be granted to any person refused an exemption.

Advise Lucy and Mark in the following situations:

1) Lucy, a potter, had acquired a small warehouse. She used the ground floor as a workshop and showroom and had converted the upstairs as a small flat in which she lived. In the week before the inspector called to view the premises, she had a serious flood in the flat; she had to have the contents of the showroom put into storage and had furniture, bedding etc from the flat spread out to dry in the showroom. The inspector ordered her to provide accommodation for two ambulancemen.

2) Mark has a six-roomed house in which he lives with his wife and daughter; two rooms are kept for his invalid son who lives in a residential home but is able to spend some weekends

at home. The inspector decides that Mark should have to accept two soldiers and refuses him an exemption. The original leaflet sent to every home explaining the scheme had mentioned the right of appeal but Mark was given no information after he was refused exemption.

University of London LLB Examination
(for External Students) Administrative Law June 1991 Q8

General Comment

Deal with the two cases separately. Generally a relatively straightforward question requiring knowledge of the law relating to jurisdictional error, and mandatory procedural requirements.

Skeleton Solution

Lucy

- Jurisdictional error.
- Unreasonable decision on the facts.

Mark

- Not an unreasonable decision per se, but failure to comply with procedural requirements.
- Whether notice of appeal mandatory or directory.

Suggested Solution

Lucy

Lucy should challenge the decision of the board on two grounds. First that it did not have the jurisdiction to classify her property as it has done, and alternatively that it acted unreasonably in determining the amount of space available for personnel. An administrative body, such as a Billet Board referred to in the question, will have to make decisions on factual questions. These can arise in two ways. First there are facts which must exist objectively before it can act. Secondly there are the facts that it is specifically empowered to determine. An example will illustrate the point. In the case under consideration, the board will not have power to require Lucy to take in service personnel unless her premises constitute a house or flat wholly or mainly used for domestic purposes. If the premises under consideration come within this description, the board can then make a further finding of fact as to the number of personnel to be billeted. Normally decisions of inferior bodies on questions of fact are not reviewable because, whether they get the answer 'right' or 'wrong' they are merely deciding something that they have power to determine, ie they are acting intra vires. Such decisions will be unchallengeable, therefore, unless Parliament has provided for some appellate body to consider the question afresh.

Despite this, the decisions of tribunals on certain questions of fact must be open to the courts to challenge, otherwise inferior bodies such as the Billet Board would be able to determine their own jurisdiction simply by making decisions on fact that they were themselves satisfied with. Issues that have to be determined as preconditions to the exercise of power are frequently referred to as 'jurisdictional facts'.

The leading authority on the approach of the courts to such issues is *White and Collins* v

Minister of Health (1939). The Court of Appeal considered the power of a local authority to exercise compulsory purchase powers over land not forming 'part of any park, garden, or pleasure ground'. The court concluded that the question of whether an area of land did, or did not, comprise part of a park or pleasure ground was one of jurisdictional fact.

The local authority's decision on such a matter had to be open to challenge in the courts, otherwise the local authority would have been able to exercise its powers of compulsory purchase over any land it chose, simply by determining that it did not, in their view, comprise any part of a park etc: see further *R* v *Fulham, Hammersmith and Kensington Rent Tribunal, ex parte Zerek* (1951) wherein Lord Goddard CJ stated:

'... if a certain state of facts has to exist before an inferior tribunal have jurisdiction, they can inquire into the facts in order to decide whether or not they have jurisdiction, but cannot give themselves jurisdiction by a wrong decision upon them; and this court may, by means of proceedings for certiorari, inquire into the correctness of the decision.'

The essence of Lucy's first ground of challenge, therefore, will be that her premises are not '... wholly or mainly used for domestic purposes ...'

Even if she were to fail on this ground she could further argue that the decision to billet two ambulancemen at her premises was unreasonable given the size of her property. The leading authority is *Associated Provincial Picture Houses Ltd* v *Wednesbury Corporation* (1948). She could contend that, on the basis of the evidence relating to the size of her property, no reasonable tribunal would have come to the conclusion reached by the board in the present case. This is clearly not as strong a ground of challenge as that based on jurisdictional error since unreasonableness is a far more subjective concept. In pursuing this argument, however, she will be relying on the fact that the board failed to take into account that it was her work place, and did not have before it sufficient evidence that it could accommodate two extra persons.

Mark

It does not appear as though Mark will be able to challenge the decision of the board on any substantive grounds. The board was required to come to its decision with regard to whether persons were permanently residing with the occupier of premises. Mark's disabled son is clearly not a permanent resident in his house, although his use of it on 'some weekends' is a factor that the board should have taken into account. Mark would be advised to concentrate his challenge on a failure to comply with procedural requirements.

In failing to give Mark notice of his right to appeal against its decision the board may have failed to comply with a procedural requirement laid down by statute. Whether or not such a failure is fatal to the validity of the administrative action to which it is linked is dependent upon the context in which the procedural error occurs. Procedural requirements can be crudely classified into two types. First mandatory requirements; failure to observe these will normally render any subsequent action void. Secondly, directory requirements; failure to observe these will not normally render any subsequent action void. In *Howard* v *Boddington* (1877), Lord Penzance emphasised the importance of flexibility in approaching the mandatory/directory dichotomy when he stated:

'You cannot safely go further than that in each case you must look to the subject matter; consider the importance of the provision that has been disregarded and the relation of that provision to the general object intended to be secured by the Act.'

How will the courts regard a failure to notify of a right of appeal? In *London and Clydeside*

Estates Ltd v *Aberdeen District Council* (1980), the House of Lords held a certificate issued in connection with a compulsory purchase order to be invalid, for failing to inform the plaintiff of his right of appeal, such a requirement being regarded as mandatory. Note that some doubt was cast on the traditional analysis of this problem by Lord Hailsham LC's observation that breach of a mandatory requirement always rendered an administrative act void. His Lordship considered 'substantiality of prejudice' to be an important factor. Further, in *Agricultural, Horticultural and Forestry Industry Training Board* v *Kent* (1970), it was held that not only was the requirement of giving notice of the right to appeal mandatory but also, failure to give adequate details of how to appeal could result in invalidity.

Thus far, however, one would advise that Mark could challenge the board's decision on the basis that it has failed to comply with this mandatory requirement, but it should be remembered that the courts will look at his complaint to see if it has any substance. In short they may not be minded to interfere with the decision if the evidence is that it was simply a 'technical' failure on the part of the board which did not result in any substantial prejudice to Mark, ie he knew full well of his right of appeal anyway: see *Coney* v *Choyce* (1975).

QUESTION THREE

A new statute makes it a criminal offence 'to experiment on animals except under licence from the Animal Protection Establishment' (APE). Professor Anteater applies for a licence to observe the movement of ants in their natural habitat. APE refuses her request to be legally represented at the hearing. It also refuses to take account of Hansard which shows that the Minister in piloting the Bill through Parliament had said that, 'Of course, APE will interpret this sensitively, it is hardly going to claim that observing ants is experimenting on animals.' APE considers that Parliament has given it, not the Minister, the responsibility to interpret the Act. APE also refuses to consider an international treaty, ratified by the United Kingdom, the European Convention on Animal Rights (ECAR) which specifically states that 'ants, fleas and other minor animal life are not protected under this Convention'. APE refuses to grant Professor Anteater the licence. The Act states that, 'There shall be no appeal and any decision of the Animal Protection Establishment shall be final and conclusive.'

Advise Professor Anteater whether she could successfully seek judicial review.

University of London LLB Examination
(for External Students) Administrative Law June 1990 Q7

General Comment

A complex question raising many issues. It is unclear whether or not APE is a statutory body; hence the question of its reviewability needs to be discussed.

Skeleton Solution

- Whether APE a statutory body or otherwise amenable to review.
- Grounds for review.
- Irrationality.
- Procedural impropriety in refusal of legal representation.
- Whether convention need be considered.
- Effect of ouster clause.

Suggested Solution

The first issue that falls to be considered is that of whether or not an application for judicial review would be the correct procedure by which to challenge the determinations of the APE. If the APE is created by statute then there would seem little doubt that its actions in this context are amenable to challenge by way of review. Generally, bodies exercising statutory or prerogative powers would be regarded as being public bodies and thus amenable to judicial review: see *R* v *Electricity Commissioners, ex parte London Electricity Joint Committee Co (1920) Ltd* (1924), and *Council of Civil Service Unions* v *Minister for the Civil Service* (1985). The information given, however, does not expressly state this to be the case, thus the possibility exists that the APE is a non-governmental, self-governing body. Would it nevertheless still be amenable to judicial review? The answer would be in the affirmative, provided it can be classified as a public law body. The traditional method by which this question would be resolved would be to consider the source of its power. Increasingly, however, the courts have decided the question by reference to a body's functions. In *R* v *Panel on Take-overs and Mergers, ex parte Datafin plc* (1987), the Court of Appeal felt that regardless of the fact that, in the view of the Master of the Rolls, the panel had 'no visible means of legal support', the court was justified in intervening to examine the legality of its actions on the basis of the enormous de facto power that it exercised to make decisions affecting the interests of the public, or at least sections of the public. On this basis it is submitted that the decisions of APE would be challengeable by way of judicial review.

Assuming this first conclusion to be correct, the question of the grounds of the application needs to be considered.

a) *Irrationality and illegality: failure to take into account relevant considerations*

The professor could contend that by failing to consider the comments of the minister in piloting the Bill through Parliament, APE has failed to take into account a relevant consideration, namely the aims and objects of the legislation. No prohibition on the use of Hansard exists in regard to the exercise of discretion by administrative bodies. It is submitted that the view taken by the APE as to the extent of its jurisdiction is one that no reasonable body would have adopted, and hence it has acted ultra vires: *Associated Provincial Picture Houses Ltd* v *Wednesbury Corporation* (1948). The courts are reluctant in any event to allow any administrative body to become the sole judge of whether it has exercised its power properly, as landmark decisions such as *Secretary of State for Education and Science* v *Tameside Metropolitan Borough Council* (1977) indicate.

It should not be assumed from this that the courts will take any opportunity to intervene and invalidate administrative action. As Lord Brightman stated in *R* v *Hillingdon London Borough Council, ex parte Puhlhofer* (1986), the courts should only intervene where it becomes obvious that the public body, consciously or unconsciously, has acted perversely. It is submitted that the present is just such a case.

As regards the refusal of APE to have regard to an international convention, it should be remembered that the convention as such does not form part of English law.

In *R* v *Secretary of State for the Home Department, ex parte Brind* (1991), the House of Lords rejected the contention that the power of the Home Secretary, to issue directives prohibiting the broadcasting of any matter, had to be construed so as to ensure their compliance with the European Convention on Human Rights. This was seen as an attempt to introduce the Convention into English law by 'back door' means. It is submitted, therefore, that failure to advert to the convention, might not of itself be a successful ground of challenge.

b) *Procedural impropriety: refusal of legal representation*

The professor is unlikely to succeed with an application for review based solely on the ground that a breach of natural justice has occurred following the denial of her request for legal representation. Whether a fair hearing requires the granting of legal representation depends largely on the circumstances of each case. The APE presumably has a discretion to allow such representation and the key question is that of whether or not such discretion has been exercised properly: see *R* v *Secretary of State for the Home Department, ex parte Tarrant* (1984). Given that the professor is applying for a licence, rather than contesting the revocation of an existing one, it is submitted that the denial of representation is unlikely to amount to procedural impropriety: see further *McInnes* v *Onslow-Fane* (1978).

The provision that the decision of the APE should be final and conclusive is unlikely to prevent the courts from investigating the legality of the decision if they so wish. The House of Lords' decision in *Anisminic Ltd* v *Foreign Compensation Commission* (1969), casts a long shadow. Lord Diplock in the course of his speech in *O'Reilly* v *Mackman* (1983) referred to the effect of *Anisminic* as having been to:

'... virtually abolish the distinction between errors within jurisdiction that render voidable a decision that remained valid until quashed, and errors that went to jurisdiction and rendered a decision void ab initio ...'

Subsequent decisions such as *R* v *Registrar of Companies, ex parte Central Bank of India* (1986) indicate that some types of ouster clause may still be proof against the *Anisminic* doctrine.

Under s98(2) of the Companies Act 1948, a registrar's certificate of the registration of any charge was stated to be conclusive evidence that the requirements of the Act had been complied with. The Court of Appeal *held* that a 'conclusive evidence' clause of the type found in the 1948 legislation is unaffected by the *Anisminic* principle. As Wade and Forsyth comment (7th edn) at p740, this produces the paradox that the strongest form of ouster clause may fail to protect some ultra vires decision or act, whereas the weaker sort may succeed in doing so!

In conclusion it might be pointed out that as the work of the professor does not appear to require the granting of a licence she might just as easily ignore the decision of the APE and continue with her work. If she is prosecuted for carrying out unlicensed work, she can raise the lack of jurisdiction of APE by way of defence under the collateral proceedings exception to the general rule of *O'Reilly* v *Mackman*, above.

QUESTION FOUR

The (fictitious) Education Reform Act 1996 makes every state school an autonomous legal entity managed by its governors. Under s2, governors must provide 'an efficient, integrated and economic education' to their pupils. Section 2(1) requires governors to pay particular attention to equipping children with skills in maths and science. A circular from the central government's Department of Education suggests this requires schools to employ experienced teachers. Under s3, each school's basic running costs are met by central government; this sum enables schools to employ a mix of experienced and inexperienced teachers, although per s3(2) governors may spend it 'as they think fit'. Under s4, local authorities may make such payments 'as they consider reasonable' to any school in their area. The same circular suggests that councils should attach considerable weight when allocating this money to achieving 'the essential task of promoting maths education'.

In April 1997, the governors of Austin school, located in a marginal ward in Blankshire whose Conservative councillor has just died, announced an 'Arts First' policy. All the s3 budget previously allocated to employing maths teachers is to be spent on extra music and dance teachers. At the same time, Blankshire County Council, which is controlled by the Conservative party with a majority of one, announces that it will use s4 to pay 'whatever it takes' to maintain Austin's maths teaching at its previous level since Austin is to become the county's 'leading school'.

You are approached by Smith, Chair of Governors at Morris school in another part of Blankshire. Smith's school has found that it cannot attract experienced maths teachers unless it pays them enhanced salaries. It has asked Blankshire for a s4 grant for this purpose. Blankshire declines to make the grant, saying that experienced teachers are unnecessary. Smith alleges that Blankshire and Austin are trying to 'bribe the electorate' in the forthcoming Austin ward by-election to maintain Conservative control of the council.

Advise Smith as to:

a) the legality of the Blankshire's grant to Austin school, and of the Austin governors' 'Arts First' education policy;

b) whether Blankshire must provide Morris school with a sufficient s4 grant to enable it to attract experienced maths teachers.

University of London LLB Examination
(for External Students) Administrative Law June 1995 Q7

General Comment

This question concerns the lawfulness of the exercise of discretionary powers. The discretion granted to the governors and the council appears to be unlimited. Identify the limits that the courts have placed upon the exercise of discretion, and the circumstances in which its exercise will be unlawful. Some discussion of the effects of circulars and legitimate expectations is also required.

Skeleton Solution

a) • Apparently unlimited discretion.
   • The circular and legitimate expectations.
   • Proper and improper purposes.

b) • *Wednesbury* unreasonableness.
   • Legitimate expectations.

Suggested Solution

a) At first glance the Blankshire grant and the Austin governors' policy both appear to be perfectly lawful. The Act has conferred upon both what appears to be complete discretion in the allocation of their funding. Furthermore, Blankshire appears to have followed central

Government policy suggesting that they give weight to the promotion of maths education. It is well established that it is lawful to develop policies for the exercise of discretionary powers and it will be rare that following such policies will be unlawful: *British Oxygen Co Ltd* v *Minister of Technology* (1971). Despite the apparent lawfulness of their actions, however, there are grounds on which the court may find that the respective decisions are ultra vires.

Unlike Blankshire, Austin governors appear to have disregarded the policy advice given in the circular. It is implicit in their decision that they will no longer use their central Government grant to employ maths teachers at all, let alone experienced teachers. Such policy advice is not binding in law, but a person affected by the policy may have a legitimate expectation that the policy will be carried out: *R* v *Secretary of State for the Home Department, ex parte Khan* (1984). Such a legitimate expectation, if it existed, would give rise to a right to challenge the decision. It is unlikely, however, that Smith could be said to have a legitimate expectation that Austin governors would carry out the policy in the circular, as Smith does not have a direct interest in the matter.

Despite the apparent breadth of the discretion conferred upon Blankshire and the Austin governors, the exercise of their discretion will be subject to the control of the courts. In *Bromley London Borough Council* v *Greater London Council* (1983) it was held that even where the language of a statute appears to confer complete power upon an organisation, that power will be subject to some limitations. A limitation identified in that case was that the organisation must not use its power in a way that conflicts with the objects of the statute. Blankshire's decision would not appear to be in conflict with the purpose of the statute, but the policy adopted by Austin governors is in conflict with s2(1) of the Act which requires them to pay particular attention to education in maths and science. The 'Arts First' policy may therefore be unlawful on this basis. There may also be questions about the extent to which the policy infringes the general rubric of s2, namely that the governors must provide 'an efficient, integrated and economic education'. While the Act clearly requires them to promote maths and science above other subjects, it is arguable that to promote the arts above other subjects infringes the requirement of an integrated education.

Other cases have gone further than the negative statement in *Bromley London Borough Council* v *Greater London Council*. There is a line of authority which states that, where they are exercised, discretionary powers must be used positively to promote the policy and objects of the statute conferring them: *Padfield* v *Minister of Agriculture Fisheries and Food* (1968). Again, on the face of it, Blankshire are promoting the policy and objects of the Act inasmuch as they are making their funding available for maths education at Blankshire. But there is clearly a mixture of motives in the allocation of the grant. It is not one of the objects of the Act that Blankshire should promote Austin at the expense of the other schools by paying Austin 'whatever it takes' in order that Austin might become the county's 'leading school'. Clearly, this motive has materially influenced the decision to fund Austin, its presence will thus make the funding decision unlawful: *R* v *ILEA, ex parte Westminster City Council* (1986). If Blankshire and Austin governors are attempting to bribe the electorate that will be a fortiori an improper purpose which will make their respective decisions unlawful. The court is unlikely to make such a finding in the absence of strong evidence to support that allegation.

Both these decisions are, therefore, open to legal challenge. In Austin governors' case the decision would appear to contravene the policy and objects of the Act. Blankshire are attempting to use their powers to promote a policy that is clearly not contemplated by the Act. Both decisions are thus unlawful.

b) As stated above, Blankshire appears to have a complete discretion in the allocation of its grants. There is no duty to provide Morris school with a sufficient s4 grant to enable it to attract experienced maths teachers. As has been pointed out, where Blankshire exercises its discretion to make a grant, it must do so in such a way as to promote the policy and objectives of the Act. This principle cannot apply in such a way as to create an obligation to make grants in particular cases: if it did so that would contravene the overriding principle that discretion must not be fettered. The central Government circular will also not create such an obligation, for the same reason.

Blankshire's decision not to make the grant to Morris may be open to challenge, however, on two bases. The first of these is that the decision is unreasonable on the basis of *Associated Provincial Picture Houses* v *Wednesbury Corporation* (1948). Blankshire's decision is based on the proposition that experienced maths teachers are not necessary. This appears to ignore the relevant considerations that the circular has advised on: namely that schools should employ experienced maths teachers, and that councils should attach considerable weight to the promotion of maths teaching in the allocation of their grants. This failure to take into account relevant considerations may lead the court to quash the decision and order the council to reconsider, but the court cannot order Blankshire to pay a grant to Morris, and it will still be open to them to refuse it having taken into account all relevant considerations.

The second ground of challenge that Smith may have is that, as Chair of Governors of Morris school, he may have a legitimate expectation that the circular will be followed: *ex parte Khan* above. It must be pointed out, however, that the circular is an advisory document which is not binding on the Council. Legitimate expectations usually arise in the context of a promise made or policy held by the authority being challenged. Since the circular represents central Government policy, rather than council policy, it may not give rise to a legitimate expectation that Blankshire will act upon it, unless they have adopted it as their own policy. Even if it does so, the effect will not be to impose a duty on Blankshire to make a grant, only to give Morris a right to make representations in the event that Blankshire decides not to follow the policy.

The decision not to award Morris a grant may therefore be open to challenge, but such a challenge will not necessarily be effective since there is no statutory duty to make a grant to Morris.

QUESTION FIVE

Following the inclusion of beach volleyball as an exhibition sport at the 1998 Olympics, two national sporting bodies, the British Beach Volleyball Association (BBVA) and Brits on the Beach (BOB) are established in 1993. The International Olympic Committee recognises both organisations as legitimate governing bodies of the sport, jointly responsible for selecting the British Olympic team. Olympic competitors must join one or other organisation.

The BBVA is run by private individuals, but receives financial support from the Department of the Environment. The Minister for Sport is quoted as saying that she considers it important that the government 'keeps and eye' on BBVA's activities to maximise the chances of Britain increasing its tally of Olympic medals. In its first publicity campaign, the BBVA stresses that skilled players might soon earn a substantial living from the sport. BOB is run and and financed entirely by private individuals: it stresses that it rejects the commercialism of the BBVA.

In January 1997, Faith, one of Britain's top players, following her recent successes on the American circuit, applies to join both BOB and the BBVA. Her applications are accepted; she pays the £10 membership each body requires and signs contracts with each organisation which state that membership may be granted, renewed or revoked on such terms as the organisation thinks fit. On 1 May 1997 she is expelled from the BBVA. No reason is given.

Hope, who plays beach volleyball for fun, applies on 12 March 1997 to join BOB. Her application is rejected without explanation on 17 March. She then goes on holiday and thinks she will do something about her application when she gets back.

Faith and Hope come to you for advice today. Advise them whether they can challenge the decisions made by BOB and the BBVA via an application for judicial review. (You are not asked to comment on the merits of their respective cases.)

University of London LLB Examination
(for External Students) Administrative Law June 1995 Q8

General Comment

This problem is directed at several questions that exist in administrative law. First is the question whether the BOB and BBVA are amenable to judicial review at all, since they are essentially private bodies. If they are, then on what basis could their decisions be challenged? Arguably, because of the Olympic Games aspect, they are analogous to licensing authorities and principles governing those authorities can be applied. Note carefully the dates contained in the problem, and that Faith and Hope come to you for advice today. 'Today' may mean that Hope is outside the three-month time limit for challenging the decision made against her.

Skeleton Solution

- Are the BOB and BBVA subject to judicial review?
- Analogy with licensing cases.
- Applicants distinguished from licence holders.
- Contracting out of natural justice.
- Hope's delay.

Suggested Solution

One of the first considerations to be applied to the claims of Faith and Hope is whether the BBVA and the BOB will be amenable to judicial review at all. On the face of it they are private clubs and such organisations are not normally subject to judicial review, even where they are able to exercise extensive regulatory powers: *R* v *Disciplinary Committee of the Jockey Club, ex parte The Aga Khan* (1993). It may, however, be arguable that the BOB and/or the BBVA are exceptions to this rule. The main reason for this relates to their function. In effect, because of the International Olympic Committee requirement that Olympic competitors must join one or other organisation, the BOB and BBVA are not ordinary clubs that volleyball players may join. Membership of one of these organisations effectively operates as a licence to compete in the Olympics. These two bodies are therefore exercising powers that are similar to public law licensing functions, and the courts may be persuaded to apply existing principles regulating the conduct of licensors by analogy to these organisations. The courts do permit judicial review of the decisions of other licensing agencies that have a sufficiently public function: see, for instance, *R* v *Gaming Board for Great Britain, ex parte Benaim and Khaida* (1970). Although the BOB and BBVA do not have any statutory basis, the recognition of their functions by the Olympic Committee may give a sufficient public law (though not statutory) underpinning to justify the availability of judicial review: *R* v *Panel on Take-overs and Mergers, ex parte Datafin plc* (1987). The possibility of judicial review may be stronger in the case of the BBVA because of the involvement of the Minister for Sport. In both cases, a further argument for the availability of judicial review is that there is no alternative remedy available to a mere applicant because a mere applicant will not have a contract with the organisations. Given the breadth of their powers there should be some regulation of their activities by the courts.

If judicial review is available against the BOB and BBVA then an appropriate challenge to their decisions would be on the basis of a failure to observe the rules of natural justice, the grounds being that neither organisation has given reasons for its decision, or any opportunity for Faith and Hope to be heard prior to making the decisions. There is some authority to suggest that these rules will apply differently to Faith and Hope. In *McInnes* v *Onslowe-Fane* (1978) applications for a licence were distinguished from revocations of licences. It was held that the rules of natural justice only applied in a weak sense to mere applications, and in the absence of any character slur there is no duty to give reasons for the refusal of an application. The only duty to a mere applicant is to consider the application fairly. The rules of natural justice will apply in a stronger way to the revocation of licences, and in such a case there will at least be a duty to give the licensee a hearing before revoking the licence. That hearing will entail sufficient reasons being given so that the licensee may know the case against her and have a proper opportunity to respond.

If *McInnes* applies in these cases, then Hope may be unable to challenge the decision to refuse her application unless she can show some specific unfairness in the decision. There is no evidence of such unfairness in this case. *McInnes* was decided on the basis of contract, however, and it has been suggested in other administrative law cases that a right to be heard must be given even to first time applicants: see *R* v *Devon County Council, ex parte Baker* (1995) per Simon Brown LJ. It is submitted that this view is to be preferred in relation to the BOB and the BBVA. Their broad powers of a public nature resemble the licensing powers of bodies like the Gaming Board, and the same principles of natural justice should apply. If this is correct then Hope will have a right to be heard in relation to the refusal of membership by BOB.

Even if Hope does have the natural justice rights contended for above, Faith should have stronger rights still as an existing member of BBVA. Her rights appear to have been diminished by the contract she has signed: it may be argued that the provision that membership may be granted, renewed or revoked on such terms as the BBVA shall think fit gives them total discretion as to membership, and precludes any access to natural justice. It is very doubtful whether Faith and BBVA could contract out of the provisions of natural justice. The courts have been very reluctant to give effect to legislative provisions restricting the rights of natural justice. Notwithstanding the wording of the BBVA contract, therefore, it is likely that Faith will still be able to challenge BBVA on the basis of breach of natural justice. Indeed, if the BBVA could contract out of natural justice that would lead to the curious result, assuming the *Gaming Board* case is followed, that Hope, who is a mere applicant, would have greater natural justice rights than Faith, a member of an organisation. This may provide some logical support for Faith's position.

One final word needs to be said about Hope. As of the date when this advice is given she is outside the three-month time limit for bringing an application for judicial review. If she can show some good reason for the delay, or why leave should be granted, then she may be able to persuade the court to extend the period pursuant to its discretion under O.53, r4(1). The fact that she has been on holiday is not a good reason for the delay, but the court may be persuaded to grant leave because of the issues of public importance involved in her case and provided no detriment to good administration would be caused by extending the usual time limit.

There may be grounds on which both Faith and Hope might challenge the decisions made by the BOB and the BBVA respectively by way of judicial review, if the court can be persuaded to treat these organisations as effectively public law bodies carrying out quasi-licensing functions and to apply the rules of natural justice to them. Faith's claim has greater prospects of success partly because of the ministerial involvement in the BBVA and partly because she had membership which was revoked, giving rise to stronger rights of natural justice than Hope's application. Furthermore, Faith's case does not suffer from the disadvantage of being out of time.

17 University of London LLB (External) 1996 Questions and Suggested Solutions

UNIVERSITY OF LONDON
LLB EXAMINATIONS 1996
for External Students
PARTS I AND II EXAMINATIONS (Scheme A)
THIRD AND FOURTH YEAR EXAMINATIONS (Scheme B)
GRADUATE ENTRY LEVEL II (Route A)
GRADUATE ENTRY THIRD YEAR EXAMINATIONS (Route B)

ADMINISTRATIVE LAW

Thursday, 6 June: 2.30 pm to 5.30 pm

Answer *FOUR* of the following EIGHT questions, including at least ONE from Part B

PART A

1 'The notion that the courts might review the legality of government action against the criterion of its compatibility with "fundamental human rights" offers both the most exciting and the most dangerous route for the development of administrative law in the late 1990s.'

Discuss.

2 'The debate over the introduction of "proportionality" into English public law is largely an exercise in wasted breath. The case law shows quite clearly that the courts are able to use the concept of "irrationality" to achieve the results that advocates of the proportionality doctrine consider desirable.'

To what extent do you agree with this analysis?

3 In what circumstances will a decision of an adminsitrative body be found unlawful because of bias on the part of the decision-makers? Is this area of the law in need of clarification and/or reform?

4 'The central and local government Ombudsmen serve no purpose that could not be better performed by the courts.'

Discuss.

5 In what ways and for what reasons do the courts distinguish between decisions which are void ab initio and those which are merely voidable?

PART B

6 Seaside District Council is currently experiencing considerable pressure on its housing resources. It decided to raise all of its tenants' rents by 50 per cent on 6 April 1996.

Brian refused to pay the whole rent increase. He instead paid his old rent plus ten per cent. When the council finally began possession proceedings against him in the County Court in April 1997, Brian wished to claim that he was not in breach of his tenancy agreement because the rent rise was *Wednesbury* unreasonable. However his barrister advised him that the judge would not hear his argument, as it raised a public law matter which could only be addressed via Order 53 proceedings. The barrister observed that *Wandsworth* v *Winder* could no longer be considered good law.

Freda, her husband and her two young children applied to Seaside Council as homeless persons in May 1997. The council accepted that Freda was entitled to be rehoused under the terms of Part III of the Housing Act 1985. However the council told Freda that it had no housing left, and could therefore not assist her. Freda wished to challenge this decision through an action for breach of statutory duty in the County Court. However her solicitor has advised her that council decisions relating to the homelessness legislation can be challenged only via Order 53.

Advise Brian and Freda whether their lawyers have analysed their legal positions correctly.

7 In May 1996, control of Woodside District Council passed by a narrow majority to the 'Independent Ratepayer' party. The Independent Ratepayers had based their election manifesto on the need to expand care facilities for the elderly in the area. The manifesto also pledged that the Independent Ratepayers would ensure that all decisions relating to the administration of new care initiatives would be processed with the utmost efficiency.

In February 1997, The Sunshine Old People's Club – relying on the manifesto commitment – spent £10,000 on renovating its premises in the expectation that the council would offer it a grant to open a subsidised meal canteen for local old age pensioners when the Social Services Committee met in May.

On 1 April, the Chair of the council Social Services Committee told the Managing Director of Old Age Care Services Inc at a party that the council was sure to award the company the contract to manage two new nursing homes that the council was planning to open. On the strength of this assurance, Old Age Care Services snapped up a consignment of furniture to equip the two homes (at a cost of £50,000).

In May, two days before the Social Services Committee met, three members of the Independent Ratepayers defected to the opposition Conservative Party, which thereby gained control of the Council. The Social Services Committee subsequently awarded the nursing home contract to the Happy Granny Nursing Company and decided not to offer any grant to the Sunshine Old People's Club.

However the junior clerk responsible for drafting the Committee's decisions was so outraged by the Committee's decisions that he deliberately sent letters to Old Age Care Services and The Sunshine Old People's Club telling them their applications had been successful. Both organisations immediately spent significant sums on their respective projects before the clerk's unauthorised action was discovered.

Advise the Sunshine Club and Old Age Care Services Inc as to the remedies, if any, they might successfully seek before a court against the council. (You are not asked to advise on the availability of non-judicial remedies.)

8 The (fictitious) Police Act 1995 empowers local police authorities to dismiss their Chief Constables if the officers perform their duties negligently or dishonestly. In May 1997, Blankshire Police Authority dismissed its Chief Constable, Mrs Smith. The Authority did not offer any reasons for its decision, nor was Mrs Smith given any opportunity to question the decision before it was made. Because she has been dismissed, Mrs Smith loses her

entitlement to a police pension. But she has for some unknown reason decided that she will not challenge the sacking.

However, Mrs Smith's husband wishes to challenge the Authority's decision. He wishes to ensure that his wife receives her pension so that he and their three children will be provided for financially in the event of her death.

Similarly, the Police Federation and the local law centre wish to challenge the Authority's action. The Police Federation claims that it is in its members' interests to establish whether such secrecy in the administration of the police service is lawful, while the law centre claims that promoting good administration in the police service is a matter in which all members of the public have a profound interest.

Advise the Police Federation, Mr Smith, and the law centre if they have standing to challenge the Police Authority's decisions.

QUESTION ONE

'The notion that the courts might review the legality of government action against the criterion of its compatibility with "fundamental human rights" offers both the most exciting and the most dangerous route for the development of administrative law in the late 1990s.'

Discuss.

University of London LLB Examination
(for External Students) Administrative Law June 1996 Q1

General Comment

A very challenging question which demands a detailed conceptual analysis of the role of judicial review as a constitutional fundamental. Constitutional doctrines such as the sovereignty of Parliament and the separation of powers form the essential context in which to discuss critically the expanding functions of judicial review. The role of the judge as a defender of basic human rights needs to be assessed and weighed against the possible risks to judicial independence and impartiality. A useful method by which to develop these themes is to use the red light and green light theories as a key to appreciating judicial attitudes on judicial review in the modern British state. These theories are discussed at length in the first two chapters of *Law and Administration* by Harlow and Rawlings (2nd edition, 1997), Butterworths.

Skeleton Solution

- Definition of the red light and green light theories of judicial review.
- Why a green light approach is safe and cautious.
- Why a red light approach can be both exciting and dangerous.
- Examples of conflicting judicial attitudes to the purposes of judicial review in the modern British constitution.

Suggested Solution

In their influential work *Law and Administration* (2nd edition 1997) Harlow and Rawlings identify two conflicting theories as to the role of judicial review in the modern British constitution. The 'red light' theory contends that the aim of judicial review should be to protect fundamental human rights against the ever-growing power of the executive. According to this theory the judge should be primarily concerned with the redress of individual grievances. Such an approach encourages the judge to be activist in developing the common law principles of ultra vires so as to ensure that as much public power as possible is brought within the court's controlling jurisdiction on as wide a review basis as practicable. In contrast, the 'green light' theory contends that the aim of judicial review is limited to ensuring that the executive acts lawfully within the defined boundaries established by statutes. According to this theory, the judge should not interfere with a technically lawful exercise of discretionary power even though he or she strongly believes such exercise to have been oppressive in the particular circumstances and a threat to individual human rights. Such an approach encourages the judge to facilitate executive action by leaving it to Parliament to establish the framework of regulation which in turn is entrusted to the executive to implement. Safeguards for the citizen are in the form of internal structuring of discretion (through the use of circulars, memoranda and the like) and external devices such as consultation with interested parties.

The green light theory is more acceptable as a matter of constitutional orthodoxy since, if followed, it minimises the risk that judicial review might be transformed into an appeal process on the merits of particular executive decisions. It 'keeps the judge in his or her place' by ensuring that the judge does not infringe the separation of powers by trespassing onto sensitive policy areas in which the ultimate decisions are ones for accountable officials to take and for Parliament to supervise and to change if necessary. This approach also ensures that the judge does not put at risk the appearance of impartiality, which might be lost if he or she is seen to be acting politically rather than judicially.

Judicial support for the green light approach can be found in those cases in which judges have emphasised that judicial review should not be used to undermine the powers and discretions properly vested in public authorities by Parliament. For example, there is the famous view of Lord Brightman that judicial review is concerned not with the decision but with the decision-making process: *Chief Constable of North Wales Police* v *Evans* (1982).

In a recent controversial case concerning the prioritisation of medical care facilities Sir Thomas Bingham MR (as he then was) expressed his sympathy for the 'difficult and agonising' judgments that medical authorities sometimes had to make, commenting that:

'the courts are not ... arbiters as to the merits of cases of this kind. Were we to express opinions as to the likelihood of the effectiveness of medical treatment, or as to the merits of medical judgment, then we would be straying far from the sphere which under our constitution is accorded to us. We have one function only, which is to rule upon the lawfulness of decisions. That is a function to which we should strictly confine ourselves': *R* v *Cambridge District Health Authority, ex parte B* (1995).

That case concerned a 10-year-old girl suffering from leukemia who had been refused further medical treatment on the grounds, inter alia, that the likelihood of her recovery was very small and the cost of the treatment very high. It was in a very real sense a 'right to life' case, the sort of case which red light theorists contend should be reviewed from the perspective of protecting fundamental rights rather than from the perspective of economic realism and administrative efficiency. Indeed, at first instance it appears that Laws J in the Queen's Bench Division adopted this approach when reaching the conclusion that the refusal of treatment was unlawful (a decision speedily reversed by the Court of Appeal). In a memorable passage Laws J observed that when a patient's life was at stake 'the responsible authority must do more than toll the bell of tight resources'.

Although the red light approach received a setback in *ex parte B*, there have been indications that judges are becoming more sympathetic to it and less deterred by constitutional orthodoxy. It may be that some of the judiciary are taking the view that the sovereignty of Parliament is a legal theory which no longer matches the political reality, namely executive dominance of the legislature as the result of the practices of crude power politics. In the absence of a written constitution and a Bill of Rights it is left to the imaginative evolution of common law to produce new and better safeguards for the citizen against the encroachments of an over-powerful bureaucracy. This is an exciting view for many judges because it gives them a creative role. In the judicial review context there have been dramatic developments, eg the extension of review of statutory bodies to many other kinds of public body (the 'functions' rather than 'source of power' test), which led some academics such as Professor Oliver to question whether the ultra vires rule was still the basis of judicial review: [1987] PL 543. In regard to grounds of review it has been suggested by the Law Lords that in cases involving fundamental human rights, such as the right to life and liberty, judges should be prepared to go beyond the technical grounds of irrationality, illegality and procedural impropriety and instead take a 'hard look' at the quality of the decision which affects such rights, thereby requiring the public authority in question to demonstrate a substantively rational decision based on moral and ethical values: *Bugdacay* v *Secretary of State for the Home Department* (1987). Such an approach has encouraged the emergence of novel doctrines such as substantive legitimate expectation, and may eventually allow in the doctrine of proportionality: see the judgment of Sedley J in *R* v *MAFF, ex parte Hamble* (1995):

'it is the court's task to recognise the constitutional importance of ministerial freedom to formulate and reformulate policy; but it is equally the court's duty to protect the interests of those individuals whose expectation of different treatment has a legitimacy which in fairness outtops the policy choice which threatens to frustrate it'.

However, these observations were later overruled, being described as 'hearsay' by more green-light minded judges in the Court of Appeal: *R* v *Secretary of State for the Home Department, ex parte Hargreaves* (1997).

Nevertheless it does appear that a general judicial view seems to be emerging to the effect that there should be no areas of public power which are completely unreviewable, but that the intensity of review should vary depending on the subject matter and the expertise of the courts. The view may be an exciting one but it carries dangers, notably of provoking clashes with the executive over the determination of sensitive policy decisions. Indeed, carried to its logical conclusion the red light theory would, if fully implemented, produce a judge-made constitution against which the legality not only of executive action but also parliamentary law itself could be tested. Two judges (Lord Woolf and Sir John Laws) have gone so far as to venture this possibility, arguing that some rights are so fundamental that not even an authentic Act of Parliament should be assumed capable of interfering with them: [1995] PL 57 and 72.

Such observations alarm constitutional purists and concern politicians. The Shadow Lord Chancellor, Lord Irvine, has recently warned the judiciary of misuse of the weapon of judicial review: [1996] PL 59. In this article he echoes the views of some ministers, eg the Home Secretary, Michael Howard (a QC as well as a politician), who has criticised some review judgments on the ground that the judges are substituting a form of appeal from decisions of the Home Office on sensitive issues such as sentencing, immigration, etc. Yet red light theorists would argue that such areas are among the ones in which fundamental rights are most threatened and which therefore deserve the 'hard look' treatment from the judges of the Divisional Court of the Queen's Bench Division. Even so, the red light theorists face the uncomfortable fact that judicial review occupies a weak constitutional position in the absence of a written constitution and a Bill of Rights clearly delimiting the sovereignty of Parliament. Judges must be careful not to give the good idea of judicial review a bad name!

QUESTION TWO

'The debate over the introduction of "proportionality" into English public law is largely an exercise in wasted breath. The case law shows quite clearly that the courts are able to use the concept of "irrationality" to achieve the results that advocates of the proportionality doctrine consider desirable.'

To what extent do you agree with this analysis?

University of London LLB Examination
(for External Students) Administrative Law June 1996 Q2

General Comment

The quotation in question is deliberately provocative since it flies in the face of orthodox understandings as to the differences between proportionality and irrationality as grounds of judicial review. The examiner is therefore probably expecting the student to contest the quotation vigorously by drawing upon appropriate judicial authorities. The object of the exercise is to demonstrate the subtle and sophisticated differences between the two concepts. It is the confusion over these differences which have sometimes led judges to use the words proportionality and irrationality interchangeably as if they were the same thing, lending some basis for the quotation in question. However, the constitutional importance of drawing proper distinctions in this field remains great and needs to be fully brought out in the discussion.

Skeleton Solution

- Definitions of irrationality and proportionality.
- Why proportionality may be more constitutionally objectionable.
- Use of proportionality by European courts.
- Use of proportionality in a domestic context: disproportionate penalties classified as irrational.
- The *Brind* decision and its aftermath.
- Recent 'red light' attempts to introduce proportionality.

Suggested Solution

In his famous judgment in the GCHQ case, in which he reclassified the modern grounds of judicial review, Lord Diplock defined an irrational decision as 'a decision so outrageous in its defiance of logic or of accepted moral standards that no sensible person who has applied his mind to the question to be decided could have arrived at it': *Council of Civil Service Unions* v *Minister for the Civil Service* (the GCHQ case (1984)). This definition was designed to give greater precision to this controversial ground for review, since Lord Diplock believed that the classic language of total unreasonableness (the *Wednesbury* test: *Associated Provincial Picture Houses* v *Wednesbury Corporation* (1948)) had on occasion been misunderstood as giving the judge a power to consider the rightness or wrongness of an administrative decision, whereas judicial review should be concerned only with whether the decision was lawful or unlawful. Lord Diplock's own re-definition has not been without controversy since he emphasises not only illogicality (the dictionary definition of irrationality) but also immorality: see further Walker's excellent critique ([1995] PL 556).

In the GCHQ case Lord Diplock expressed the view that the doctrine of proportionality might one day become a ground for review, thereby clearly distinguishing it from his test of irrationality. In other jurisdictions, notably on the continent, proportionality is a device used to set judicial standards against which to measure administrative action. This approach demands that the executive authority shows a reasonable proportion between the administrative objective and the means used to achieve it. For red light theorists, who believe that the redress of grievances and the protection of individual rights should be the primary aims of judicial review, proportionality carries the additional attraction of requiring that the administrative action should be the least restrictive of fundamental human rights compatible with the objective being pursued. The primary judgment, subject only to a limited 'margin of appreciation', is for the court not the executive. Therein lies the constitutional importance of distinguishing correctly between irrationality and proportionality, since under the former the courts exercise only a secondary judgment in reviewing the legality of administrative action. Under proportionality the constitutional balance shifts by allowing the courts to evaluate the merits or quality of the decision in order to assess whether an appropriate response to a problem has been taken. The proportionality concept is found in many of the judgments of the European Court of Human Rights and the European Court of Justice, and since the UK courts are influenced indirectly by the former and directly by the latter the implications for UK judges are significant and, some would say, it is tempting to import the doctrine into English common law.

Turning to the quotation in question, it is apparent from the discussion so far that irrationality has a much more limited scope than proportionality and cannot, as the quotation contends, achieve the same results. Admittedly there is some case law in which judges have classified as irrational action which they have also described as disproportionate, but in these cases the disproportionality has been so great that it was easy for the judges to classify the action as so manifestly absurd on its face as not to be what Parliament intended when conferring the executive discretion, eg the wage rise which was really a charity handout in *Roberts* v *Hopwood* (1925), or the disproportionate penalty of depriving a man of his livelihood for a trivial infringement of the rules of his occupation in *R* v *Barnsley Metropolitan Borough Council, ex parte Hook* (1976). On occasions judges have been rather lax in terminology and used the expressions *Wednesbury* unreasonableness/irrationality/ propor-tionality as if they were all the same thing: *R* v *General Medical Council, ex parte Colman* (1990). This lends some credence to the quotation in question, but on closer analysis it can be seen that the judges in these cases were not behaving like their European counterparts in evaluating policy and weighing competing public interests.

Indeed, any doubts as to the differences between irrationality and proportionality were removed when all five Law Lords agreed that there was an important conceptual and constitutional distinction to make between them in *R* v *Secretary of State for the Home Department, ex parte Brind* (1991). Admittedly three expressed no decided views as to whether it was desirable for proportionality to become a ground for review, for, like Lord Diplock in the GCHQ case, they preferred pragmatically to leave the door open. But two Law Lords, Lords Ackner and Lowry, forcefully repudiated the proportionality doctrine for being constitutionally dangerous. They thought to use it would turn judicial review into an appellate process and that if this was desirable it was for Parliament to authorise it, eg by incorporating the European Convention on Human Rights into English law. In a telling passage Lord Ackner said that for the judges to use proportionality as a ground for review would be tantamount to incorporation of the Convention by the back door and would involve the judges in a wrongful usurpation of power.

Effectively this settled judicial attitudes in the immediate aftermath of the decision. The primary judgment was still for the executive. Nevertheless, *Brind*'s case did not prevent the review court, in exercising its secondary judgment, from taking a 'hard look' at decisions affecting important civil liberties and from requiring the executive to show an important competing public interest to justify its action: per Neill LJ in analysing the effects of the *Brind* judgments in *NALGO* v *Secretary of State for the Environment* (1992). Neill LJ also voiced his concern as to the possible future use of proportionality since, while it allowed decision-makers a margin of appreciation, it did not confer as generous a discretion or latitude as that afforded by *Wednesbury* unreasonableness/irrationality. Clearly Neill LJ was thinking about the risks to the judge of getting involved in the policy merits of decisions.

Since proportionality is part of the jurisprudence of the European Court of Justice, UK courts must use it in appropriate EC contexts because of s2 of European Communities Act 1972. However, the red light theorists have argued that even where no direct application of EC law is involved there is much to be said for applying common standards in fields such as judicial review and civil liberties. As English judges become more familiar with the doctrine of proportionality as a result of their use of it in EC-related cases, so they may become more willing to extend its use to the purely domestic context. Academic support for this view was expressed recently by Beyleveld ([1995] PL 577), and judicial support for it can be found in the judgment of Sedley J in *R* v *Secretary of State for the Home Department, ex parte McQuillan* (1995). Indeed, Sedley J contends that the 'hard look' approach of judicial review in cases involving fundamental rights effectively achieves the aims of proportionality and was authorised by *Bugdacay* v *Secretary of State for the Home Department* (1987):

'Whether this in itself is a doctrine of proportionality I do not now pause to ask: if it is, the House of Lords has long since contemplated its arrival with equanimity' (per Sedley J at pp422j–423a).

Hence, what was once regarded as inimical to constitutional orthodoxy may be on the point of receiving formal judicial blessing. If that is the case the view expressed in the quotation under discussion is not as misguided as may at first sight have appeared.

QUESTION THREE

In what circumstances will a decision of an adminsitrative body be found unlawful because of bias on the part of the decision-makers? Is this area of the law in need of clarification and/or reform?

University of London LLB Examination
(for External Students) Administrative Law June 1996 Q3

General Comment

A reasonably straightforward question on bias, calling first for a narrative of the categories of bias and the circumstances in which they apply, and second for a critical appraisal of the state of the existing law. In the critical analysis use could be made of the red light and green light theories of judicial review as a basis for arguing for and against reform of this area of the law. There is considerable recent case law calling for discussion.

Skeleton Solution

- The three categories of bias.
- The real danger of bias test and whether it is applicable to decisions of administrative bodies.
- Red light arguments for subjecting administrative bodies to more rigorous tests for bias.
- Green light arguments against such reform.

Suggested Solution

Common law has established three categories of bias:

a) *Actual bias*

This may take the form of either financial or non-financial bias. The category was explained by Sir Thomas Bingham MR (as he then was) in *R* v *Inner West London Coroner, ex parte Dallaglio* (1994):

'There are cases in which a decision-maker is shown, in fact and for whatever reason, to have been influenced in his decision-making by prejudice, predilection or personal interest. Such cases are very rare ... But the law is very clear and emphatic: where a decision is shown to have been tainted by actual bias it cannot stand.'

There would appear to be no reason of principle to distinguish between judicial and administrative decision-making for this purpose, although in regard to the latter the review judge may prefer to use the language of 'bad faith' (a category of *Wednesbury* (1948) unreasonableness) rather than actual bias, but in practice there is no difference and the outcome would be the same: the decision would be liable to be set aside for being ultra vires.

b) *Apparent bias in the form of a direct financial interest*

Traditionally this has been a ground for automatic disqualification of an adjudicator involved in any kind of judicial-type decision-making. The modern test is to ask whether there is a 'real danger of bias' in cases involving apparent bias, and clearly there would be no difficulty establishing such danger regardless of the status of the adjudicator and the amount involved because 'the nature of the interest is such that public confidence in the administration of justice requires that the decision should not stand': per Lord Goff in *R* v *Gough* (1993). However, until recently it was thought that this rigorous approach was not appropriate to administrative decision-making and this point is considered further below.

c) *Apparent bias in the form of a non-financial interest*

Again, *R* v *Gough* has settled that in regard to judicial-type decision-making of any kind the test is to ask whether there was a real danger of bias arising as a result of the operation of a non-financial interest. This test replaced alternative tests which had arisen over a long stretch of common law development, namely the 'reasonable suspicion of bias' test (eg, as used in *R* v *Sussex Justices, ex parte McCarthy* (1924) and the 'real likelihood of bias' test (eg, as used in *R* v *Rand* (1866)). The former test put the emphasis on an appearance of bias and presented the applicant with a fairly low standard of proof. In that sense it could be described as a 'red light' test in giving priority to the protection of individual rights. By contrast, the real likelihood test required more than proof of a mere appearance of bias: the applicant had to produce evidence to satisfy the review court that the non-financial interest was of such a kind that, having regard to the context of the decision, it was 'really likely' or 'probable' that it had affected the mind of the adjudicator. This was a much higher standard of proof and could be regarded as a 'green light' test in that it protects public decision-making from 'casual' challenges based on insubstantial or flimsy grounds. Not surprisingly, therefore, judges differed as to which test was best depending on their individual attitudes as to the primary purposes of judicial review. For example, in *Metropolitan Properties Co (FGC)* v *Lannon* (1968) Lord Denning MR favoured the real likelihood test on the ground that a lower standard would encourage a flood of applications undermining public confidence in the judicial system, whilst Edmund-Davies LJ favoured the reasonable suspicion test on the ground that it demonstrated to the public judicial confidence in the administration of justice.

In *R* v *Gough* the House of Lords resolved the conflict of authority by producing a new test, the 'real danger' of bias test which seems to come closest to the real likelihood of bias test, although the new formula puts the emphasis on a 'real risk' of bias or a 'real possibility' of bias rather than on a probability of bias. This was explained by Simon

Brown LJ in *R* v *Inner West London Coroner, ex parte Dallaglio*, above, in analysing the effects of *R* v *Gough*. Hence the new formula may be said to be slightly less 'green light' in character than the real likelihood test but certainly more 'green light' than the reasonable suspicion of bias test. Red light theorists would object to the new formula on the ground that it undermines the rights of the citizen to an appearance of fair proceedings, a right famously summed up in Lord Hewart's dictum that justice must not only be done but must be seen to be done: *R* v *Sussex Justices, ex parte McCarthy*, above. Indeed, in *R* v *Inner West London Coroner*, above, Sir Thomas Bingham MR observed that this famous dictum is no longer good law following *R* v *Gough* because

'if, despite the appearance of bias, the court is able to examine all the relevant material and satisfy itself that there was no danger of the alleged bias having in fact caused injustice, the impugned decision will be allowed to stand.'

In regard to purely administrative decision-making it had been thought that the approaches on bias adopted in regard to judicial decision-making would not be appropriate or in the public interest. Instead allowance was made for the needs of administration and the practical operation of such public bodies as local authorities, for example. A doctrine of necessity was formulated under which, eg, a direct financial interest was not fatal provided that the administrative body had engaged in a genuine exercise of discretion and had not fettered its discretion by having such an interest. This permitted local authorities to have a contractual or other financial interest in land development over which it was the local planning authority: *Steeples* v *Derbyshire County Council* (1984) and *R* v *Amber Valley District Council, ex parte Jackson* (1984).

From a red light perspective this area of common law cries out for reform because the use of the doctrine of necessity in this context seems to promote administrative expedience to the point of denying to citizens their fundamental right to fair administration: see, for example the critique of Tracey ([1982] PL 628). On the other hand, green light theorists would contend that to subject administrative bodies to the same standards as judicial bodies would impose intolerable stresses on public administration which would be in danger of grinding to a halt if caught up in numerous applications for review. In a recent decision the red light approach has received a boost in the decision of Sedley J to extend the real danger of bias test to administrative bodies: *R* v *Secretary of State for the Environment, ex parte Kirkstall Valley Campaign Ltd* (1996). Sedley J took the view that the *R* v *Gough* test should be uniformly applied to all kinds of decision-making. There were, he thought, sound grounds of principle in modern public law for this new approach because in the modern state the interests of individuals or of the public might be more radically affected by administrative decisions than by the decisions of courts and judicial tribunals.

It remains to be seen whether this breakthrough, made by a judge famous for his 'red light' attitudes on the functions of judicial review, will be sustained by other judges in similar cases, but if it is so sustained it will probably obviate the need for reform of this area of the law: the reform will have come about as another dramatic evolution of the common law!

QUESTION FOUR

'The central and local government Ombudsmen serve no purpose that could not be better performed by the courts.'

Discuss.

University of London LLB Examination
(for External Students) Administrative Law June 1996 Q4

General Comment

A standard question on the ombudsman system, requiring critical analysis of the issue of whether judicial review could provide a fully comprehensive substitute for the work of the ombudsmen. A brief summary of the scope of judicial review should be given, followed by a detailed scrutiny of the areas of work of the main ombudsmen, bringing out the comparisons and contrasts with the role of the courts.

Skeleton Solution

- Brief summary of scope of judicial remedies.
- Definition of maladministration and its relationship with the concept of illegality.
- Examples of 'non-justiciable' work performed by ombudsmen.
- Comparisons and contrasts between remedies available from the courts and those recommended by ombudsmen.
- Critical conclusions as to the value of ombudsmen.

Suggested Solution

The statutory framework expressly prohibits the ombudsmen from investigating matters which can be dealt with by the courts unless the particular ombudsman is satisfied that in the particular circumstances it is not reasonable to expect the party aggrieved to pursue his remedy at law: Parliamentary Commissioner Act 1967 and Local Government Act 1974. Clearly Parliament's intention was that the ombudsmen should supplement the work of the courts, and this implies that there were certain kinds of work which Parliament believed would be better performed by ombudsmen than by a court of law. Those kinds of work are covered by the umbrella concept of 'maladministration' which is not per se a justiciable concept, since judicial review is comparatively narrowly defined and depends upon proof of some specific act of illegality, irrationality or procedural impropriety, whilst private law remedies depend upon proof of specific breaches of established tortious or contractual duties.

Parliament deliberately avoided providing a definition of maladministration in order to give the ombudsmen as wide a discretion as possible in developing their jurisdiction. The famous 'Crossman catalogue' of examples of maladministration show that it is much wider than illegality, though there may be an overlap in some areas: 'bias, neglect, inattention, delay, incompetence, ineptitude, perversity, turpitude, arbitrariness and so on'. Whilst such matters as bias and perversity could clearly be dealt with under a judicial review, matters such as inattention and delay are less likely to give rise to sufficient grounds for a remedy from the courts. Further, even where a remedy from the courts might be available, the ombudsman might use his discretion to deal with the complainant's case on the ground that judicial review is so wide, uncertain and technical that it is unreasonable to expect the citizen to take out such an application when he or she can have the matter dealt with simply, in private and for free by the ombudsman.

Certain areas of public administration appear to be non-justiciable and therefore eminently suitable for investigation by an institution such as the ombudsman. A classic example is 'quasi-law' such as departmental rules, circulars and memoranda which may lack sufficient substance to be subject to the ultra vires rule yet are crucial in helping officials to structure their decision-making. The Parliamentary Commissioner in particular has been found to be effective in dealing with cavalier disregard of such rules and guidance: Mowbray conducted research which led him to the conclusion that the role of the Parliamentary Commissioner had been particularly valuable in cases where the relevant guidance had not been published and where consequently it would have been almost impossible for the citizen to seek a judicial remedy: [1987] PL 570.

The work of the Local Commissioners is concerned with much of the 'small change' of administrative work which, even if justiciable, would be an inappropriate burden for already overworked courts to handle, eg, giving misleading information to applicants for housing grants, delaying in making emergency repairs to council tenants' properties, failing to protect an alleged public footpath, etc.

Even where maladministration and illegality overlap, going to court may eventually prove a less attractive option for the person aggrieved in terms of the remedies available. In private law the main remedies are damages, injunctions and declarations, and in public law orders of certiorari, prohibition and mandamus (in addition to the private law remedies). A right to damages will depend upon proof of an established cause of action such as a tort or breach of contract. There is no remedy in damages for ultra vires decisions or for pure maladministration falling short of an excess of power. This point was noted by Schiemann J in *R* v *Knowsley Metropolitan Borough Council, ex parte Maguire* (1992), who observed that the general absence of a right to compensation for administrative wrongdoings made going to law 'notoriously unsatisfactory' from the claimant's point of view.

By contrast, although the ombudsmen cannot enforce their findings the persuasive weight of their recommendations is often so great that ex gratia payments are frequently made, even where the central or local authority has hotly contested the findings of maladministration, for example, most memorably, when the Department of Trade and Industry agreed to make voluntary payments of several million pounds to the aggrieved investors in the Barlow-Clowes company: see further [1991] PL 192 and 408.

Ombudsmen also have greater scope than the courts in choice of remedy, and may be able to propose an individualised course of action which may truly redress the citizen's grievance, eg, where delay in paying housing benefit has caused the individual to lose a private tenancy, the local ombudsman may well propose not only money compensation but also that the council in question should grant the complainant a public sector tenancy.

Hence the value of the ombudsmen in comparison to the courts can be established by thousands of individual cases at central and local levels. The issue can also be considered as a matter of principle. From a 'red light' perspective, the paramount need to protect individuals from oppressive bureaucracy demands as wide a range of relief as possible. Mowbray's research (above) persuaded him that the Parliamentary Commissioner has helped to protect the vital interests of citizens from some of the adverse effects of the creation and application of administrative guidance, and that therefore the Parliamentary Commissioner deserves a central place in lawyers' understanding of the mechanisms that provide relief in this area. No doubt the same can be said of the Local Commissioners. Further, the jurisdiction and procedural operation of the ombudsmen permit them to investigate the innermost workings of the administrative and political process. Many of the holders of the offices of ombudsmen have been former officials, and as 'insiders' know the people they question and know where to look in the departmental files for likely evidence of maladministration. No one has challenged the integrity of individual ombudsmen and hence it can be assumed that they will arrive at independent and objective views. Inside knowledge of the workings of officialdom is therefore not likely to compromise their independence but rather to ensure friendly co-operation in helping to restore the good name of public administration. If the only remedy was a judicial one the consequent formalisation of investigatory procedures might put such officials onto the defensive and make them minimalist in their response. This was the conclusion of researchers from Sheffield University ([1988] PL at 259), and also of a former Local Commissioner, Dr David Yardley ([1983] PL at 531).

QUESTION FIVE

In what ways and for what reasons do the courts distinguish between decisions which are void ab initio and those which are merely voidable?

University of London LLB Examination
(for External Students) Administrative Law June 1996 Q5

General Comment

A straightforward question requiring a narrative of the case law concerning the conceptual basis underlying the effects of ultra vires, what some have called the void/voidable distinction. It should be noted that some judges, eg Lord Hailsham, have disapproved of this terminology and therefore the use of it in the question is open to challenge.

Skeleton Solution

- Early classifications of the effects of ultra vires.
- Green light trends away from the concept of absolute nullity.
- Emergence of the concept of limited interim validity.
- Red lights objections to this concept.

Suggested Solution

Traditionally judges have had no hesitation in declaring a decision void ab initio for ultra vires, eg, a breach of natural justice was said to render a decision a 'complete nullity' in *Anisminic* (1969). The reason for such a robust approach seems to have been based on simple logic: how can a decision reached in excess or abuse of power be anything other than totally invalid? The decision-maker has acted in excess of jurisdiction and, accordingly, his decision lacks any formal or legalistic basis to be recognised as having any shred of validity. The strict logic of this position was reasserted by Lord Reid in *Ridge* v *Baldwin* (1964) and, most famously, in *Anisminic* (1969), where an ouster clause protecting the Commission's 'determinations' from judicial review was held not to be operative in regard to an ultra vires determination. The logic of this approach also underpinned a red light approach in the use of judicial review, since red light theorists saw it as the best means of safeguarding citizens' rights against an overpowerful executive. Indeed, in *Dunlop* v *Woollahra Municipal Council*

(1982) Lord Diplock went as far as to advise citizens that an ultra vires decision could be safely ignored as it could not affect their rights!

The wisdom of such advice came to be challenged, however, when it was appreciated that apparently ultra vires decisions could in practice be operative and affect many people unless challenged by a party with legal standing. If no party came forward, or if one did so only after a considerable lapse of time (eg, several months), then the reality was that the decision had acquired a kind of legitimacy and it might be against the public interest to treat it as if it had never been made.

A more flexible approach to the effects of ultra vires would put the emphasis on judicial discretion in granting public law remedies, so that if, in the exercise of such discretion, the judge takes the view that the public interest would be prejudiced by a finding of absolute nullity then instead the judge should grant prospective relief, ie effectively treating the decision as valid unless and until declared void by the court, what some have described as a 'voidable' decision per Schiemann LJ in *Percy* v *Hall* (1996). Such an approach treats the concept of voidness as a relative rather than absolute one, what Professor Wade described as a concept of 'limited interim validity': (1974) 90 LQR 436.

This approach departs from the logic of jurisdiction and undermines the shelter given to citizens faced with an excess of jurisdiction. But from a green light perspective it is defensible for being more in accordance with the realities and necessities of public administration. Indeed, the safeguard for the citizen lies in the exercise of wise judicial discretion and for this reason some judges have even disapproved of using such rigid labelling as void/voidable, preferring instead to emphasise the context-based character of judicial review under which the effects of ultra vires might need to depend upon the nature of the function being exercised: per Lord Hailsham in *London & Clydeside Estates Ltd* v *Aberdeen District Council* (1980).

A significant context in which the void/voidable distinction may crucially affect citizens' rights is that of a disciplinary hearing. Frequently in a domestic context, such as the pursuance of a trade or occupation, breach of professional obligations results in a hearing before a disciplinary tribunal, from which there is usually a right of appeal to another kind of tribunal established by the rules of that trade or occupation. If the first instance tribunal acts unfairly and exceeds its powers the logic of absolute nullity would suggest that the citizen affected can obtain judicial review even though in the meantime there has been an appeal at which the citizen received a fair and lawful hearing . Logically there is no 'decision' from which an appeal could be taken (using the *Anisminic* reasoning by analogy). However, such a rigid and formalistic approach would make nonsense of many domestic internal appeal structures and undermine the objective of settling such disputes outside the formal court structure. For these reasons the judges have preferred to adopt a more pragmatic attitude, under which a defect at the initial hearing can be treated as 'cured' by a full and fair hearing de novo on an appeal prior to the application for review. This happened in *Calvin* v *Carr* (1979) where a decision taken in breach of natural justice by local racecourse stewards was held sufficiently valid so as to permit an appeal. Since the appeal procedure had observed natural justice there was nothing left for the applicants to complain about in their request for judicial review. In this case Lord Wilberforce observed that,

'there may be instances where the defect is so flagrant, the consequences so severe, that the most perfect of appeals and rehearings will not be sufficient to produce a just result'.

Lord Wilberforce also thought that the protection of absolute nullity might be needed in trade union cases, 'where movement solidarity and dislike of the rebel, or renegade, may make it difficult for appeals to be conducted in an atmosphere of detached impartiality and so make a fair trial at the first, probably branch, level an essential condition of justice'.

Apart from such cases, Lord Wilberforce preferred to use the concept of limited interim validity as a means of discouraging too much formal judicialisation of domestic disputes which ought, in his view, to be left to be settled by the agreed methods of the trade or occupation in question. This kind of exercise of judicial discretion has certainly diluted the concept of absolute nullity in public law. Indeed, rigid labelling of any kind seems to be discouraged lest it limit judicial discretion in the granting of public law relief.

However, red light theorists would strongly object to such developments on the ground that the citizen is entitled to resist unlawful decision-making as a matter of fundamental right and to live under the rule of law, not the rule of discretion. The movement away from the concept of absolute nullity also undermines the certainty concerning the legal nature of an act done in excess of power. In a vividly striking analogy Stephen Sedley has written that ultra vires acts resemble the undead in a horror movie:

'Unlike the undead, however, this prospect is not mere fantasy ... it is comparable to a doctor attempting to revive a dead patient by refusing to sign the death certificate.': [1989] PL 32.

Hence, from the points of principle and practicality the present state of the law as to the effects of ultra vires is far from satisfactory.

QUESTION SIX

Seaside District Council is currently experiencing considerable pressure on its housing resources. It decided to raise all of its tenants' rents by 50 per cent on 6 April 1996.

Brian refused to pay the whole rent increase. He instead paid his old rent plus ten per cent. When the council finally began possession proceedings against him in the County Court in April 1997, Brian wished to claim that he was not in breach of his tenancy agreement because the rent rise was *Wednesbury* unreasonable. However his barrister advised him that the judge would not hear his argument, as it raised a public law matter which could only be addressed via Order 53 proceedings. The barrister observed that *Wandsworth* v *Winder* could no longer be considered good law.

Freda, her husband and her two young children applied to Seaside Council as homeless persons in May 1997. The council accepted that Freda was entitled to be rehoused under the terms of Part III of the Housing Act 1985. However the council told Freda that it had no housing left, and could therefore not assist her. Freda wished to challenge this decision through an action for breach of statutory duty in the County Court. However her solicitor has advised her that council decisions relating to the homelessness legislation can be challenged only via Order 53.

Advise Brian and Freda whether their lawyers have analysed their legal positions correctly.

University of London LLB Examination
(for External Students) Administrative Law June 1996 Q6

General Comment

The problem requires discussion of the procedural exclusivity principle of *O'Reilly* v *Mackman*. This decision created a procedural minefield because of the technical and sophisticated exceptions that were developed to circumvent the general principle. In the two cases arising in this problem two of these exceptions need to be analysed in the light of recent case law: the 'collateral issue' exception and the 'collateral proceedings' exception. Whilst the general rule and these two exceptions to it have generated much academic debate and criticism, it is important in giving advice to the clients to adhere to the settled authorities and not give way to the temptation of assuming that some cases are no longer good law in the light of such academic comment.

Skeleton Solution

- Definition of the procedural exclusivity principle of *O'Reilly* v *Mackman* and a brief summary of the reasons for it.
- The collateral issue exception as worked out in subsequent cases.
- The collateral proceedings exception as worked out in subsequent cases.
- Application of existing state of the law to cases of Brian and Freda.

Suggested Solution

In *O'Reilly* v *Mackman* (1982) the House of Lords held that the judicial review procedure under RSC O.53 is an exclusive procedure for public law cases and that use of private law proceedings in such cases would be regarded as abuse of process and liable to be struck out. The reason for procedural exclusivity of O.53 is to be found not in any statutory language surrounding the procedure but rather in the view taken by the court under its inherent jurisdiction that use of alternate means of process would frustrate the public interest which lay behind the reforms of O.53. These reforms came into force on 1 January 1978, and involved improved procedural rights for applicants balanced against procedural safeguards for public authorities to protect them from frivolous or tardy applications.

However, the House of Lords recognised that an absolutely rigid distinction between public law and private law cases was unlikely to work in practice, and hence Lord Diplock spoke of exceptions to the 'general rule' of procedural exclusivity. These exceptions were expected to be worked out on a case by case basis as judges at High Court level became more sensitive to the public/private dichotomy. The basic test was to be whether the chosen procedure in a particular case was an 'abuse of process'. Lord Diplock said, obiter, that, for example, if the public law issue is merely subsidiary to or 'collateral' to the private law issues in the case then a plaintiff would not be acting in abuse of process by issuing a writ or an originating summons to protect the predominant private law rights.

This became known as the 'collateral issue' exception, created by a 'narrow' interpretation of the general exclusivity principle. Application of it gave rise to much difficulty since it involved the 'disentangling' of public and private law issues to decide which were predominant, and this task was made harder by the conceptual confusion that persisted over the public/private divide. Traditionally English law has not recognised such a distinction because of the Diceyan influence in trying to treat public bodies as if they were the same as private individuals, amenable to the same courts and same sets of proceedings. Nevertheless, despite the difficulty of the task it appeared to be accomplished in *Cocks* v *Thanet District Council* (1982), in which an action for breach of statutory duty in respect of a decision of a housing authority was struck out on the ground that since the 'condition precedent' to establishing the plaintiff's private law rights was an analysis of the public law discretion of the housing body, the public law issue was predominant and not collateral, and therefore the general rule of procedural exclusivity applied.

However, doubt has been thrown onto the continuing authority of this decision as a result of an apparent modification of the *O'Reilly* v *Mackman* principle in *Roy* v *Kensington and Chelsea and Westminister Family Practitioner Committee* (1992) in which the House of Lords seemed to accept many of the academic criticisms which had been made of this area of the law. Lord Lowry suggested a 'broad' approach to the interpretation of the general rule, so that a plaintiff would be permitted to utilise private law proceedings so long as some kind of private law right was clearly involved, ie whether it was predominant or not should no longer matter. Effectively this would mean abandonment of the 'narrow' approach suggested by Lord Diplock, which had given rise to the decision in *Cocks* v *Thanet*. Hence it could be argued that the latter decision, although not expressly overruled in *Roy*, need no longer be followed if judges follow Lord Lowry's new advice on a broad interpretation of the relevant principles.

A further exception to the procedural exclusivity principle arose in the permitted use of 'collateral proceedings' to determine public law issues, ie proceedings before either an ordinary civil court (as distinct from the Divisional Court of the Queen's Bench Division) or a tribunal or a criminal court. This exception is based on the view that the collateral proceedings should not be stayed to allow an application for judicial review to be brought if the particular court or tribunal is competent to resolve the public law issues, ie the exception recognises the public interest in encouraging 'one-stop' litigation, particularly as there is at present no procedural mechanism for transferring a private law case to the Divisional Court to obtain its advice on public law matters. It follows that, in deciding whether the exception can apply, the collateral court or tribunal must correctly decide whether it has the necessary skills and enforcement powers to deal adequately with the particular public law issues before it: *Chief Adjudication Officer* v *Foster* (1993).

A further complication to the collateral proceedings exception is the dimension added to it by the controversial decision in *Wandsworth London Borough Council* v *Winder* (1985). In this case the House of Lords held, inter alia, that where the public law issue of ultra vires was raised as a defence, rather than as a cause of action, it could be settled in collateral proceedings since it was an historic right of a defendant to choose whatever form of defence was legitimately open to him/her, and it would therefore be both nonsense and a threat to such an historic right to classify such a defence as an abuse of process. However, this aspect of the collateral proceedings exception attracted much criticism for apparently creating a loophole through which citizens could more easily circumvent the *O'Reilly* v *Mackman* rule and thereby frustrate public administration. In *Wandsworth* v *Winder* the decision to permit a tenant to contest the legality of a rent rise by way of a defence to ordinary civil proceedings for possession led to a delay of some five years before the local authority was able to discover with certainty whether their budgets and spending plans were lawful. The whole purpose of O.53, according to the *O'Reilly* reasoning, is to safeguard public bodies from precisely this kind of risk. It is notable that Lord Woolf, a supporter of the collateral proceedings exception when based on the skills and enforcement powers of the collateral body, is a fierce critic of *Wandsworth* v *Winder* for creating an inappropriately wide dimension to the exception: [1986] PL 220.

Turning to the cases in issue in the light of the above advice, it can be seen that Brian's case falls squarely within the *Wandsworth* v *Winder* exception and that since that decision has not yet been overruled his lawyer is simply wrong in advising that it is no longer good law. Indeed, its continuing authority was recently reaffirmed by Laws J in *British Steel plc* v *Customs and Excise Commissioners* (1996). Freda's case may be caught by *Cocks* v *Thanet*, upon which her lawyer was probably relying when giving the advice in question. This advice may be correct, since *Cocks* v *Thanet* was not overruled in *Roy*, and it may be that High Court judges will feel themselves bound to go on applying the narrow approach advocated by Lord Diplock in *O'Reilly*. Indeed, Laws J in the *British Steel* case, above, appears to accept the continuing validity and applicability of *Cocks* v *Thanet*. However, the lawyer's advice to Freda does not take account of the possible use of the broad approach advocated by Lord Lowry in *Roy*.

Also, it may be that Freda's case can be distinguished from *Cocks* v *Thanet* on the ground that the Seaside District Council has exercised its public law discretion in deciding that she is entitled to rehousing, and that its decision not to rehouse her becomes a purely 'operational' one attracting private law liability if, for example, there is evidence that it overlooked some available housing. Freda's action would then be a straightforward one for breach of statutory duty, and would not depend on the 'condition precedent' (Lord Bridge's words in *Cocks*) of analysing the exercise of a public law discretion.

QUESTION SEVEN

In May 1996, control of Woodside District Council passed by a narrow majority to the 'Independent Ratepayer' party. The Independent Ratepayers had based their election manifesto on the need to expand care facilities for the elderly in the area. The manifesto also pledged that the Independent Ratepayers would ensure that all decisions relating to the administration of new care initiatives would be processed with the utmost efficiency.

In February 1997, The Sunshine Old People's Club – relying on the manifesto commitment – spent £10,000 on renovating its premises in the expectation that the council would offer it a grant to open a subsidised meal canteen for local old age pensioners when the Social Services Committee met in May.

On 1 April, the Chair of the council Social Services Committee told the Managing Director of Old Age Care Services Inc at a party that the council was sure to award the company the contract to manage two new nursing homes that the council was planning to open. On the strength of this assurance, Old Age Care Services snapped up a consignment of furniture to equip the two homes (at a cost of £50,000).

In May, two days before the Social Services Committee met, three members of the Independent Ratepayers defected to the opposition Conservative Party, which thereby gained control of the Council. The Social Services Committee subsequently awarded the nursing home contract to the Happy Granny Nursing Company and decided not to offer any grant to the Sunshine Old People's Club.

However the junior clerk responsible for drafting the Committee's decisions was so outraged by the Committee's decisions that he deliberately sent letters to Old Age Care Services and The Sunshine Old People's Club telling them their applications had been successful. Both organisations immediately spent significant sums on their respective projects before the clerk's unauthorised action was discovered.

Advise the Sunshine Club and Old Age Care Services Inc as to the remedies, if any, they might successfully seek before a court against the council. (You are not asked to advise on the availability of non-judicial remedies.)

University of London LLB Examination
(for External Students) Administrative Law June 1996 Q7

General Comment

A challenging problem-type question on grounds of judicial review. The problem puts the emphasis on the doctrine of legitimate expectation, the rule against fettering discretion, and the place, if any, of estoppel in public law.

Skeleton Solution

- Definition of the concept of legitimate expectation.
- Procedural and substantive expectations.
- Relationship of legitimate expectation to the rule on the fettering of discretionary power.
- The role of estoppel in public law.
- Availability of remedies, if any, for the clients in the problem.

Suggested Solution

The success of any applications for judicial review in this case will depend on whether the applicants can invoke either the doctrine of legitimate expectation or the doctrine of estoppel. Each doctrine has a number of complicated aspects and each comes into conflict with another aspect of the ultra vires rules, namely, the fettering of discretionary power, which in general is unlawful. So for the purposes of exposition the relevant law will first be examined, and then the position of the various claims will be considered in the light of that advice.

Legitimate expectation is a concept of relatively modern origin in public law in this country. It has two established limbs, each with their own line of authority. One limb concerns reliance upon a regular practice of consultation, which does not arise for discussion on the facts given. The other limb, which is relevant here, concerns reliance on public statements or assurances from public officials. This aspect of the doctrine has traditionally been regarded as procedural in character, giving rise to a right to a fair hearing before the statement can be lawfully changed or the assurance lawfully broken. However, recent cases have suggested that there may be a substantive character to the doctrine under which the court might enforce a reasonable expectation that a decision will not be changed or a promise broken. This doctrine of 'substantive' (or 'reasonable') expectation can apply only where the public body has promised to embark on an intra vires course of action, since it is well established that a public body cannot extend its jurisdiction or otherwise act ultra vires through the operation of promissory estoppel or anything that resembles it.

The emergence of a doctrine of substantive or reasonable expectation is one of great controversy in modern public law. It is far from being a settled doctrine, and there are authorities which expressly repudiate it on the ground that it conflicts with the rule that a public body cannot fetter the exercise of its discretionary powers through contracts with or promises to individual citizens: see the judgment of Laws J in *R* v *Secretary of State for Transport, ex parte Richmond-upon-Thames London Borough Council* (1994). Nevertheless, there are several authorities to the contrary which suggest that a public body may be unable to go back on its statement/assurance unless it is in the overriding public interest to do so. These authorities tend to involve cases where breach of the public body's representation would cause severe hardship to individuals and damage the name of good public administration: *R* v *Secretary of State for the Home Department, ex parte Khan* (1984); and *R* v *Secretary of State for the Home Department, ex parte Ruddock* (1984). This line of authority is outweighed by other cases in which the doctrine of legitimate expectation was held to have only a procedural character, entitling an applicant to a fair hearing before the decision could be changed but not entitling the applicant to be guaranteed that the decision would never be changed (these authorities are reviewed in Laws J's judgment in *ex parte Richmond*, above).

In two recent cases the doctrine of substantive/reasonable expectation has received a considerable boost. In *R* v *Devon County Council, ex parte Baker* (1995) Simon Brown LJ compared the doctrine to estoppel in its effect and acknowledged that it could operate to protect the citizen against unfairness in public administration provided that 'there is a clear and unambiguous representation upon which it was reasonable to rely', and provided such representation involved an intra vires course of action. In *R* v *MAFF, ex parte Hamble* (1995) Sedley J also took the view that such a representation might be binding, though he preferred to emphasise the need to prevent unfairness, and discouraged use of the doctrine of estoppel. He pointed out that estoppel requires knowledge of the reliance upon the representation, whereas the doctrine of legitimate expectation in its substantive character did not.

How can such a doctrine be reconciled with the general rule that it is ultra vires for a public body to fetter its discretionary powers? Sedley J's answer in *ex parte Hamble* (above) is clearly based on a 'red light' perception of public law, for whilst he acknowledges the constitutional importance of a public body's freedom to formulate and reformulate its policy, it was in his view equally the court's duty to protect the interests of those individuals whose expectation of different treatment has a legitimacy which in fairness out-tops the policy choice which threatens to frustrate it. Hence, depending on the circumstances, there may be some kinds of public statement that cannot be changed so as to override the individual's prior expectation because there is no overriding public interest requiring such change. This, he said, is as near as public law is able to approach an estoppel.

However, Sedley J's observations in *ex parte Hamble* have since been condemned as 'hearsay' and overruled by the Court of Appeal: *R* v *Secretary of State for the Home Department, ex parte Hargreaves* (1997).

The modern judicial trend is to discard any attempt to import into public law the private law doctrine of promissory estoppel. Instead the doctrine of legitimate expectation has been developed as a shield for the citizen against oppressive use of public power. This is not surprising, because the use of estoppel in public law was effectively killed off in a series of decisions repudiating Lord Denning's attempts to use it in the creative way he had used it in private law. Indeed, the objection to the 'Denning approach' was that if flagrantly offended the principle that statutory powers cannot be extended by an estoppel, eg the novel doctrine of 'estoppel by ostensible authority', under which advice from a public official on a matter which his status appeared to give him authority to advise upon was held capable of binding his employers: *Lever Finance Ltd* v *Westminister (City) London Borough Council* (1971). This was later drastically modified so as to apply only to those rare cases in which there was clear evidence of a formal delegation of authority to the particular official: *Western Fish Products Ltd* v *Penwith District Council* (1981).

Turning to the cases in question in the light of the above advice, it appears that the following positions emerge:

a) The £10,000 spending by the Sunshine Old People's Club was on the basis of a hope of getting a grant from the Woodside District Council. This hope was based on generalised statements of party political intent contained in an election manifesto which could not be implemented because of a change of party control of the Council. The Club's hope therefore fell far short of any kind of legitimate expectation, which requires a clear and unambiguous representation upon which it was reasonable to rely. Further, it is not ultra vires for a change of policy to take place, whether or not there has been a change of partly control, since manifesto promises, although relevant to the exercise of discretionary power, cannot be enforced as otherwise they would be unacceptable fetters on public administration, which requires room to modify or change its policies in the public interest: *Bromley London Borough Council* v *Greater London Council* (1982) and *Secretary of State for Education and Science* v *Tameside Metropolitam Borough Council* (1977).

b) The £50,000 spending by Old Age Care Services Inc was based on informal advice from the Chair of the relevant Council Committee. This again seems to fall short of a clear and unambiguous representation upon which it was reasonable to rely, and hence it is very doubtful whether it is sufficient to give rise to any kind of legitimate expectation. Whilst the Chairman clearly had ostensible authority to speak on the issue, the circumstances in which he did so (at a social occasion) were so informal that it must be doubtful whether even the limited doctrine of ostensible authority could be invoked in such circumstances.

c) The further spending by both the Sunshine Old People's Club and Old Age Care Services Inc was based on an apparently formal letter notifying them of the Council's decision, which was sent by a junior clerk acting maliciously against his employers. It is possible that the doctrine of ostensible authority could be invoked here, but as the clerk was only a 'junior' clerk it is doubtful whether there would be evidence of a formal delegation of decision-making power to give rise to an estoppel: *Western Fish* case (above). There is, however, a better chance of establishing a legitimate expectation based on a clear and unambiguous representation upon which it was reasonable to rely. At minimum this will give the two organisations a right to be heard on the matter, and possibly a right to prevent a change of policy under the substantive aspect of the doctrine, but the latter must be considered doubtful in view of the overriding public interest in the efficient management of social care facilities, which demands flexibility of operation. Nevertheless, the clerk's letter at least gives rise to a basis for an application for judicial review in which a declaration of the legal position is the most likely individual remedy.

QUESTION EIGHT

The (fictitious) Police Act 1995 empowers local police authorities to dismiss their Chief Constables if the officers perform their duties negligently or dishonestly. In May 1997, Blankshire Police Authority dismissed its Chief Constable, Mrs Smith. The Authority did not offer any reasons for its decision, nor was Mrs Smith given any opportunity to question the decision before it was made. Because she has been dismissed, Mrs Smith loses her entitlement to a police pension. But she has for some unknown reason decided that she will not challenge the sacking.

However, Mrs Smith's husband wishes to challenge the Authority's decision. He wishes to ensure that his wife receives her pension so that he and their three children will be provided for financially in the event of her death.

Similarly, the Police Federation and the local law centre wish to challenge the Authority's action. The Police Federation claims that it is in its members' interests to establish whether such secrecy in the administration of the police service is lawful, while the law centre claims that promoting good administration in the police service is a matter in which all members of the public have a profound interest.

Advise the Police Federation, Mr Smith, and the law centre if they have standing to challenge the Police Authority's decisions.

University of London LLB Examination
(for External Students) Administrative Law June 1996 Q8

General Comment

This problem raises three aspects of the law of locus standi: personal interest standing, associational standing and public interest standing. Although the question is only on the standing of the relevant parties, there will need to be some discussion of the likely grounds of review and remedy since these may affect the issues of standing in some of the cases in the problem. There is much recent case law which can be utilised, especially on the concept of public interest standing.

Skeleton Solution

- The context of the case and how it may affect issues of standing.
- Mr Smith: does he have sufficient personal interest standing to apply for judicial review?
- The Police Federation: does it have sufficient associational standing to apply for judicial review?
- The law centre: does it have a sufficient basis for claiming public interest standing so as to apply for judicial review?

Suggested Solution

The facts indicate that Mrs Smith may have been unfairly dismissed. Whilst this would usually be a matter of private law, her status as a Chief Constable elevates the matter into the field of public law, and examples of procedural impropriety, such as denial of the right to make representations and, arguably, the failure to give reasons for her dismissal, will render the decision ultra vires and give rise to relief under RSC O.53, the most appropriate remedy being certiorari to quash the decision: *Ridge* v *Baldwin* (1964) – dismissal of Chief Constable of Brighton.

a) *Mr Smith*

The issue here is whether, as husband of the victim of apparent procedural impropriety, Mr Smith can apply for review if his wife chooses not to do so. Mr Smith can show that the dismissal will have adverse financial consequences for the Smith household since loss of pension rights follows the dismissal. This would appear to give Mr Smith sufficient personal interest so as to have standing to apply for relief in his own name. Section 31(3) Supreme Court Act 1981 and O.53 provide that the court shall not grant leave to apply unless it considers that the applicant has 'a sufficient interest in the matter to which the application relates'. The last eight words indicate that, in deciding this question, the court will normally grant leave to apply and decide the issue of standing at the full hearing because the question of standing is bound up with the context of the application. Leave would be refused only where it was obvious that the applicant was a complete 'stranger' to the context of the application.

Mr Smith is certainly no such stranger and would therefore be given leave to apply. At the full hearing he would probably be able to satisfy the court of his sufficient personal interest in the context of his wife's dismissal and would probably be granted certiorari to quash the decision:

'... prohibition and certiorari lie on behalf of any person who is "person aggrieved" and that includes any person whose interests may be prejudicially affected by what is taking place. It does not include a mere busybody who is interfering in things that do not concern him: but it does include any person who has a genuine grievance because something has been done or may be done which affects him.': per Lord Denning MR in *R* v *Liverpool Corporation, ex parte LTFOA* (1972).

The last sentence of the quotation is probably reflected in the modern statutory formula for establishing sufficient interest. Whilst it is curious that Mrs Smith does not intend to contest her dismissal, her failure does not itself prevent others personally affected by it from doing so.

b) *The Police Federation*

The Federation is in a very different position from Mr Smith, who has a personal interest in his wife's dismissal. The Federation is effectively claiming 'associational standing' to represent its members in order to contest what it claims is a matter affecting all its members, namely the 'secrecy' surrounding the handling of Mrs Smith's dismissal. A possible difficulty facing the Federation is its status: if it is unincorporated it will lack the capacity to apply for review and will be struck out at the leave stage. Assuming it is incorporated, the problem will be in establishing sufficient interest, since the mere fact of incorporation will not in itself give the Federation such interest and, indeed, the court appears reluctant to recognise the concept of associational standing at all: *IRC* v *National Federation of Self-Employed and Small Businesses* (1982) – Federation denied standing to represent self-employed over tax treatment of individual citizens.

The only apparent way round this difficulty is for the Police Federation to argue that the treatment of Mrs Smith involved very serious abuse of power with implications for the whole police service. In *IRC*, above, Lord Diplock recognised that there might be 'extreme' cases where a representative group (or perhaps even a single individual) would be granted standing to challenge flagrant and serious breaches of the law. This makes it likely that, on the present facts, the Police Federation will be successful at the leave stage since, on a 'bird's eye view' of the case the judge at that stage will probably assume the Federation has standing. But at the full hearing the Federation may have difficulty sustaining its claim to standing because Mrs Smith's individual treatment may not be symptomatic of widespread unlawful secrecy in the police service: it may have been a 'one-off' episode of impropriety, similar to the peculiar background that had led up to the dismissal of the Chief Constable of Brighton in *Ridge* v *Baldwin*. Its only hope may be in seeking the remedy of the declaration which appears to have the most relaxed test of standing of all the remedies under O.53. In *Royal College of Nursing of the United Kingdom* v *DHSS* (1981) the RCN was granted standing to seek a declaration as to the legality of a DHSS circular advising on the participation by nurses in the termination of pregnancies. The RCN had associational standing to represent nurses, and one of its special functions was to advise its members on relevant law. Since it genuinely disputed the legal advice in the DHSS circular it was appropriate for the court to grant a declaration as to the formal legal position to the RCN. However, in the present case the Federation is not contesting an interpretation of substantive law but rather is challenging procedural impropriety surrounding a dismissal, and it is doubtful whether the court would apply the *Royal College of Nursing* decision so as to grant standing to the Federation here.

c) *Law centre*

The law centre is claiming 'public interest standing' on the ground that Mrs Smith's case reveals defects in the administration of the police service. The law centre is therefore not claiming associational standing in the sense of seeking to represent a defined membership with common interests, but rather is seeking to represent the general public interest. If it tried to bring ordinary civil proceedings for this purpose (eg, for an injunction to stop the Police Authority from hearing further similar cases), the law centre would be told that it must obtain the Attorney-General's consent, since only the Attorney-General can constitutionally claim to represent the general public interest in such proceedings: *Gouriet* v *Union of Post Office Workers* (1978).

However, if the law centre applies for judicial review under O.53 it simply faces the same test as Mr Smith and the Police Federation, namely of showing sufficient interest in the context of the case. Traditionally it has been difficult for special interest groups or concerned citizens to seek review on the basis of 'public interest': the court has been wary of encouraging a flood of applications if it adopted too liberal a test of standing. But in recent cases there has been a trend towards recognition of the concept of public interest challenges, particularly where the remedy was a declaration, as this enjoys the most relaxed test on standing of all the O.53 remedies: see the *Royal College of Nursing* case.

In several cases a special interest group has been granted standing, apparently on the basis of its special expertise/experience in the field in question and because of the serious nature of the illegality alleged: see *R* v *Inspectorate of Pollution, ex parte Greenpeace Ltd (No 2)* (1994) and *R* v *Secretary of State for Foreign and Commonwealth Affairs, ex parte World Development Movement Ltd* (1995). A statutory body set up to protect citizens against sex discrimination was also recognised as having public interest standing on this basis: *R* v *Secretary of State for Employment, ex parte Equal Opportunities Commission* (1994).

However, it must be doubtful whether a law centre can lay similar claim to the long experience and expertise in their particular subject areas of such bodies as Greenpeace, the World Development Movement and the Equal Opportunities Commission. A law centre is often dependent on a few full-time salaried officials and a host of part-time volunteers; it tend to involve itself in a wide range of social welfare cases and cannot claim expertise in any particular area. Indeed, it is not a 'special interest' group of the sort recognised in the above trilogy of recent cases. Further, Mrs Smith's case by itself may not be evidence of widespread illegality in the operation of police administration, and for that reason it is also distinguishable from the recent trilogy of public interest cases, which all involved very real and substantial allegations of illegality, on matters of nuclear waste disposal, foreign aid and sex discrimination respectively.

For these reasons it is suggested that the law centre will not be successful at the leave stage in seeking to apply for judicial review. Whilst it may have a genuine concern on the matter, its interest is too generalised and too remote from the context of Mrs Smith's dismissal to be classified as 'sufficient'.

Old Bailey Press

The Old Bailey Press integrated student library is planned and written to help you at every stage of your studies. Each of our range of Textbooks, Casebooks, Revision WorkBooks and Statutes are all designed to work together and are regularly revised and updated.

We are also able to offer you Suggested Solutions which provide you with past examination questions and solutions for most of the subject areas listed below.

You can buy Old Bailey Press books from your University Bookshop or your local Bookshop, or in case of difficulty, order direct using this form.

Here is the selection of modules covered by our series:

Administrative Law; Commercial Law; Company Law (no Single Paper 1997); Conflict of Laws (no Suggested Solutions Pack); Constitutional Law: The Machinery of Government; Obligations: Contract Law; Conveyancing (no Revision Workbook); Criminology (Sourcebook in place of a Casebook or Revision WorkBook); Criminal Law; English Legal System; Equity and Trusts; Law of The European Union; Evidence; Family Law; Jurisprudence: The Philosophy of Law (Sourcebook in place of a Casebook); Land: The Law of Real Property; Law of International Trade; Legal Skills and System (Textbook only); Public International Law; Revenue Law (no Casebook); Succession: The Law of Wills and Estates; Obligations: The Law of Tort.

Mail order prices:

Textbook £11.95

Casebook £9.95

Revision WorkBook £7.95

Statutes £9.95

Suggested Solutions Pack (1991–1995) £6.95

Single Paper 1996 £3.00

Single Paper 1997 £3.00

To complete your order, please fill in the form below:

Module	Books required	Quantity	Price	Cost
		Postage		
		TOTAL		

For Europe, add 15% postage and packing (£20 maximum).
For the rest of the world, add 40% for airmail.

ORDERING

By telephone to Mail Order at 020 7385 3377, with your credit card to hand.

By fax to 020 7381 3377 (giving your credit card details).

By post to:

Old Bailey Press, 200 Greyhound Road, London W14 9RY.

When ordering by post, please enclose full payment by cheque or banker's draft, or complete the credit card details below.

We aim to despatch your books within 3 working days of receiving your order.

Name

Address

Postcode Telephone

Total value of order, including postage: £

I enclose a cheque/banker's draft for the above sum, or

charge my ☐ Access/Mastercard ☐ Visa ☐ American Express

Card number

☐☐☐☐ ☐☐☐☐ ☐☐☐☐ ☐☐☐☐

Expiry date ☐☐☐☐

Signature: ....Date: ....